CRITICAL INSIGHTS

Horton Foote

CRITICAL INSIGHTS

Horton Foote

Editor
Robert W. Haynes
Texas A&M International University, Laredo

SALEM PRESS
A Division of EBSCO Information Services, Inc.
Ipswich, Massachusetts

GREY HOUSE PUBLISHING

Publisher's Cataloging-In-Publication Data
(Prepared by The Donohue Group, Inc.)

Names: Haynes, Robert W. (Robert William), 1951- editor.
Title: Horton Foote / editor, Robert W. Haynes, Texas A&M International
        University, Laredo.
Other Titles: Critical insights.
Description: [First edition]. | Ipswich, Massachusetts : Salem Press, a division
        of EBSCO Information Services, Inc. ; Amenia, NY : Grey House
        Publishing, [2016] | Critical insights | Edition statement supplied by
        publisher. | Includes bibliographical references and index.
Identifiers: ISBN 978-1-61925-840-2 (hardcover)
Subjects: LCSH: Foote, Horton--Criticism and interpretation. | American drama-
        -20th century--History and criticism.
Classification: LCC PS3511.O344 Z66 2016 | DDC 812/.54--dc23

First Printing

PRINTED IN THE UNITED STATES OF AMERICA

Contents

Resources _____

About This Volume

Robert W. Haynes

After Horton Foote's death in 2009, he was honored not only by memorial services but also by an increase in the number of performances of his plays across the United States. As a man of the theater, he would certainly have appreciated that kind of tribute, and with Cicely Tyson's 2013 Tony for her role in *The Trip to Bountiful* and the 2015 Emmy for Outstanding Television Movie that went to *Bessie*, a film based on a Foote screenplay, it is clear that his contributions to drama and cinematic art are going strong. In this book, thirteen essays by eleven Foote scholars discuss a variety of aspects of the plays and films we have inherited from this American master, with commentary on works ranging from his first one-act play, staged in 1940, to the amazing nine-hour sequence *The Orphans' Home Cycle*, which he was still working on at the time of his death.

Authors whose works are assembled here range from seasoned senior scholars to graduate students, and they work in places ranging from Connecticut to Colorado to China, with, of course, a few of Foote's fellow Texans making their voices heard. Some of these contributors know Foote only through his work, and others were his close friends, but all share a deep respect for an author who maintained both artistry and integrity during a long and challenging journey through his country's theatrical life. No doubt many of the writers here would disagree over certain points of literary judgment and even over the merits of Horton Foote's numerous plays, teleplays, screenplays, and other works, yet here the reader will find critical differences set forth for what they are worth, with each writer's main objective being to add to the reader's knowledge. That, we believe, is the kind of critical attitude appropriate for a work about Horton Foote.

One writer here notes that Foote was forty-six, halfway through his life, when the film of *To Kill a Mockingbird* put his screenplay before an audience of millions. In 1962, the battle for civil rights was still raging, and it was actually late in Foote's life that open opposition to racial equality faded from view. With this in mind, readers of Rebecca Briley's chapter here will benefit from her energetic study of this author's treatment of race and prejudice in his works. Jan Whitt's perceptive assessment of the alterations Foote made in adapting Harper Lee's novel for the film version of *Mockingbird* also touch on this issue, and she goes on to muse on what it means to adapt a work from one genre to another.

Robert Donahoo takes on a theoretical appraisal of aspects of one of this country's most underestimated plays, Foote's Pulitzer Prize-winning *The Young Man from Atlanta*, a work that, even more than *The Actor*, constitutes a major retrospective on *The Orphans' Home Cycle*. Robert W. Haynes also discusses this play as he considers the role of memory and memorials in Foote's drama. He has another essay here on Foote's films, in which he argues that Foote saw, even among his fellow Texans, the hope of a kind of sanity that, when it can be achieved, offers an escape from desperation.

Two different kinds of comparative studies are included here. Xueying Wang juxtaposes Foote's *The Trip to Bountiful* with a short story by the famous Chinese writer Lu Xun, pointing out similarities in the protagonists' desire to recover spiritual peace and radical differences in their relative capacities to do so. Roy J. Gonzáles, Jr., analyzes Foote's early play *The Chase* and examines ways the writer altered the fictional circumstances as he converted the dramatic story into a novel.

In his essay, Terry Barr explores Foote's role as southern writer, relating his artistry to that practiced by authors who, unlike Foote, are actually discussed at conferences on southern literature. Barr, no mean creative writer himself, wrote the first doctoral dissertation ever on Horton Foote. Crystal Brian, whose hefty doctoral dissertation on Foote contains many jewels of insight, presents a fascinating impressionistic collage of observations and experiences supported by her conviction that this playwright is a mystic of the theater.

Gerald C. Wood, whose works on Horton Foote are essential to any study of the man from Wharton, has two essays here. One is an assessment of Foote's critical reputation, a survey of criticism from the 1980s (when Foote scholarship began) up to Marion Castleberry's invaluable literary biography of 2014. The other essay presents a detailed account of the development of the screenplay for *Tender Mercies*, the 1983 film that won Foote his second Oscar.

Gertrude Stein scholar and high modernist Elizabeth Fifer provides an engaging essay here focusing on the awareness and memory of three aging women and making a powerful case for the range of Foote's artistic vision.

In a different kind of chapter, Cynthia Franco, librarian at the DeGolyer Library at Southern Methodist University (and author of the library's finding aid for the Horton Foote Archive), describes the materials held at SMU.

The authors of these chapters hope that their contributions will be helpful to those interested in Horton Foote and his work.

CAREER, LIFE, AND INFLUENCE

On Appreciating Horton Foote_____

Robert W. Haynes

Horton Foote, the quiet Texan whose dramatic career extended through nearly seven decades of American literature, remains best known for his Academy Award-winning screenplay for the film classic *To Kill a Mockingbird* (1962). This film was based on one of the best-selling books in English, a novel that was published in 1960, just as the American civil rights movement gathered strength to push aside institutionalized prejudice and open new doors for millions of citizens long denied the fundamental rights promised by their nation. Harper Lee's book drew on the implications of Mark Twain's fictional friendship between Huckleberry Finn and Jim and showed that the promise of fair and honorable relations between races was still poisoned by the dishonesty implicit in racial discrimination. Horton Foote's screenplay expresses its author's deep concern about the South's reluctance to re-think its social habits and its adherence to a sentimentalized, romantic illusion of a noble antebellum plantation society. The film appeared in a bloody and anxious year on the American civil rights front, and the year that Foote turned forty-six. Since he died in 2009, just short of his ninety-third birthday, 1962 was the mid-point of his life, and, with the film's release, it was, professionally speaking, the high point of his life up until then. Though much remained in the way of achievement as the Texas playwright worked steadily through the years, building a solid record of work in television, in film, and in works for the stage, it is only quite recently that the remarkable quality (and, incidentally, the quantity) of his work is being widely acknowledged.

On April 16, 1940, drama critic Arthur Pollock of the *Brooklyn Daily Eagle* published a rather informal review of three one-act plays he had recently seen in a makeshift theater over a garage. He says has lost his notes on the performances and adds that the low-budget theatrical group could not afford to print programs, so that he has to do the review from memory. His article begins:

At 256 W. 69th St., Manhattan, is a garage and over the garage are actors. Young actors, mostly, with here and there an adult. They have no stage, do not need one, for they can imagine. Part of the floor over the garage is cut off from the rest of it by a curtain, which is drawn between actors and an audience of about 40. That is, the curtain is drawn before the play begins and after it ends. Between the acts they don't bother to draw it. The actors simply stop acting and shift the simplest scenery while the audience looks on. They call themselves the American Actors Company. (Pollock 15)

Pollock goes on to praise the talents and attitudes of the group, mentioning that he has previously seen the American Actors put on Paul Green's play "Shroud My Body Down," which he had some difficulty understanding, and proceeds to describe the company's current program of three one-act plays, commenting "Two of them are by Thornton Wilder and, being empty, are clearer than Paul Green's play. The third is by a young man in the company, not so complacent as Wilder's but friskier. None of the names of the plays come to mind at this moment" (Pollock 15).

The young man in the company who wrote that third play was Horton Foote, and the play was "Wharton Dance," his first. It must have been slightly embarrassing to the young playwright to have his name forgotten by this critic, but Pollock's words about Foote's acting group and the critic's evident enjoyment of the play itself must have been some compensation. And Foote tells us himself that another critic, Robert Coleman, of the *New York Mirror*, attended the plays, explaining, "He was impressed with my play, praised Mary's direction, and liked all the actors, giving me a special mention" (*Farewell* 199).[1] Yet there is something in Pollock's lapse of memory that seems to predict a pattern for Horton Foote, who remains one of the world's best-kept literary secrets. The successes of recent works associated with him—notably, the 2014 stage and film production of *The Trip to Bountiful*, with Cicely Tyson, and the 2015 film *Bessie*, based on a screenplay written by Foote in the 1970s, as well as the publicity associated with the fifty-year anniversary of *To Kill a Mockingbird*—have increased the public's familiarity with his name, but the academic bibliography on Foote remains much less developed than that found for Tennessee Williams, Eugene O'Neill, or Arthur Miller. An interesting feature of Foote scholarship is the fact that most of those in academia who have written about him are individuals who knew him personally and have a regard for him that approaches reverence, for Foote was a kind and generous man whose character stood out as exemplary in the world of which academics write—and even more in that in which they work. His genuine modesty, which did not preclude his confidence in the artistic vision shaping his works, matched his devotion to writing, and the telling impact of his trademark dramatic understatement reflected a level of control that is unique among writers for the stage.

Geraldine Page, receiving the Academy Award for her remarkable performance in Foote's film *The Trip to Bountiful*, was unable to restrain her gratitude to him. Not only had she been able to earn this high recognition, but she had done so with a part she had been able to make completely her own in one of film's most memorable performances. Foote's affinity for actors arose no doubt in part because of his own experience on the stage, but, even as playwright, he remained deeply conscious of the challenges faced in the collaborative process between actor, writer, and others engaged with making a play work. In the 2011 commemorative volume *Farewell: Remembering Horton Foote, 1916–2009*, editors Marion Castleberry and Susan Christensen assembled memorial statements from many show-business celebrities, academic scholars, and other friends of the playwright, producing a substantial variety of perspectives which show the respect and admiration felt for him. Contributions from stage and screen personalities include those from Bruce Beresford, Betty Buckley, Ellen Burstyn, Robert Duvall, Lois Smith, Jean Stapleton, and Harris Yulin. Writers include Edward Albee, Jacques and Marguerite Barzun, John Guare, Wilborn Hampton, and Romulus Linney. Many others, Foote family members and associates, theater professionals, and academics, are also represented. The age of the youngest of these contributors is unknown, but Jacques Barzun was 104 in the year of the book's publication, so there is a considerable range of age groups here. This impressive list of participants would undoubtedly include, if they were still among the living, Stark Young, Kim Stanley, Geraldine Page, Lucy Kroll, Rosamond Pinchot, Tamara Daykarhanova, Jerome Robbins, Fred Coe, and a host of others. In short, the reputation of Horton Foote, though not as popular (or notorious) as that of more flamboyant or controversial writers, is grounded in his acknowledged artistic achievement and personal character, as the testimonials in this book make clear. If that reputation has not yet been shaped by the sensational or become the theme of superficial enthusiasm, perhaps that is because the subject matter of his plays works wisely against such responses. This statement does not, of course, mean that Foote's artistic impulse or his drama is somber or Puritanical any more than is the work of Samuel Clemens or Flannery O'Connor. In fact, a comic spirit is infused throughout Foote's work, for real humans do often err, making false steps, wrong turns, and bad investments. One of the fine touches in Geraldine Page's performance in *The Trip to Bountiful* is her managing to keep Mrs. Watts a little ludicrous, while unfolding her formidable spiritual power. And, if anything negative can be said about Robert Duvall's interpretation in *Convicts* of the half-crazed plantation owner Soll Gautier, it is that the comic possibilities of the part prove a bit too tempting and overshade the old man's essential savagery.

Though academic criticism of Foote is still minimal compared to the massive assemblages of elucidation and ideology compiled so far on other playwrights by the publish-or-perish Myrmidons, an impartial assessment of what has appeared so far will acknowledge that much remains to be done in Foote scholarship. Good foundations have been laid by such scholars as Gerald Wood, Marion Castleberry, and Laurin Porter, but Foote's family history, so relevant to his work, is rich and complicated. As Abram W. Foote showed in his 1907 book, *Foote Family*, one of Horton Foote's ancestral relatives in Philadelphia was a friend and associate of Benjamin Franklin. The playwright was also a distant relative of Harriet Beecher Stowe, whose mother was a Foote and whose powerful novel *Uncle Tom's Cabin* (1852) compares interestingly to Harper Lee's *To Kill a Mockingbird*, for which Foote wrote his Oscar-winning screenplay. In Foote's early life in small-town Texas, incidentally, Stowe would not have been a relative to boast about, and the same would have been true in Wharton as the civil rights movement gained strength in the 1960s.

Foote's extensive archive at the DeGolyer Library at Southern Methodist University in Dallas now has a finding aid, and the library now has a policy permitting digital photography—which would have been a welcome convenience several years ago for those struggling to decipher the playwright's penciled correspondence. There can be no doubt that many significant discoveries remain to be made, both in established archives and in materials yet to become available for research. Foote was a letter writer of the old school, and much of his correspondence remains to be located and considered.

The area of scholarship dealing with early television has gained in popularity and promises recovery of valuable resources, quite probably including recordings of programs significant for Foote scholarship, as he was one of the most insightful and respected of the writers of the "Golden Age of Television." Two possible investigative options among many possibilities are: (1) work on information about the version of Foote's play *Only the Heart* which was broadcast on TV in 1948, and (2) a search for further facts about a February 4, 1940, telecast described in the *New York Times* as follows: "Play. 'The Long Christmas Dinner,' by Thornton Wilder, presented by the American Actors Company" ("Notes on Television"). The American Actors Company, of course, included Horton Foote. This area of research offers some exciting options for literary detective work.

It is the remarkable extent of Foote's creative career both in time and across genres that makes it difficult to accurately assess his achievement, but surely that assessment is well under way, even as new productions of his work (or productions based on his work) continue to appear. For basic facts, Marion Castleberry's 2014 literary biography *Blessed Assurance: The Life and Art of Horton Foote* supplements and extends the information provided in Charles Watson's earlier work. As electronic searches of old publications and archives become more accessible, and as the relevant materials in the archives of Foote's friends and contemporaries are made available, a clearer picture will emerge. The scholar working in a reading room with a computer and a digital camera must sincerely admire (and sympathize with) his predecessors, whose work, at best, required a clumsy and tedious (and sometimes expensive) photocopying process and, at other times, meant trying to capture, with pencil, the essence of a text. Technology marches on, however, and no doubt the very function of the reading room will be, for some needs, transferred to the electronic realm. Still, however, work is needed in biographical investigation, in recovery of defunct publications and forgotten videos, in identification of correspondence and connections, and in sorting out the mass of documents and other items already available. As Cynthia Franco, librarian at the DeGolyer Library, indicates in her chapter of this volume, much of what is held in the Horton Foote Archive, including unpublished works and numerous versions of screenplays not chosen for use by filmmakers, remains to be evaluated.

Another significant area of scholarship on Foote that calls for development is the history of critical responses to his works. This essay included in its opening paragraphs some of Arthur Pollock's half-remembered impressions of Foote's first play, a work which—though its ill-considered accuracy made no difference in New York—used the actual names of people living in Wharton. Other relevant contemporary comments on Foote and his associates will no doubt surface as technology advances. Here, as elsewhere, the online *New York Times* article archive is essential for scholars, as is the online *Brooklyn Daily Eagle*. Yet there are issues needing clarification that do not involve the availability of electronic resources, and such matters must be investigated at least mainly by means of traditional approaches. Here is such a matter.

In a letter to Lillian Vallish, dated October 19, 1944, Horton Foote writes: "I missed the Van Druten article but if you still have it—send it on—also Nathan's new book is out, + I'm warning you there is a devastating attack on me in it—Ho Hum, didn't even get me mad—This one. (about Only the Heart.)" (Letter). Horton Foote, already having had, at twenty-eight, four plays (one was a one-act, and another consisted of four short dramatic presentations) on the

New York stage, one of them on Broadway, wrote this passage in a letter to his fiancée, noting that the well-known theater critic George Jean Nathan had included in a recent book a negative review of Foote's Broadway play. Though the young playwright had come a long way since arriving at the Pasadena Playhouse in 1933, fresh from Wharton, Texas, his putative nonchalance about Nathan's comments must have masked some disquiet, for the critic after all had long been conspicuous as an uninhibited observer of the New York theater world, and Foote knew well the power of criticism to affect the play-going public. There is some bravado in Foote's tone here, as he is aware that Lillian's mother opposes their planned marriage and may take advantage of any evidence that he will not be able to make a success of his writing career. He must know as well that Nathan's judgments are not always approved by others,[2] and the dismissive response he writes here may well have been to some extent an answer in kind to Nathan's not having mentioned Foote's name except at the top of the review, where "*A play by Horton Foote*" follows the title.

The book containing the "devastating attack" is Nathan's *The Theatre Book of the Year 1943–1944: A Record and an Interpretation*, and the relevant chapter is titled "ONLY THE HEART. April 4, 1944" (275). In his study *George Jean Nathan and the Making of Modern American Drama Criticism*, Thomas F. Connolly says of Nathan's significance on Broadway, "through the 1920s, 1930s, and 1940s, he was as fiery a presence as ever" (121). Connolly notes later of Nathan that after World War II, "He had been the most erudite and demanding critic for two generations" (136). Thus this critic's blast against *Only the Heart* could not have been welcome to Foote as a response to the playwright's first Broadway play.[4] Yet in having incurred the disapprobation of Nathan, Foote joined a distinguished company of authors, directors, and actors, including some individuals he greatly respected. Eva Le Gallienne, whose touring Ibsen sequence Foote had seen in Los Angeles in 1934, much to the young actor's admiration, was one of these persons, and her biographer Robert A. Schanke has called Nathan "LeG's nemesis" (177). Connolly, discussing the relationship between Nathan and

Tennessee Williams, cites the latter as referring to the critic as "my nemesis." So the attack by Nathan did not necessarily mean that Foote did not belong among New York theater people, though the impersonality of the review suggested that the playwright was not worthy of more than the most casual mention. Nathan's review actually focuses on his aversion to non-Broadway theater, finding this play to be an overrated product of an upstart system lacking in professionalism and thus undeserving of its production on Broadway. His list of professionals he believes to have been misguided in their enthusiasm for Foote's play includes Katharine Cornell, Margaret Webster, Howard Lindsay, Eva Le Gallienne, Hume Cronyn, Peggy Wood, and Thornton Wilder, and he suggests that none of these may have seen the play. Nathan, of course, opposed Le Gallienne's Civic Repertory Theatre, which had sought to establish a noncommercial company that would produce classic plays at reasonable prices, and her interest in Foote's play possibly diminished any inclination he may have had to give it a fair hearing.

On the other hand, the play's lack of success, emphasized in italics at the top of the chapter, was not due to Nathan's negative response to it. The heading reads:

> *A play by Horton Foote, tested in December, 1942 by the same group in the Provincetown Playhouse. Produced to sparse audiences for a forced run of 47 performances by the American Actors' Theatre in the Bijou Theatre.* (Nathan, *Theatre Book of the Year 1942–43*)

Thus, by the time the critic's views were published, *Only the Heart* had expired of natural causes, not that this would have made Foote feel any better upon reading these comments. Of the play and the playwright himself, Nathan noted some alterations between the Provincetown Playhouse version and the Broadway version, continuing:

> Even with some studious revisions of the original script, including the reduction of the characters from six to five, the transformation of the husband's mistress from a Negress to a Bohemian woman, and the changing of the period from 1935 to 1921, and with the further cautious

recruiting of a largely professional acting company, the play proved again to be just about what it was in the earlier appraisal of the less inebrious reviewers. Which is to say a monotonous and painfully dull rehash of the theme of the domineering mother who brings unhappiness and worse to her family through her uncompromising selfishness. The author writes without imagination and with metronome insistence; he manages to bring to the old and stale materials no sense of dramatic life, no fresh observation; and his play, except for a single scene between the daughter and her young husband, plods its course with the heavy emotional repetition of a juke-box blues song. (Nathan, *Theatre Book of the Year 1942–43* 276)

Two years earlier, on the first anniversary of Pearl Harbor, in fact, *New York Times* drama critic Lewis Nichols had said of the earlier version of the play: "'Only the Heart' is not a great play, probably it is not even a good play as they would reckon those things uptown." The reviewer, though generally encouraging, also notes that the play "is not yet ready for the bitter winds of Broadway." Thus Foote must have realized in 1942 that this work signaled a continuation of his apprenticeship, and, when Nichols reviewed the improved and recast version of the play on April 5, 1944, the critic sadly pronounced it to be "talky, old-fashioned and dull." The performance reviewed was the same as that reviewed by Nathan (April 4), and it is significant that Nathan opened his comments with the statement: "Charge off this error to some of the reviewers," justifying this assignment of blame by asserting that critics overstated the quality of works presented at the Provincetown Playhouse and thus encouraged the inappropriate migration of such works to Broadway.

After drawing attention to the weaknesses of Foote's play in the long paragraph cited above, Nathan concludes his discussion with three paragraphs on "these local experimental organizations" (*Theatre Book of the Year 1942–1943* 276), the theatrical groups such as the American Actors' Company, who "founder on their lack of purely theatrical skill" (277). It is possible that Nathan's alert reading of theater columns and reviews had developed his skepticism about Foote and his group, for the sequence of *New York Times* entries about Foote and his plays in the early 1940s was not, taken

---

all in all, encouraging. Even Brooks Atkinson's favorable review of *Texas Town* (1941) had found fault with Foote's acting, and the sequence of false starts, title and cast changes, and interruptions that marked the stage history of *Only the Heart* (formerly *Mamie Borden*) might have prejudiced a more patient critic than Nathan. After all, Horton Foote had come east to act, not to write, and his emergence as playwright had, to some extent, surprised even him, if one may judge from his memoirs. Since his publishing career went into a hiatus of several years after the closing of this play, it may be useful to review the work, in so far as can be done from a reading of the 1944 Dramatists Play Service edition, to ascertain whether such reviews as those by Nathan and Nichols were fair to the playwright. One cannot recover the all-important effects of the stage production, but it is certainly possible to evaluate the play itself as published.

The fact that a good play can be badly produced, directed, or acted has never been in doubt, and it should be kept in mind that Sophocles' *Oedipus Rex* did not win the Athenian competition in which it was originally staged. Yet, there are definitely moments in *Only the Heart* in which the credibility of action and dialogue is strained, thus posing extra challenges for the actors. Since the version produced on Broadway had been recast as well as revised after the cool reception of the play staged at the Provincetown Theater, this aspect of the drama must have been recognized, at least to some extent. In the process of development, the play's focus appears to have been weakened somewhat, as can be seen, as Nathan notes, in the alteration of Mr. Borden's mistress, who was originally an African American woman but has been converted to a "Bohemian" one. One wonders how scandalous it would actually have been in rural Texas for a man to have had a Bohemian mistress. It may be that any scandal would have been due more to the stigma of adultery than of social rejection of inappropriate ethnic interaction, and the role of the Ku Klux Klan seems substantially less of a threat in the revised play. In accord with this observation is the alteration of the title, which applied to both versions. Foote wanted *Mamie Borden* as his title, but it was feared that Mamie might be confused with Lizzie, and he was forced to accept the vague and essentially irrelevant phrase from Heine's poem (as if Heine and his poetry would be familiar to a Broadway audience).[3] A reading of the play quite justifies Foote's original title, for the dramatic action of the play is Mamie Borden's self-destructive effort to neutralize Fate by keeping herself and her loved ones busy. Her obsession with work is an effort to counter a vulnerability she cannot accept, and it distorts her naturally generous and sympathetic personality to the extent that she resorts to bullying and cruel threats in an effort to preserve her fantasy of a happy family made safe by unstinting labor.

The title *Mamie Borden* suggests that of *Hedda Gabler*, a play which had changed Foote's view of drama some ten years before *Only the Heart* reached Broadway, and it shares with the Ibsen play a central focus on a strong woman who battles her own vulnerability at the cost of those around her. Another Ibsen play titled with the name of the central character is *John Gabriel Borkman*, whose protagonist has, like Mamie, destroyed his family because of an obsession, and Borkman's preoccupation with underground minerals even parallels Mamie's visions of the power of oil to bring happiness.

Nathan was not the easiest of critics to please in any case, and he often told his readers that the duty of the critic was to tell the truth about plays as a means of quality control. A reading of *Only the Heart* many decades after its Broadway closing suggests that the play would have required a better-than-average level of acting and production to have been a success, and neither Nathan nor Lewis Nichols reported such ability in their reviews. Though Mildred Dunnock, who played India Hamilton, appeared in a number of contemporary plays, she does not appear to have distinguished herself in this one.[3]

It was generally known to Nathan's readers at the time that he disliked non-Broadway plays from New York. He had certainly made this aversion clear in the 1942–1943 *Theatre Book* (130), in which he had also disparaged an earlier effort by Horton Foote's own group, the American Actors Company. Referring to the group's production of Ben K. Simkhovitch's *The Playboy of Newark*, Nathan declared:

Another random example of the activities of the amateur experimental groups, it re-established the lamentable fact that these present groups are a far cry from those which a score or more years ago contributed so handsomely to the advancement of the American stage and its drama. (*Theatre Book of the Year 1942–1943* 258)

Though Shirley Frohlich also condemned this play in *The Billboard*, Nathan's main point is that non-Broadway theater should generally be discouraged. Foote was probably referring to this review in the letter to Lillian quoted earlier when he wrote, "Ho Hum, didn't even get me mad—This one…." The phrase "This one" indicates an earlier provocation by Nathan that did anger the young playwright, and perhaps the critic's attack on the Simkhovitch play did that. Foote had good reason to defend his non-Broadway company, for it had not been long since Agnes De Mille had suggested to Foote, then an aspiring actor, that he write for the stage, and indeed his first two plays "Wharton Dance" and *Texas Town* had soon earned him some attention, along with the ambivalent designation "promising." Since Brooks Atkinson and Arthur Pollock, two established critics, had found his dramaturgy worthy of favorable comment, it is not surprising that Foote would resist discouragement from such a controversial figure as George Jean Nathan.

Foote was soon to seek employment elsewhere, however, as he had a new wife and no doubt felt some inclination to work under more normal expectations than came with being a promising New York playwright. He had recognized the dramatic material that empowered his imagination, but he seems also to have felt distraction from his environment and from family considerations. He certainly wanted to convince his mother-in-law that he would be a good husband to Lillian and thus alleviate some of his wife's anxiety about her mother's feelings. He also saw his friend Tennessee Williams, several years older than himself, returning to New York, after years of wandering, with a play *The Glass Menagerie*, which would soon assure his professional success. The opportunity to do theater work at the King-Smith School in Washington, DC, offered Foote relief from some pressures and an opportunity to develop his skills and, above all, to continue writing. He had left his Texas home in 1933 and had led a typically improvident theatrical life for over ten years. Now married and with a clear sense of his own objective as writer, he was ready for relative stability. It may have been relevant as well that, as the war reached its climax in 1944, and as he dealt with the news that his brother was missing in action in Europe, he felt more strongly impelled than ever to establish the value of his own calling by seeking the perfection of his art.

Thus the reader wishing to understand Horton Foote's work as fully as possible can take into consideration the implications of literary history and apply them as appropriate to bring light to the composition of that work. Keeping in mind the essentially collaborative nature of theater, a sensible reader will also seek out relevant circumstances of that collaboration as possible sources of clarification. The writer's two Academy Awards, his Pulitzer Prize, and his many other distinguished awards are significant indications of his achievement, but so are many of his yet-uncelebrated plays and programs, which invite scholarly attention. As one contemplates the long and productive life of Horton Foote, it becomes evident that much remains to be clarified. Fortunately, as can be seen in the tone and mood that characterizes most Foote criticism, that process is itself often invigorating and conducive to a philosophic state of mind.

Notes

1. An attempt to locate Coleman's review was unsuccessful, although NYPL Senior Reference Librarian Matthew J. Boylan did find an article in which Robert Coleman mentioned that "Wharton Dance" would be performed that evening (April 9, 1940). Boylan checked a number of subsequent editions and found no review by Coleman. Though Coleman may have reviewed the play later, it is also possible that Foote's memory of this review is erroneous.

2. In the previous year's edition of *The Theatre Book of the Year*, Nathan had mocked, among others, Paul Horgan, Vincent Price, Katherine Hepburn, William Saroyan, Thornton Wilder, Phillip Barry, and fellow critics John Mason Brown, Robert Coleman, and Brooks Atkinson.

3. Lizzie Borden figured in a number of popular treatments in the 1930s and 1940s, including the 1933 Broadway play *Nine Pine Street*, in which Lillian Gish played Lizzie.

4. In his 1942–1943 *Theatre Book*, Nathan discussed three plays in which Dunnock was a member of the cast: *The Cat Screams*, *Vickie*, and *Richard III*.

Works Cited

Atkinson, Brooks. "American Actors Company Produces Horton Foote's 'Texas Town' in Sixteenth Street." *New York Times*. (30 Apr. 1941): 22. *ProQuest Historical Newspapers*. 18 Oct. 2015.

Boylan, Matthew J. "Follow-up on request for Robert Coleman review." Message to Robert W. Haynes. 7 Dec 2015. Email.

Connolly, Thomas F. *George Jean Nathan and the Making of Modern American Drama Criticism*. Rutherford, NJ: Fairleigh Dickinson UP, 2000.

Foote, Abram William. *Foote Family, Comprising the Genealogy and History of Nathaniel Foote, of Wethersfield, Conn., and His Descendants*. Vol. 1. Rutland, VT: Marble City Press, The Tuttle Co., 1907.

Foote, Horton. *Farewell: A Memoir of a Texas Childhood*. New York: Scribner 1999.

_____, screenwriter. *Convicts*. Dir. Peter Masterson. Perf. Robert Duvall. MCEG, 1991.

_____. Letter to Lillian Vallish, 19 Oct. 1944. Unpublished letter in Horton Foote Collection, De Golyer Library, Southern Methodist University.

_____. *Only the Heart*. New York: Dramatists Play Service, 1944.

_____, screenwriter. *The Trip to Bountiful*. Dir. Peter Masterson. Perf. Geraldine Page. Island, 1985.

_____, screenwriter. *To Kill a Mockingbird*. Dir. Robert Mulligan. Prod. Alan J. Pakula. Perf. Gregory Peck. Universal, 1962.

_____. "Wharton Dance." Unpublished Playscript in Horton Foote Collection, DeGolyer Library, Southern Methodist University.

Frohlich, Shirley. "Off-Broadway Opening" Review of the AAC production of *The Playboy of Newark*, by Ben. K. Simkhovitch. *The Billboard* (10 Apr. 1943): 10.

Lee, Harper. *To Kill a Mockingbird*. New York: Lippincott, 1960.

Nathan, George Jean. *The Theatre Book of the Year 1942–1943*. 1943. Rutherford, NJ: Fairleigh Dickinson UP, 1971.

_____. *The Theatre Book of the Year 1943–1944*. New York: Knopf, 1944.

Nichols, Lewis. "The Play: *Mamie Borden*." Review of early version of Horton Foote's *Only the Heart* (formerly *Mamie Borden*). *New York Times* (7 Dec. 1942): 22. Web. 18 Oct. 2015.

_____. "The Play: Pistol Packin' Mama." Review of Horton Foote's *Only the Heart*. *New York Times* (5 Apr. 1944): 17. Web. 18 Oct. 2015.

Pollock, Arthur. "Actors at Work over a Garage: Plays by Paul Green, Thornton Wilder Done by the American Actors Company." *The Brooklyn Daily Eagle*. (16 Apr. 1940): 15. Web. 18 Oct. 2015. <http://bklyn.newspapers.com/image/52777103>.

Schanke, Robert A. *Shattered Applause: The Eva Le Gallienne Story*. New York: Barricade Books, 1992.

Stowe, Harriet Beecher. *Uncle Tom's Cabin*. 1852. Ed. Elizabeth Ammons. Norton Critical Edition. New York: Norton, 2010.

Biography of Horton Foote_____

Robert W. Haynes

Born on March 14, 1916, Albert Horton Foote, Jr., was the son of two natives of the small cotton town of Wharton, Texas, located sixty miles southwest of Houston. Foote's father was the great-grandson of a distinguished Texas pioneer and planter named Albert Clinton Horton, a Georgia native who had been a significant political figure in Alabama before moving to Texas.

Horton Foote's mother was the daughter of an astute businessman, Tom Brooks, who was a leading figure in Wharton. Brooks refused to allow his daughters to marry, and he particularly opposed Albert Foote's courtship of his daughter Hallie. The young couple eloped, however, and no reconciliation was made until Hallie became pregnant, at which time the Brooks parents put aside their reservations about Albert and sought to restore normal relations. Albert, however, though he admired and respected his father-in-law, was never willing to accept assistance from Hallie's father and could never forget Brooks' earlier hostility toward him. This story became an important part of Horton Foote's most ambitious dramatic composition, the cycle of nine plays he called *The Orphans' Home Cycle*.

Childhood

Born into this family situation, young Horton thrived, and he has described his early years in detail in *Farewell: A Memoir of a Texas Childhood* (1999). Life in the small town was simple in many ways, as Wharton's primary activity had to do with cotton farming. Though the town did have its rough elements, and racial bias, drunkenness, and violence were common, the boy who found kindred spirits in Mark Twain's Tom Sawyer and Huckleberry Finn spent many pleasant hours by the Colorado River in his home town.

At school, young Horton did fairly well, though his love of reading was often a stronger incentive for learning than were the exhortations of his teachers. In high school, however, a new teacher, who shared her enthusiasm for the stage, found him eager to learn more about plays and acting. Though the Great Depression had struck when Horton was thirteen, his father's thrift and diligence, along with, probably, some quiet assistance from his mother's prosperous family, meant that the economic hard times had not been devastating for the Footes. Horton's father strongly hoped that his son would go to college. Horton's mother had attended Kidd-Key College in Sherman, Texas, where she had studied music. However, as Horton approached his high-school graduation, he told his parents he wished to go to acting school and not to college. At this point in the Depression, with his father's store barely making a profit, this request seemed outrageous, but when Mr. Foote got over his initial disbelief and fury, his love for his son eventually triumphed, and he agreed, reluctantly, to provide tuition for two years' study in California at the Pasadena Playhouse.

Pasadena

Graduating in the spring of 1932, Horton worked that summer in his father's store, and, in the fall, he joined his grandmother in Dallas, where he attended a drama school run by a Miss Woodrow that fall and the following spring. In the following autumn, the young man took the bus to California and enrolled in the acting school at the Pasadena Playhouse, where he spent two years working on basic skills, the first of which was to eliminate his heavy Texas accent. In the first year, he had little opportunity to specialize, but in the second year, he performed in a number of plays and was treated as something of a veteran.

One of his most important experiences in Pasadena occurred when his grandmother came out from Texas for an extended stay. Daisy Brooks had received a comfortable inheritance upon her husband's death, and she intended to keep an eye on her grandson as he found his way in the new environment of urban California. As his eighteenth birthday approached, she learned that he wanted to see a play that was coming to Los Angeles, and she offered to take Horton to the performance. The play was Henrik Ibsen's *Hedda*

Gabler, and it was to be put on by Eva Le Gallienne's traveling troupe. Foote never forgot the effect of Le Gallienne's performance, and Mrs. Brooks, moved by the play, but possibly even more by her grandson's profound appreciation of it, took the young man back to Los Angeles to see two more Ibsen plays, *A Doll's House* and *The Master Builder*, performed by the group. Foote indicated many years later that these plays gave him his first real understanding of the theater's emotional power.

Beginning in October 1934, Foote acted in twelve plays, with the last one performed in June 1935. He played the part of Mimos in *Pygmalion and Galatea*, that of Joseph in *The Coventry Nativity Play*, Robert Audley in *Lady Audley's Secret*, and Lord Augustus Lorton in *Lady Windermere's Fan*. Aside from these productions, Foote made some personal connections in Pasadena that would be beneficial to him later. His fellow students included John Forsht, who would accompany him east after he completed the second year, and Joseph Anthony, who would much later direct the film *Tomorrow* (1972), based on a Foote adaptation of a Faulkner story. Foote also met actress Rosamond Pinchot, who was performing at the Pasadena Playhouse. Two of the teachers at the Playhouse, Blanch Townsend and Louise Lorimer, who worked during summers at a drama school on Martha's Vineyard, invited some of the students to accompany them in the summer of 1935 to assist in play productions. Horton Foote was included, and this invitation opened to him the opportunity of getting to the East Coast and the environs of New York, the destination he had long dreamed of.

The East Coast and New York

At the Phidelah Rice Institute of Drama, Foote and his friends from Pasadena earned only token salaries, but they were given some professional indoctrination and were able to learn more about the options open to struggling novices in the theater. Foote acted onstage in *Up Pops the Devil* and in a dance production, and he played the lead part (in blackface) in a version of the Paul Green play "The No 'Count Boy." As the summer ended, Foote and some of his friends left Martha's Vineyard for New York, where he would begin a struggle to establish himself in the acting profession. Though times were challenging, he was able to secure enough small parts to survive, as he regularly toured agents' offices seeking work. When his budget permitted it, he attended plays, seeing onstage such stars as Burgess Meredith, Judith Anderson, Alla Nazimova, and Pauline Lord. As he was completing his first winter of hardship as an aspiring actor in Depression-racked New York, he accidentally met, on Broadway, Rosamond Pinchot, whom he had befriended in Pasadena, and she immediately invited him to join her as a student of the Russian drama teacher Tamara Daykarhanova, offering to pay his tuition if he would help her as a scene partner. This gracious gesture marked an important moment in Foote's life, as his resulting connection with the Russians Daykarhanova, Vera Soloviova, and Andrius Jilinsky, all veterans of the Moscow Art Theater, would shape his life and art and bring him in touch with persons whose friendship and abilities would inspire and challenge him. And, like the generosity of his father, who somehow managed to send Horton to acting school despite the seeming folly of such an effort, Rosamond's kindness strengthened her younger friend's appreciation of the value of generosity, a quality for which Foote himself would become legendary.

The Russian teachers, though at first dubious about Foote's Pasadena training, became fond of him, as he found their teaching much in accord with his own instincts. Though Rosamond Pinchot unexpectedly left New York for work in California, he was allowed to continue his studies. In the fall, he was invited to join the large cast of a Franz Werfel play titled *The Eternal Road*. The part was non-speaking, but it paid twenty-five dollars a week, and it enabled him to work on a production directed by Max Reinhardt and choreographed by Benjamin Zemach. As he continued working with the Russians, one of his fellow students, Mary Hunter, decided to start an acting company, and Foote, Forsht, Anthony, and others were invited to join. The group called itself the American Actors Company, and its first production, Euripides' *The Trojan Women*, performed in January 1938, was condemned by the critics, but the group persisted, deciding to focus on American plays. During some practice improvisations based on the regional origins of the actors, Horton drew on his Wharton background, and Agnes de Mille suggested that he try his hand at writing. Interested in creating parts for himself, he went home and wrote a one-act play titled "Wharton Dance," which the group staged early in 1940. A well-known drama critic attended the performance and praised the work, and thus began the career of a writer whose productivity would extend over nearly seventy years.

Pleased with this recognition, and quite probably recognizing an unsuspected affinity for writing plays, Foote decided to pursue dramaturgy, and he returned to Wharton where he could live comfortably while composing a full-length play. This work, *Texas Town*, was favorably assessed by Brooks Atkinson in the *New York Times*, and though the play itself had a short run, Horton Foote became known as a man to watch in the field of theatrical writing. Though he continued to act when possible, it was not long before he realized that writing was what he wanted to do, and his desire to perform onstage faded away.

Foote's next dramatic presentation was a sequence of four short plays he titled *Out of My House* (1942). This experimental work, atypical of Foote's drama, has strong political overtones directed at small-town aristocracy, and the fragmented structure works against coherence. Foote decided to make his following play more conventional, and, when *Only the Heart* was staged later in 1942, it received some encouraging reviews. The author reworked the play, taking some bad advice in the process, and, when the work opened on Broadway in April 1944, it was arguably a weaker play than the earlier version. It ran for forty-seven performances and received mostly negative reviews. Since Foote had been writing plays now for several years and had been called a promising playwright too long for his own comfort, he took a job managing a Doubleday bookstore in New York, where he met and courted a Radcliffe student named Lillian Vallish, who became his wife in 1945. Horton and Lillian, recognizing the need of a stable income, looked for new employment, and, when Horton was offered a position teaching drama at the King-Smith School in Washington, DC, Lillian also joined the staff, managing administrative tasks effectively. The Footes remained at the school for four years, with Horton writing and directing and staying in touch as much as possible with matters in the New York theater world.

Writing for Television

In 1949, Horton and Lillian moved back to New York, where a friend helped Horton get a job writing for a western TV show for children. The pay was acceptable and much needed, and Foote's expertise in handling plot and character served him well. He became known to others in the television industry and was asked to write dramatic scripts for other programs. He had seen a TV broadcast of a performance of his *Only the Heart* back in 1948 but had not liked the program very much, and in fact, he had not worked on the TV version. Soon, however, he found the challenges interesting, and he realized that he could develop some of his ideas quite well in the television studio. The pay, about a thousand dollars per show, was a substantial improvement over his previous salaries. Lillian had her first child in 1950, and Horton found a rhythm of artistic productivity that enabled him to work on multiple projects while maintaining a comfortable income. Some early teleplays were *Ludie Brooks* (1951), *The Old Beginning* (1952), *A Young Lady of Property*, *The Tears of My Sister*, and *The Trip to Bountiful* (all 1953), *The Dancers* (1954), *The Roads to Home* (1955), *Flight* (1956), *The Traveling Lady* (1957), *The Old Man* (1958), *The Shape of the River* and *Tomorrow* (both 1960), and *The Night of the Storm* (1961). Though television was, in many ways, still somewhat crude by later standards, these programs brought Foote into close contact with gifted actors and directors, some of whom had not yet achieved the reputations they would later have and some of whom were already legendary, as, for example, Lillian Gish. Others working in his teleplays included Kim Stanley, Geraldine Page, Joanne Woodward, Estelle Parsons, Hume Cronyn, Jean Stapleton, Julie Harris, James Earl Jones, E. G. Marshall, Sterling Hayden, Franchot Tone, Richard Boone, Steven Hill, Mildred Dunnock, Chill Wills, Eva Marie Saint, and Wendy Hiller. Among those directing his programs were Vincent

Donehue, Arthur Penn, John Frankenheimer, Robert Mulligan, and Delbert Mann, and producers included Fred Coe, David Susskind, and Herbert Brodkin.

Television programs at this early period were filmed live. Videotape had not yet been developed, so the only recording of a TV show was the kinescope, made by directing a movie camera at a monitor. For actors, then, television work was much like acting on stage, though little mobility was permitted by the cameras of the day, and sets had to be kept simple and accessible. From Foote's earliest days, there was a background of potential conflict between sponsor and artist, but by the time he went to work for Fred Coe, Foote liked writing for television, with its stresses and deadlines made tolerable by collegiality and the pleasure of working with gifted actors and imaginative directors. At the same time, however, Foote's family was growing, and as he himself approached middle age, he wished to advance in his artistic profession and to achieve security for his loved ones. He still wished above all to succeed in the theater, and he had ideas and play scripts he hoped to develop. One play, titled *The Chase*, had been begun in Washington, DC, and Foote was able to get it produced in New York in 1952.

This play, featuring the inner conflicts of a small-town Texas sheriff, opened on Broadway to unenthusiastic reviews and closed after thirty-one performances. Foote, who was being encouraged to try his hand at prose fiction, later converted the play into a novel, which was no more successful than the play had been. Television had put his name into wide circulation in the entertainment business, and in 1956, he was asked to adapt a crime novel into a screenplay. The resulting film *Storm Fear*, though it gave Foote little desire to repeat either the process of adaptation or that of writing for the big screen, marked the beginning of a career in screenwriting that would bring him two Academy Awards.

Mockingbird and Hollywood

By the late 1950s, Foote had matured as playwright and as television writer. In TV, he was at the top of his profession, though that profession was changing rapidly, and the days of live television drama were ending as videotape made possible the pre-editing of programs. He had been able to engage his own memories and concerns in many teleplays and in his stage plays as well. In 1960, he wrote the script for a program ("The Shape of the River") on Mark Twain, one of his literary heroes, and adapted a story ("Tomorrow") by another hero, William Faulkner. He also worked that year on *Roots in a Parched Ground*, a teleplay about his father's childhood that foreshadowed the great dramatic cycle he would write many years later. This play, retitled *The Night of the Storm*, was broadcast in 1961.

As the nation began to feel the internal stress of racial discrimination and the need for its remediation, Alabama author Harper Lee published a novel that would make her one of the most famous of American writers. Her work *To Kill a Mockingbird* (1960) enjoyed enormous success, and still does, more than half-a-century later. The novel focuses on the conflicts associated with the denial of justice to a black man in a small southern town and features three children and an honest local lawyer. After some negotiation, it was decided that Horton Foote would write the screenplay for the film version of the novel. He met Harper Lee, and they became good friends. Both were from small southern towns, and each instinctively trusted the other. Gregory Peck was cast in the lead role as Atticus Finch, with Mary Badham as his daughter Scout and Brock Peters as Tom Robinson. The film was released late in 1962, and it was an immediate success, earning eight Oscar nominations, including one for Horton Foote's screenplay. Both Foote and Peck won Academy Awards (though Foote did not attend the ceremony).

The *Mockingbird* Oscar not only brought Foote into the national spotlight, but it also associated him with the southern group of intellectuals who supported civil rights. In 1963, this was no small matter, as southern opposition to the civil rights movement was fierce, even among those appointed to uphold the law. The year 1963 brought Medgar Evers' murder as well as that of the children who died in the Birmingham church bombing. With the assassination of President Kennedy in November, however, and the assumption of the presidency by Lyndon Johnson, a wave of emotional shock swept through the nation, including, as Marion Castleberry has explained, the set in Texas where Steve McQueen and Lee Remick were filming *Baby, the Rain Must Fall* (1965), a film based on Foote's play *The Traveling Lady* (231).

Producer Sam Spiegel, having read Foote's novel *The Chase*, decided to make a film based on it. He hired seasoned screenwriter Lillian Hellman to adapt the work and recruited a cast of stars, including Marlon Brando, Robert Redford, Jane Fonda, Robert Duvall, and E. G. Marshall. Hellman seems to have disliked Foote, or at least his work, and she developed a plan of her own, aimed at making the film satirize Texas. Spiegel had ideas of his own, which conflicted with Hellman's, and their mixed intentions produced a hodgepodge of a screenplay that Foote himself was at last asked to improve, a task he tried to execute, despite the script's having been altered beyond recognition. The result was released in 1966, confirming Foote's conviction that Hollywood's system was destructive to art.

Foote's film work brought him offers to adapt a number of works, and, at times, the stipends were substantial. Often, the film company would hire several writers and then select the version thought likeliest to make money, so a number of Foote's versions, not used by those who paid for them, remain unpublished in his archive at Southern Methodist University. One film for which Foote was reluctantly credited despite his non-contribution was Otto Preminger's *Hurry Sundown* (1967).

Family Matters

As his four children, all born in the 1950s, grew up and went to school, Horton and Lillian made some adjustments. Having lived in Nyack, New York, since 1956, they relocated in 1966 to a remote rural home near New Boston, New Hampshire. The turbulence of the 1960s was very evident in the theater, and Foote felt that there was no contemporary audience for his kind of drama. He wrote a script for a musical version of *Gone with the Wind*, which was staged in London in 1972–73, but this show, despite much publicity, did not make money and was shut down.

Foote's aging parents brought anxiety to his household. He brought them to New Hampshire, but his father, confused but still energetic, was miserable there, and, when Horton and Lillian realized that the couple would find life easier to manage back in Wharton, his parents returned home. His father died in 1973, followed in the next year by his mother. Thus as he approached sixty himself, Horton—coping with the seeming incompatibility of his work with current film and theater, seeing his children depart to make lives for themselves, and grieving over the loss of his beloved parents—had to return to his old home in Wharton to deal with property issues and other arrangements. In his parents' home, looking through the records of their lives, he began thinking of new plays in which he could deal with his own emotions and his parents' lives, and, in the next few years, he composed a sequence of nine plays he called *The Orphans' Home Cycle*, a work dealing with his father's struggle from childhood to maturity. Each play was conceived as an independent work, which could be staged alone, but no one reading through the *Cycle* will fail to notice that the work's cumulative effect makes it one of the most powerful works of American literature. This work signaled a kind of artistic recovery for Horton Foote as he moved from personal grief to a resumed confidence in his mastery of his dramatic art.

With his family finances posing problems in the early 1980s, Foote sought a movie contract to be based on a screenplay of his own composition. Numerous difficulties occurred, but, with encouragement from his actor friend Robert Duvall, Foote persisted, putting together a script about an alcoholic country singer seeking to recover sanity. Australian director Bruce Beresford agreed to join the effort, and the film *Tender Mercies*, a movie very different from Hollywood's usual productions, was released in 1983, receiving five Academy Award nominations and winning Oscars for Robert Duvall and for Horton Foote. Pleased with this outcome, Foote pushed on in independent filmmaking with a long-cherished project, a film of his play *The Trip to Bountiful* (1985). This movie starred Geraldine Page, who won an Oscar for the part of Mrs. Watts, the elderly countrywoman who runs away from Houston to return to her old farm in Bountiful. Foote was also nominated for an Oscar for his screenplay.

Having tasted success with his participation in making films, Foote sought to produce cinematic versions of the plays from his *Cycle*. Film versions of these plays appeared as follows: *1918* (1985), *On Valentine's Day* (1986), *Courtship* (1986), *Convicts* (1991), and *Lily Dale* (1996). The filming of these was sometimes a family matter, with several relatives taking part, most notably his daughter Hallie Foote, actress, and his wife Lillian, who coproduced two of the movies.

The success of *Tender Mercies* and *The Trip to Bountiful* brought Foote back into the professional circles from which he had once felt excluded, and his plays began to find theaters that welcomed them. The 1980s brought forth productions of *In a Coffin in Egypt* (1980), *The Man Who Climbed the Pecan Trees* (1982), *The Old Friends* (1982), *The Road to the Graveyard* (1982), *The Roads to Home* (1982), his trilogy *Harrison, Texas* (1985), *Land of the Astronauts* (1988), *The Habitation of Dragons* (1988), and *Dividing the Estate* (1989), along with some productions of individual plays from the *Orphans' Home Cycle*. In 1987, PBS broadcast a series of programs based on three of the *Cycle* plays.

Though Foote turned seventy in 1986, his artistic skill remained impressive, and he continued his work into the 1990s. His screenplay for the 1992 film of John Steinbeck's *Of Mice and Men* connected him to another major twentieth-century writer, and, in 1995, Foote's stage play *The Young Man from Atlanta* was awarded a Pulitzer Prize. His enthusiasm and energy kept him writing, and, as the century wound down, he published a volume of memoirs (*Farewell* 1999). As usual, he kept writing plays, with *The Last of the Thorntons* staged in 2000. He went on to publish a second autobiographical volume (*Beginnings*) in 2001.

The Twenty-First Century

Foote received much recognition of his artistic contributions late in his life. One of his most treasured was the National Medal of Arts awarded to him in 2000 by President Clinton. Other awards he had accumulated included his two Oscars, an Emmy, and membership in the Theatre Hall of Fame and the American Academy of Letters, along with numerous others. Going into the twenty-first century, it was known that he continued to produce excellent work, and the theatrical world remained attentive to his productions. His plays *The Carpetbagger's Children* (2002) and *The Actor* (2003) showed that he remained open to innovation, and his participation in rehearsals showed his delight in the theater. When a project was developed to produce a marathon production of his *Orphans' Home Cycle* at Hartford Stage in Connecticut, he joined the project and worked on adapting his nine-play original for three three-hour performances that could be seen in one day. As he devoted himself to this project, however, his strength failed him, and, just short of his ninety-third birthday, Horton Foote died.

The life and work of this distinguished playwright was commemorated in many ways by the nation's artistic community and those touched by his teleplays, stage plays, and films. Dallas, home of his literary archive at SMU, held a Horton Foote Festival in which many of the city's theater groups participated, and a special exhibit was put on at the DeGolyer Library, where so many of his manuscripts are held. The year 2016 marks the hundredth anniversary of Foote's birth, and it will surely remain clear that this writer has given the world much to remember and much to reflect upon.

Acknowledgments

Ellen Bailey, archivist at the Pasadena Playhouse, and Hilary Wall, archivist and librarian of the Vineyard Gazette Media Group, kindly provided valuable information for this study.

Works Cited

Castleberry, Marion. *Blessed Assurance: The Life and Art of Horton Foote*. Macon, GA: Mercer UP, 2014.

Foote, Horton. *Farewell: A Memoir of a Texas Childhood*. New York: Scribner, 1999.

CRITICAL
CONTEXTS

All Lives Matter: African Americans in Horton Foote's South

Rebecca Luttrell Briley

When Horton Foote died on March 9, 2009, the first African American president of the United States had scarcely taken the oath of office. Today, with Foote a scant seven years in the grave, "Black Lives Matter" is a household debate, Ferguson a nationally acknowledged powder keg, and a young black man in a hoodie the poster child for presidential sympathy. Indeed, the Confederate flag no longer flutters defiantly above the capitol of South Carolina, and statues of Confederate heroes that have stood like stone walls throughout the South are finding their footing to be less than stable. What the Texas native might have to say about these recent occurrences can only be imagined; what is certain, however, is that whatever Horton Foote might say, it would be polite, thoughtful, and charitable in the voice of the soft-spoken gentleman he immovably was. While it is precarious to suppose Foote's stance on any of these controversial events, the time is right for reexamining his legacy through dark-colored glasses, so to speak: to focus the spotlight on his depiction of black characters and his personal philosophies in light of the reality of racism still smoldering throughout America.

My initial study on Foote, *You Can Go Home Again: The Focus on Family in the Works of Horton Foote* (Lang, 1993), examined the father-son relationships so evident in all his works, including those works he adapted for other writers. From his first one-act play produced for the 1939–40 season by the American Actors Theatre to his Pulitzer Prize–winning *The Young Man from Atlanta* (1995), Foote was not only "always doing Texas," as he once told a reporter, but consistently examining familial relationships taken directly from his personal frame of reference (Jones). When he died, his *Dividing the Estate* (1989) was in a revival production for the Hartford Stage; even here, its author's gaze had not wavered from the interactions among kinfolks prevalent in all the previous works.

This preoccupation with his own family portraits may account for the lack of minority figures in his casts of characters or explain Foote's seeming lack of interest in African Americans in general, as he includes blacks infrequently in his *dramatis personae* and only as they interact with the dominant white families, never as protagonists. When choreographer Agnes DeMille advised the young actor to "write what you know," Foote took her literally, setting his work then—and later—in Harrison, his barely disguised hometown of Wharton, Texas (Briley 20). Here, although the population at the time was nearly equally black and white, its entrenchment in the segregated South would wrap the young Foote in a sheltering cocoon as long as he made Wharton his home, thus providing him a well-meaning, but naive and self-absorbed perspective upon the world. He was raised on a steady diet of family stories, so the expected artistic outcome could only be an imitation of that life itself.

Lest one assume Foote was rarely in the company of blacks or never claimed any as friends, Foote recalls in *Farewell* (1999), the first of two published memoirs, growing up with "almost as many blacks as whites," numbering among his close acquaintances sundry African Americans who worked for his family. "I knew many of the blacks by their given names," he recounts, from Uncle Joe, his grandfather's hired man, to Walter, who "looked almost white." One particular black man, Stant Powell, who worked in his father's haberdashery left an indelible impression on the young Horton:

> As a child I loved Stant … I remember always feeling very safe and secure with him, for no matter how busy he was he always paid me a great deal of attention. Sometimes carrying me around in his arms, calling me his boy, and bragging on me, making me feel very loved, and I thought he would surely be a part of my life forever. (*Farewell* 75–76)

After his father sold his cleaning and pressing shop and Stant found employment elsewhere, Foote wondered why the black man went from addressing him as "Little Horton" to "Mr. Horton" when they saw each other occasionally in town. Unsettled by the new dynamic in their relationship, he asked his father. Foote didn't understand his father's reply, "That's because you're both in the South and that's how things are done in the South," and Foote continued to think about Stant long after he disappeared from Foote's circle, as did so many other blacks he "felt close to as a boy" (*Farewell* 76). Foote remembers many relationships he enjoyed with African Americans whom he "knew intimately" (82), including a boy with whom he played nearly every day before they were separated by segregated schooling. He was to mourn the loss of these friends the rest of his life.

The companionship Foote shared with many members of Wharton's black community was exemplified by his immediate family. Although his ancestors admittedly had owned hundreds of slaves, by the time Horton came along, the relationship between the two races had greatly changed. Now most of the blacks he encountered worked as tenants on the family's farms, a seemingly satisfactory collaboration. He recalls that his "grandparents were always generous to the poor and needy, black and white" (*Farewell* 25), and the black community spoke highly of the Brookses and their kin, welcoming them into their homes. As a boy, Foote's father, Albert Horton Foote, Sr., even preferred to live with a black couple after his own father died, as this is where "he was happiest" (45).

Albert Foote conducted his business as evenly as Texas allowed, serving African Americans with equal civility in his store, taking care to shake their hands and "thank them for coming" (*Farewell* 181), and many black customers would solicit his tailoring skills long after they moved away (190). If ever pressure from presumptuous white customers forced Mr. Foote to defer to their demands of preferential treatment, his son noted the consternation it caused his father, who was always apologetic to his acquiescing black clients. Though not observing any bitterness on their part, Foote later ruminated about "how they stood all the restrictions of segregation" (181).

One disturbing situation he did raise with his father involved a prominent white doctor in town who "bragged openly" about manipulating black farm owners out of their mineral rights. Foote asked himself, "How ... could this kind, generous man openly cheat ignorant people, many of whom couldn't read or write, and didn't even know what they were signing?" (*Farewell* 133). In a recalled conversation not unlike many Scout might have had with Atticus in *To Kill a Mockingbird*, his father explained:

> "Well," my father said, "you better learn now that some people, good people it would seem, don't mind taking advantage of poor ignorant Negroes. To them, Negroes have no feelings, no sense, and wouldn't know how to take care of the money if they got it."
> "That's terrible, Daddy."
> "Of course it's terrible."
> "Could you do something like that?"
> "No, not if I was starving and my wife and children were starving. I couldn't."
> And I believed that was so, because my father spent a great deal of his life helping black people who couldn't read or write figure out forms and legal documents, for which he got no kind of payment, except the loyalty and affection of the whole black community, most of whom addressed him in the plural as Mr. Footes.... (*Farewell* 133–134)

This scene, reminiscent of scenes in *To Kill a Mockingbird*, may explain how readily Foote connected with Lee's characters later and how lovingly he could sculpt her father figure, having had his own model from which to draw inspiration. Incidentally, while Foote may have preferred to concentrate on his own father's story, this influence may actually have produced the freedom from prejudice so admirable in both father and son.

To highlight only the positive aspects of childhood is a dishonesty Foote would not endorse. He turns his attention to the less positive when he recalls in *Farewell*, "The Ku Klux Klan was a real political force in Texas during my childhood," relating how as a child he watched the Klan march down the street in front of his house in their robes with their torches. He was aware his father "had no use for the Klan," abhorring their violence against blacks, Jews, and Catholics (*Farewell* 28–29). He remembers, too, that a white man rumored to have a black mistress was tarred and feathered by the Klan and that a White Man's Union existed to keep anyone other than whites from voting. In his introduction to the volume containing the first four plays of *The Orphans' Home Cycle*, Foote explains the "harsh time" in which his father grew up,

> a time of far-reaching social and economic change in Texas.... But in spite of political and social acts to hold onto the past, a way of life was over, and the practical, the pragmatic were scrambling to form a new economic order. Black men and women were alive who knew the agony of slavery, and white men and women were alive who had owned them. (xii-xiii)

Foote admits,

> I took all of this for granted, if I wondered about it at all, as I accepted all evils of segregation: separate schools, drinking fountains, toilets.... Lynching ... had mostly ended by 1914, but once in a while one lynching or another would be recalled.... I don't remember anyone saying how terrible they were, or seeming glad they had ended. The tales were told with no apparent moral concerns. (*Farewell* 32)

There were moral concerns, though, regarding miscegenation; not only were mixed marriages not allowed, verification of sexual affairs between the races was more than frowned on even by the Foote family. A great-aunt's prospective marriage was discouraged when it was discovered her suitor had "outside children," a euphemism for illegitimate black progeny (*Farewell* 46–48).

Perhaps the most momentous early memory Foote describes is of finding a Klan robe in his own kitchen while he was playing and his mother was cooking supper:

> "Mother?... What's this?" I said, holding up the robe.
> "Give me that," she said, and I could tell she was very upset.
> "I don't know why your daddy didn't burn this. Where did you find it?"
> "Under here in the cabinet. What is it, Mother?"
> "It's a Ku Klux Klan robe."
> "Where did Daddy get it?"
> "Oh, Lord. There are a lot of members of the Klan here and he and Papa got pressured to go to one of their meetings, and they went

together.... Anyway, both Papa and your daddy were disgusted by what they saw and heard."

"Why were they disgusted?"

"Because they didn't agree with what was being said or who was saying it."

"What was being said?"

"Lord, honey. Just a lot of foolishness. Anyway, they were so disgusted they never went back." (*Farewell* 28–29)

This single instance stands out as symbolic of the position the Foote family maintained, planted in the traditionally racist South while maintaining an attitude of cooperation and sympathy between the races. Relatively unique, this personal environment went a long way in nurturing the young Horton, protecting him from the taint of bigotry he might have absorbed from the outside community and cultivating in him instead the healthy blend of *logos* and *pathos* that was to define the rest of his life and color the portraiture of his characters.

There was much for the unassuming young Foote to realize, and it would take moving away from the South before he could put his protected upbringing into perspective. In his second memoir, *Beginnings* (2001), Foote explains, "the political climate in New York at the time [1936] was radically different from anything I had known in Texas or Pasadena," where he first went to study acting. "In New York City I was soon assailed on every side with the politics of change" (189), he remembers. Receiving a life-time education in a few months surrounded by a diverse and liberal-minded group of actors, artists, writers, and activists, the young actor was to learn of the "enormity of the Depression," Communism and Socialism, labor unions and the American Labor Party, Nazis and Fascists, and even the thorn in his own southern side: racism. On a mission to confront his family with this newly acquired information during his next trip home, he recalls how he "began a diatribe on the unfairness of the tenant system and the exploitation of blacks in the South" (*Beginnings* 191), aware his grandmother's six cotton farms, on which black tenants sharecropped, were managed by his father. His father's only reaction when his son stopped to catch his breath was to ask if he were still a Democrat, and, when he replied in the affirmative, his father, relieved, responded, "I could forgive you almost anything except your voting the Republican ticket" (192). Encouraged by an open-minded father, Foote was to return to New York with a sense of having been absolved of the southern sin.

This awakening to the racial prejudice he had been oblivious to throughout his childhood did not dissipate, though it was never his style to mount a soap box or join the marching mob in protest of the injustices suffered by African Americans in the South. For a brief period, he did try his hand at agit-prop theatre, trending at the time, and explored "the issue of racial friction among blacks" in *People in the Show*, which Foote finished in 1945. Wilborn Hampton calls this work the "most overtly political play" Foote was ever to write, but in spite of the inclusion of two black characters at odds with one another over civil rights, the focus of the piece was primarily anti-Semitism (98).

Whatever his deep-felt convictions were, he played them close to the vest, though this underlying thread of egalitarianism, as an actor, a writer, and a human being would continue to course through the rest of his career. After marrying, moving to Washington, DC, for a time, and founding his own acting company, he recalls with a quiet satisfaction that, while "Washington theatres were segregated in those days, … from the beginning our school and theatre were not" (*Beginnings* 268). For the ever-modest Foote, the mention of this one particular accomplishment—one that testifies to his principles for racial equality—speaks louder than anything.

The most famous, perhaps, and certainly the most beloved work of his entire canon is Foote's screenplay for the film version of Harper Lee's novel *To Kill a Mockingbird*, for which he won the 1963 Academy Award for adaptation. The collaboration was so successful that even the exacting novelist could find little to criticize, declaring "If the integrity of a film adaptation is measured by the degree to which the novelist's intent is preserved, Mr. Foote's screenplay should be studied as a classic" (Lee v). Indeed, Foote was at home in Lee's milieu. According to *New York Times* theatre critic Wilborn Hampton, Foote "knew and understood [Lee's characters] as well as his own family and neighbors" (145). Among the many notable characters, Calpurnia, the black cook who helps the widowed Atticus raise his motherless children, is handled skillfully by an adaptor who grew up surrounded by similar figures. Other black characters form a soft, dark background to the white Maycomb community and are rendered compassionately, even reverently, as the falsely accused Tom Robinson remains atop a sympathetic pedestal, and his subdued family, firmly ensconced in its ragtag place, is portrayed as polite and deferential. Lee's black community is depicted no less benignly than Foote's, but the longer novel provides a greater sense of realism than the film's few select scenes allow. However, one scene alone covers a multitude of omissions. Taken directly from Lee's pages, the iconic moment in the film comes when the black Reverend Sykes urges Scout to stand with the rest of the "colored balcony" to honor her father for his courage, integrity, and human decency: "Miss Jean Louise, stand up. Your father's passin'." This is one of the most memorable scenes in all of American filmmaking, proving a single image may be mightier than the pen.

In spite of his success with *To Kill a Mockingbird* and the accolades that followed, Foote consistently preferred investing his time and talent in his original works, determined to tell the story of his own middle-class southern white family and their ancestors. When African Americans are mentioned, albeit briefly, in Foote's plays, they are always presented with the greatest care, almost as if Foote were afraid of touching something so foreign or fragile. While this gentle approach is indicative of Foote's attitude toward all living beings, it also intimates a hesitation to venture into an area where the author fears he has little knowledge, in spite of his obvious experience among the black community of his childhood. In an interview with Terry Barr and Gerald C. Wood, Foote confessed why he was reluctant to write much about African Americans:

> It's a terrible thing about the Blacks and me. And I feel badly about it because actually I owe them a great debt. They really sustained me in many ways as I was growing up... [but] I don't write about them because I really think maybe only a Black person can really write about them. And I'm afraid if I write about them in a naïve point of

view and not a real point of view. So I avoid writing about them, and it's a real loss to me. (236)

The loss, perhaps, is ours, as Foote is plainly too modest if his memoirs alone are any indication, but his disinclination is not disingenuous. He does have one play, though, in which black characters are prominent: *Convicts*, the second episode of *The Orphans' Home Cycle*. This collection of nine plays, rooted deeply and accurately in the life of Foote's father, relates the lonely journey of the fatherless Horace Robedaux from childhood to his own fatherhood. In *Convicts*, the young Horace, working in his uncle's plantation store to buy a tombstone for his father's unmarked grave, is surrounded by the black chain gang hired to cut the sugar cane on the decaying plantation. Foote takes the setting of his story not only from his father's actual experience, but also from a personal memory mentioned in his second memoir where he and a cousin witness a group of convicts working in the cotton fields outside a Texas penitentiary. "Look at those poor devils," his cousin Nannie muses. "How would you like to spend your life doing that?" she asks. Horton replies he "wouldn't like it, thank you" (*Beginnings* 86). As did his father before him, the young Foote always sympathized with the less fortunate, and this sympathy lends itself to the compassionate composition of Foote's black characters.

In *Convicts*, very little separates the Texas plantation of former Confederate Soll Gautier from its antebellum days; if the scene weren't identified as 1904, one would hardly know the difference. Mr. Soll, as everyone addresses the drunken old man, still runs his spread of land no differently than his father did before him when slaves worked the fields. Black men still quarter in the outbuildings of the property and cut the vast acres of sugar cane under the supervision of an overseer, just as they did prior to emancipation, though these particular men are convicts farmed out by the state to work off their sentences. Soll, who claims to have fought as a Confederate "in every goddamned battle they'd let me" (56), treats his workers as if they were still slaves, and, being convicted prisoners, they are no better off than their enslaved African American ancestors were.

He keeps the gun to their heads, figuratively and literally, barking profanity-laced orders at them and threatening their very lives should they dare to disobey. Perpetually intoxicated, Soll fires his rifle indiscriminately at the men who labor for him, as well as at nonexistent bears and even ghosts he imagines inhabiting his empty old house, expecting the black trustee Jackson to bury as many as he kills. Unable to keep names and dates straight in his whiskey-befuddled brain, he is most meticulous, however, in keeping the graves of the bodies separate from those in the white cemetery on the other side of the property, where his father is buried. Even when he himself dies, his black subordinates, including the couple who runs the plantation store, Ben and Martha Johnson—ordered by Soll not to bury him in his family graveyard—bury him near, but not in, the convicts' graveyard, no more released from the white man's mandate now than when he was alive.

The film opens with the escaped convict Leroy Kendricks, who has just killed fellow prisoner Jessie Wilkes, being chased by men and dogs in a scene so reminiscent of the pre-Civil War South it could just as easily be a montage from *Twelve Years a Slave*. When recaptured, Leroy is dragged back to be chained to a tree, and thirteen-year-old Horace is tasked with guarding him until the sheriff arrives. Horace has worked in Mr. Soll's plantation store for six months without receiving a cent of the promised fifty cents a week. However, he stays on because the old man keeps assuring him he'll pay him soon. It is now Christmas Eve, and the boy is reluctant to leave without his money, preferring to spend Christmas with Martha and Ben.

Few changes occur between the play and the film, released in 1991, both written by Foote, the latter directed by Peter Masterson. Robert Duvall, who debuted as the silent Boo Radley in Foote's film adaptation of *To Kill a Mockingbird*, takes on the role of the crusty old Mr. Soll. Duvall, who later won an Oscar for his role as Mac Sledge in Foote's *Tender Mercies* (1983), is comfortable with Foote's approach; his portrayal of Fentry in Foote's adaptation of Faulkner's *Tomorrow* (1972) is also memorable. He is joined in *Convicts* by his inimitable peer, James Earl Jones, in the role of Ben Johnson, along with the young Lukas Haas as the well-mannered

Horace, whose "Yes, Sir" is his ready and appropriate response to his uncle and the black workers alike.

This respect for all human beings, black or white, differentiates the young Horace from the arrogant disregard demonstrated not only by the faction Mr. Soll represents, but also by the younger white couple in the story. Soll's thirty-something niece and nephew, Asa and Billy Vaughn, are not much more admirable than the old man: equally thoughtless, racist, and drunk, their very existence exemplifies the racial prejudice that continued throughout the postwar South well into the twentieth century. Horace's deference to the Johnsons, as well as his compassion for the convicts, is a fresh breeze wafting through the Gautier property, intimating a change blowing in the wind. It is this possibility of a better future that lifts *Convicts* above its otherwise sobering realism, expanding Foote's contribution beyond just that of family recorder of ancestral anecdotes.

Horace demonstrates this consideration by learning every one's name, including those of the black convicts. Unlike his predecessors, who merely nicknamed their slaves, Horace persists in learning last names as well and who their folks were and where they are from. He is interested in knowing if Leroy went to school and generously cuts him chew after chew of tobacco before giving him the rest of his plug. Careful to withhold his knife from the desperate convict lest he attempt suicide, Horace puts himself in the unfortunate black man's place, suggesting how he would escape if it were him, and warns the man to "stay away from the river, if you can't swim" (46). Finally, he appoints himself to say a prayer over the newly dug grave of the dead convict, saying, "I feel bad he was just dumped into the ground and no prayer was said" (46).

Even Ben, obsequious as he is, is not as deferential to the convicts as is Horace. Having been born in a cabin "right over yonder," the older man explains to the boy how after Emancipation some black people, his parents included, stayed on to work for wages until convicts—also all black—were brought in. Not wanting to be associated with this fallen class of convicts, just as Mr. Soll "don't want them buried near his people," Ben explains, "I don't want them buried near my people in our graveyard" (44, 49), suggesting that even among those of shared race, there exists a caste system. Horace, like his prototype Albert, sincerely prefers Martha's company to that of his indifferent mother, and even the indubitably racist Soll, who insists on being accompanied only by a white person when he dies, elevates the "faithful and trustworthy" couple above his own despicable relatives, raving that the Vaughns will "get nothing of mine. Ben and Martha are to have it all" (56).

Though it is not mentioned in the play, the film depicts Horace clutching an old Confederate battle flag as he sits with the dying old man, reading aloud from a paper dated 1865 in which the rebellious Texas has been denied admittance back into the Union. As far as Soll is concerned, nothing has progressed beyond the Civil War, though Texas' reentry was sanctioned before 1902. When Soll, seizing the boy's hand, dies, Horace is unable to free himself from the old man's final grasp. "Ben," he cries in panic, "I can't get loose from him. He won't let me go" (63), suggesting the hold the old generations and their prejudices retained on their southern descendants well into the twentieth century. But as Ben successfully removes the boy's hand from Soll's death grip, the scene suggests that this generation and those to come will find a way to release themselves from their restrictive past to make way for a new society more bountiful for everyone.

Foote could not have predicted the recent furor over the Confederate flag or foreseen its removal from capitols all over the South, but one may surmise any such flags Foote himself may have retained as memorabilia of his people's past were quietly folded away in trunks in the attic. Regardless of pride in one's history, nothing in Foote's life or work suggests a racist penchant, and in spite of the over-wash of demeaning dialogue throughout the script, there is no use of the "n-word," and he is careful to let the egalitarian Horace speak for him. When Horace wonders what's going to happen when someone's "white daddy and colored mother… all go to heaven together" (50), taking for granted the races will spend eternity in the same place, Martha admits she doesn't know. That she hasn't considered such a conundrum is evidence of her generation's acquiescence to the status quo. Throughout *The Orphans' Home Cycle*, Horace alone represents the coming new order. Though the message is understated by limited dialogue, its meaning is firm, and it should not go unnoticed that Horace is the sole white person attending the grave of the Confederate veteran in the closing scene. While Foote may be reticent in revealing his position overtly in so many of his plays, the conviction here is unmistakable. The most direct of his scripts in presenting this ugly underbelly of his native culture, this play is not out of place among the rest of the Foote canon, nor is its voice in conflict with any of the other pieces focused on his family.

Lest there be any doubt of Foote's intentions in *Convicts*, Ben puts the situation and its significance into meaningful and poetic terms when he speaks over Soll's grave, "Six months from now you won't know where anybody's buried out here. Not my people, not the convicts, not Mr. Soll. The trees and the weeds, and the cane, will take everything… The house will go, the store will go, the graves will go, those with tombstones and those without" (65). Intoned in the resonant bass of James Earl Jones, the film imprints this prophecy, loud and clear.

The last play of *The Orphans' Home Cycle*, *The Death of Papa*, also brings final attention to the racial dynamic, highlighting Horace Junior's naiveté regarding what could be labeled as his own "white privilege," while at the same time conveying sympathy for the black people who work for his family. Laurin Porter draws a correlation between Foote's family and their black servants in her *Orphans' Home: The Voice and Vision of Horton Foote* (2003), claiming the black characters "function as a kind of shadow family to the Vaughn-Robedauxs… hint[ing] at another network of lives being lived out with its own joys and sorrows" (61).

Gertrude, the black nursemaid, knows little about her ancestors, while young Horace is a fountain of information concerning his, including a great-great-grandfather who owned one hundred twenty slaves on his plantation. His ignorance accounts for his lack of sensitivity in calling attention to this taboo topic, and Gertrude has to explain to Horace Junior that it was *her* people, *her* race, who were those slaves to whom Horace is so nonchalantly referring. Porter points out, "He is almost totally unaware of race as a social determinant, since for him, growing up white, it has never been an issue" (61). She goes on to assert that "As we watch the two of them trying to come to terms with complex historical issues…, we are aware that their young lives are shaped by those ideas to which they are exposed, both on a societal and a familial level" (62).

In his "Introduction" to the Grove Press edition of the first four plays of the *Cycle*, Foote recalls with chagrin a moment of revelation in his youth:

> I remember the first time slavery had a concrete face for me. I was on a fourteen-mile hike to complete some phase of becoming a Boy Scout. I stopped in a country store for a bottle of soda water and on the gallery of the store was an elderly black man. As I drank my soda water we got to talking and he asked me my name, and when I told him he said he had been a slave on my great-great-grandfather's plantation. I have never forgotten the impact that made on me. Slavery up until then was merely an abstract statistic that I'd heard older people talking about. "Our family had one hundred sixty slaves, one hundred twenty…" or whatever, but as I looked into that man's tired, sorrowing face, I was shocked to realize that this abstraction spoken of so lightly ("we were good to them," "we never mistreated them") was a living, suffering human being. The tales of the past had a new reality for me after that. (xiii)

Possibly still stinging from this offense committed ignorantly as a child, Foote may be playing out his own *mea culpa* in this scene from *The Death of Papa*. When Gertrude declares she is going to college to "help her people," Horace Junior wants to know if she is referring to her parents, as these are the only people he identifies; but the maid defines them as "my race," stressing that this is the reason for her education (115). Later, the boy announces to his mother that, like Gertrude, he wants to help his people (149), but it is unclear if he has moved beyond his immediate family in that assessment. Clearly, his interest is possibly still very focused on his own relatives, though the rest of his race—or all races—may benefit from this concentration, if these examples are any indication. Although understated, the intention for inclusion, rooted in his personal life, would suggest so.

Foote maintained he was not an overtly political writer, certainly not like many of his contemporaries: Odets, Miller, Hellman—or, later, Kopit, Guare, Rabe. Admitting to social points of view not "shared by a lot of people," he preferred to listen quietly and avoid quarrels. "I'm a social writer," he suggested to Samuel Freedman, "in the sense that I want to record, but not in the sense of trying to change people's minds" (Foote, *Two Plays* xix). Perhaps Foote realized that the most effective way to persuade another to one's point of view required a softer, more subtle approach, where actions speak louder than words, a practice of showing over telling, and subscribing to the advice of a Harper Lee character whose dialogue he once adapted: "Atticus said you never really knew a man until you stood in his shoes and walked around in them" (116). Just watching Foote's plays may be enough, as Scout says of standing on Boo Radley's porch.

In a 1988 interview with Marion Castleberry, Foote remembers "all kinds of people in my daddy's store... I saw blacks who were unable to write their name or unable to pay more than $1.50 down for a suit... They took me into an entirely different world than I was used to.... I learned to love these people, to look forward to Saturdays and to hear their accents so different from my family's and to listen to their stories" (21). Clearly these stories thread into and throughout the tales of his own family, less prominently, perhaps, but just as integrally. The different colors, tightly woven together, create a pattern so integrated that where one thread begins and the other ends may be difficult to determine after all.

Works Cited

Brian, Crystal. "*The Orphans' Home Cycle* and the Music of Charles Ives." *Horton Foote: A Casebook*. Ed. Gerald C. Wood. New York: Garland, 1998. 89–108.

Briley, Rebecca. *You Can Go Home Again: The Focus on Family in the Works of Horton Foote*. New York: Peter Lang, 1993.

Castleberry, Marion. "Remembering Wharton, Texas." *Horton Foote: A Casebook*. Ed. Gerald C. Wood. New York: Garland, 1998. 13–33.

Foote, Horton. *Beginnings: A Memoir*. New York: Scribner, 2001.

_____. *Convicts. The Orphans' Home Cycle Part One: The Story of a Childhood.* New York: Dramatists Play Service, 2012.

_____, screenwriter. *Convicts.* Dir. Peter Masterson. Perf. Robert Duvall. MCEG, 1991.

_____. *"Cousins," "The Death of Papa": Two Plays from "The Orphans' Home Cycle."* New York: Grove Press, 1989.

_____. *The Death of Papa. "Cousins," "The Death of Papa": Two Plays from "The Orphans' Home Cycle."* New York: Grove Press, 1989.

_____. *Farewell: A Memoir of a Texas Childhood.* New York: Scribner, 1999.

_____. *"Roots in a Parched Ground," "Convicts," "Lily Dale," "The Widow Claire": The First Four Plays of "The Orphans' Home Cycle."* New York: Grove Press, 1988.

_____, screenwriter. *To Kill A Mockingbird.* Adaptation of Harper Lee novel. Dir. Robert Mulligan. Perf. Gregory Peck. Universal, 1962.

Freedman, Samuel G. Introduction. *"Cousins," "The Death of Papa": Two Plays from "The Orphans' Home Cycle."* New York: Grove Press, 1989. xi–xxvi.

Hampton, Wilborn. *Horton Foote: America's Storyteller.* New York: Free Press, 2009.

Jones, Kenneth & Andrew Gans. "Pulitzer Prize-Winning Playwright Horton Foote Is Dead at 92." *Playbill.* Playbill, Inc., 04 Mar. 2009. Web. 13 Dec. 2015. <http://www.playbill.com/news/article/pulitzer-prize-winning-playwright-horton-foote-is-dead-at-92-158657#sthash.8qbHqWAV.dpuf>.

Lee, Harper. "A Word." *To Kill a Mockingbird.* Screenplay by Horton Foote. New York: Brentwood, 1964.

Porter, Laurin. *Orphans' Home: The Voice and Vision of Horton Foote.* Baton Rouge: Louisiana State UP, 2003.

Wood, Gerald C., ed. *Horton Foote: A Casebook.* New York: Garland, 1998.

_____ & Terry Barr. "A Certain Kind of Writer." Interview with Horton Foote. *Literature/Film Quarterly.* 14.4 (1986): 226–37.

Horton Foote's Critical Reputation_____

Gerald C. Wood

When Terry Barr and I traveled from East Tennessee to Horton Foote's apartment on Horatio Street in New York City in the summer of 1985, we knew of almost no writing about Mr. Foote. Such a lack of published criticism may have been predictable for such a humble and sometimes reclusive writer as Foote. But at the time, he was about to turn seventy years old, he had written more than forty plays, and he was a celebrated writer of the golden age of television. He had also fashioned a half-dozen movie scripts, including the classic *To Kill a Mockingbird,* for which he had won the Academy Award for Best Adaptation in 1962, and *Tender Mercies,* winner of the Oscar for Best Original Screenplay in 1983. We hoped our interview would help bring more attention to the writer. It took a while. But finally, there is a body of critical work to help establish and support Horton Foote's critical reputation.

Until the 1980s, the responses to Foote were almost exclusively reviews of his individual works, mostly in newspapers. That began to change with the fitful publication of interviews and summaries of his career. Jack Barbera wrote a piece in 1981 in the *Southern Quarterly* on *Tomorrow,* the independent film made from Foote's adaptation of a William Faulkner story. Two years later, Merrill Skaggs wrote in the *Southern Quarterly* about Foote's adaptation of Faulkner's "Barn Burning." Samuel G. Freedman's "From the Heart of Texas," published in the *New York Times Magazine* on February 9, 1986, established the influence of Wharton, Texas—Foote's hometown—on his dramas and storytelling. In that article, Freedman quotes Foote observing, "No matter how far away I've been—New York, London, Hollywood—half of me is always thinking about Wharton, trying to figure out some aspect of this life back here." The interview Terry and I conducted in Greenwich Village was placed in *Literature/Film Quarterly* in 1986. We focused on Foote's writing for film. But along the way, we touched on his reading habits (including his love of poetry), his religious beliefs, his respect for women, and the pattern of theme and variation in his writing.

These interviews were followed by two seminal articles. In Amanda Smith's "Horton Foote: A Writer's Journey," which appeared in *Varia* in the summer of 1987, Foote asserts that his work, though from Texas, seeks to revise the Texas myths and become stories that express his personal understanding of the human condition:

> I don't like professional Texans or professional Southerners. [They're] my roots by accident of birth, what I was given, and I hope that [my work] transcends that. Any writer has that job—to break down the stereotypical myth and to see things whole and to see things in their particulars, in terms of his own vision" (qtd. in Smith 20).

He also explains his relationship with his audiences. Foote adds he hopes "to get people to reexamine and to think about each other and relationships and the lives we live and not tell them what's wrong or good about it—let them decide for themselves. Being didactic doesn't interest me. I'm always trying to change my point of view, to see something fresh, to understand and to present what I perceive, and to engage whoever is watching in that process" (qtd. in Smith 27). Equally insightful and influential was Marian Burkhart's essay "Horton Foote's Many Roads Home: An American Playwright and His Characters" in *Commonweal* (February 26, 1988). Burkhart emphasized that Foote's quotidian subjects resonate as universals. Her essay also identified *The Orphans' Home* as Foote's major achievement and sensitively explored the religious questions at the heart of Foote's work: courage and the search for order and grace in the face of injustice, fear, and violence.

Over the years, play services and publishing houses have reprinted many of Foote's plays, teleplays, and screenplays. Also from time to time, individual works have been studied in detail by editors and scholars. The first such study was *Tomorrow and Tomorrow and Tomorrow*, edited by David G. Yellin and Marie Connors, published by the University Press of Mississippi in 1985, with a foreword by Judith Crist. In addition to an introductory essay,

"Faulkner and Foote and Chemistry," the editors reprint Faulkner's short story; the teleplay (first aired on March 7, 1960, at CBS); and the screenplay of the film, released in 1972. At the back of the volume are responses by Foote (called "The Visual Takes Over"), producers Gilbert Pearlman and Paul Roebling, actors Robert Duvall and Olga Bellin, director Joseph Anthony, and editor Reva Schlesinger. Also included is a selective bibliography. The artists agree that the achievement of the film was based on the writing, the efforts to be true to place, and Foote's development of the relationship between Fentry and Sarah.

Horton's lesser known works reached a wider readership with *Selected One-Act Plays of Horton Foote*, which Horton and I published with Southern Methodist University Press in 1989. This book brings together eight teleplays from the 1950s with nine one-acts from the 1980s. Its preface is from Horton, and in the introduction, I focus on Foote's humanism, pursuit of order, and use of writing to study the sources of courage and personhood. After a chronology of Foote's life and work to date, the plays follow in historical order, with each introduced by a brief statement of its contribution to Foote's style and themes. Among them are Foote's studies of dehumanizing capitalism, race relations, erosion of the agrarian ideal, social politics, and women's issues. At the same time, this collection exemplifies the movement in Foote's work from a more traditional theater, in which characters explain themselves and the stories end with some form of closure, to the later works' more troubling, dark worlds of impersonality, brokenness, and illusion.

By the time *Selected One-Act Plays* appeared, the academic community had started to discover Horton Foote. Four doctoral dissertations were crucial. Terry Barr's dissertation, "The Ordinary World of Horton Foote," from the University of Tennessee in 1987 led the way by establishing Foote's respect for and dramatization of regular people and their everyday lives. Rebecca Briley's "You Can Go Home Again: The Focus on the Family in the Works of Horton Foote" followed from the University of Kentucky in 1990 and explored the use of personal and local material in Foote's writing. In 1993, two other doctoral studies introduced major contributors to Foote scholarship. Crystal Brian, a director and scholar, wrote "The Roads to Home: Material, Method, and Meditation in Horton Foote's *The Orphans Home*" at UCLA. That same year, Marion Castleberry's "Voices from Home: Familial Bonds in the Works of Horton Foote" from Louisiana State University explored, in detail, Horton Foote's use of his family history.

In a study similar to the Yellin and Connors' examination of *Tomorrow*, Barbara Moore and David G. Yellin's *Horton Foote's Three Trips to Bountiful* (1993) reprinted three versions of the *Bountiful* story: the teleplay, which aired on Goodyear Television Playhouse (March 1, 1953); the stage play (Henry Miller's Theatre, New York City, November 3, 1953); and the screenplay (released January 24, 1986). In the introduction, the editors astutely describe the complex, unsentimental journey of Mrs. Watts and the increasing focus on the relationship of Ludie and his mother in the three scripts. Also, they note the crucial shift from a contemporary piece, directed by Vincent Donehue in the first two, to a study of a turning point in the history of Texas and the United States in the film. Afterward, Moore and Yellin include interviews, primarily about the film version, with Foote, producer Sterling Van Wagenen, director Peter Masterson, and actress Carlin Glynn. Equally useful are a chart comparing the three versions of the story, an afterword by Horton Foote, and a bibliography.

After another significant doctoral dissertation in 1995, Tim Wright's "Dancing with Shadows: Stylistic Attributes of Impressionism in Selected Works by Horton Foote" (Regent University), the work of major Foote interpreters was gathered in *Horton Foote: A Casebook* by Garland Press. As the following years have demonstrated, that little book brought together the best students to date of Foote's work in the first comprehensive format, including writers of dissertations and/or books: Marion Castleberry, Terry Barr, Rebecca Briley, Tim Wright, Crystal Brian, Laurin Porter, and Gerald Wood. Included are essays that give biographical, literary, and formal contexts; others that describe styles and themes that recur in Foote's works (especially the plays); and in-depth analyses of all four plays from the Signature Theatre Series: *Talking Pictures*,

Night Seasons, *The Young Man from Atlanta*, and *Laura Dennis*. The *Casebook* also surveyed Foote's career and offered bibliographies of his writing and significant critical work before the end of the 1990s.

Following on the heels of the casebook was LSU's publication of my *Horton Foote and the Theater of Intimacy* in 1999. In it, I described Foote's pervasive theme of loneliness in America and how it is ameliorated by redemptive attachments to community, work, family, and lovers. I link the physical pursuit of place with the psychological search for identity, the crucial role of courage, often inspired by loving women, and Foote's subtle examination of the relationship between personal intimate acts and the public political acts that reflect them. Along the way, I explored the plays and films as products of the same imagination and examined, in detail, individual works like *The Orphans' Home Cycle*, *Tender Mercies*, and *The Young Man from Atlanta*. I also pointed out the subtle role of Foote's practice of Christian Science in some of the plays and films.

In the same year that *Horton Foote and the Theater of Intimacy* appeared, Horton published the first of his two memoirs, *Farewell: A Memoir of a Texas Childhood*. Written, as is the second, in a direct, clear, personal style, *Farewell* relates Horton's family background, early years in Wharton, Texas, and the many storytellers in his immediate family. His account of these details is crucial, of course, because of the influence of this past on his own writing. The memoir also offers his memories of his first experience with the theater and his commitment to become an actor. Even in this record, Horton doesn't romanticize. He records the racism, alcoholism, and various forms of violence in his town. It includes a thoughtful study of the history and dramas of his ancestors on both his father's and mother's side of the family, many of which were the basis of later Foote plays.

Two years later, in 2001, he published *Beginnings: A Memoir*, which describes his life from the time he entered acting school at the Pasadena Playhouse until he and Lillian returned to New York from the King-Smith School in Washington, DC. In California, his interest in a more serious theater was inspired by three Ibsen plays, starring Eva Le Gallienne, which he saw at the Biltmore

Theater in Los Angeles. It was also where he met Joseph Anthony, later a member of the American Actors Company and eventually the director of the independent film production of *Tomorrow*. He describes the transition to New York as an actor and the influence of Rosamond Pinchot in his studying with Russian teachers. It was through his acting with Tamara Daykarhanova and others that he met Mary Hunter, the key figure in the creation of the American Actors Company, which eventually inspired and supported Foote's early writing. Among the most influential of his associates was Agnes de Mille, who encouraged him to write his first play, *Wharton Dance*. He explains in detail the history of *Only the Heart*, his first play to reach Broadway, and his experimentation with the use of music and dance in theater under the influence of Valerie Bettis, Martha Graham, Doris Humphrey, and Charles Weidman. The memoir closes with his meeting Lillian Vallish, their marriage, and their five years in Washington, DC, where Horton wrote and directed before returning to a more realistic theater beginning with *The Chase*.

In 2003, two books appeared that gave both breadth and depth to Foote scholarship and the writer's reputation. Charles Watson's "literary biography" first linked Foote's life and work. It includes family history, letters, and a sense of the history of southern playwrights, Watson's specialty. It is a useful place to start, though it has become a bit dated, with no reference to *The Carpetbagger's Children*; the staging of *The Orphans' Home Cycle* in Hartford, Connecticut, and New York; or other significant events that followed its publication. While not as descriptive of Foote's personal life as the later work of Castleberry and Hampton, Watson's study explores a variety of provocative subjects: Christian Science, country music, adaptation, and the one-act plays. He also gives two chapters to *The Orphans' Home Cycle*. Marion Castleberry's similar work, in progress at the time (see below), supersedes Watson's work, has far fewer inaccuracies, and boasts stronger editing than Watson's.

The other 2003 book was Laurin Porter's study of Foote's most comprehensive and definitive dramatic work *The Orphans' Home*, a nine-play cycle, generally considered his magnum opus. In *Orphans' Home: The Voice and Vision of Horton Foote*, Porter argues that the plays are driven by the search for order, meaning, and identity against the chaos of human experience. Understated plots and rich subtexts, the role of community in shaping character, and the value of language and storytelling, with theme and variation, are essential, Porter asserts, to establishing a civil and hopeful future. In her words, "Foote's emphasis is not so much on returning home as on leaving it, and ... 'home' in his works is not defined so much by a specific locale as it is a network of relationships, a family" (22). As she brilliantly summarizes, "Redemption in Foote's drama comes only through the pain of leaving home, whatever form that takes, of confronting one's sense of loss and moving forward into the future, making new connections, finding new sources of meaning. It is ... a mysterious process, one that defies precise explanation or empirical evidence" (205).

A crucial and unique contribution to Foote criticism was made by Marion Castleberry's edition *Genesis of an American Playwright*, published in 2004. With the support and approval of Foote, Castleberry collected the writer's essays and lectures, his published and unpublished nonfiction writing. Organized in a loose sense of chronology in each section, *Genesis* initially records Foote's description of his writing history. In the second section, Foote writes about "Being a Southern Writer." The following essays and lectures focus first on Foote's reflections on writing for the stage and then for film. *Genesis* concludes with the writer's "Thoughts on the American Theater." The book begins with an exhaustive chronology of Foote's life and work and ends with equally complete appendices. One is a list of casts and production credits for Foote's works in television, theater, and film. The other is a bibliography of the produced and published dramas and books from those works.

During its brief run, the *Horton Foote Review* made a major contribution to Foote criticism. It was sponsored by the Horton Foote Society and supported by Baylor University in conjunction with the Horton Foote American Playwrights Festival. The first volume, edited by Scot Lahaie and DeAnna M. Toten Beard, appeared in 2005, following the creation of the Society in 2002 and the inaugural Festival of March 3–6, 2004. The initial volume celebrated the Festival, which brought together academics, artists, and friends at Baylor University. The Festival also offered a special staging of Foote's play *The Traveling Lady*, a presentation of the film *Convicts*, and a visit by bus to Horton's home town, Wharton, Texas. Included in the first *Horton Foote Review* issue are also selected essays from the festival. Those study his view of aging in the films *Trip to Bountiful* and *Alone* and the writer's complex understanding of the past and memory as source of identify and belonging but also a powerful source of courage to live in the future. Equally valuable are studies of Horton's understanding of social and sexual politics in *The Widow Claire* and Foote's involvement in the staging of dance in the late 1940s and beyond, particularly the work of Agnes de Mille, Doris Humphrey, and Martha Graham. Also explored is Foote's writing at the King-Smith School and for the *Dance Observer*.

Volume Two, published in 2009, was especially poignant since it appeared soon after Horton Foote's death on March 4, 2009. Edited by Susan Christensen, the second issue includes a photo essay on the filming of *1918* and poems by Michael Blumenthal and Robert W. Haynes in honor of Mr. Foote. Robert Donahoo's interview with Foote focuses on the play *The Day Emily Married*, and Marian Burkhart considers *The Habitation of Dragons* as a search for a religious sense of home and forgiveness in the face of the materialism and chaos of much human experience. A number of the essays show influence of other writers on Foote's storytelling, notably Brian Friel, Henrik Ibsen, and Katherine Anne Porter. Rebekah Clinkscale examines the relationship between character and song in *The Orphans' Home Cycle*, and Laurin Porter reveals how Foote exposes the false romanticism of slavery in *Convicts*, *The Last of the Thorntons*, and *The Carpetbagger's Children*.

Essential to understanding Horton Foote's life, both inside and beyond his writing, is Wilborn Hampton's biography *Horton Foote: America's Storyteller*, published by the Free Press of Simon & Schuster in the year of Foote's death (2009). It includes insightful discussions of all Foote's major works but also explores the writer's life as no previous study had done. Hampton's book is the best place to find a clear, direct discussion of the family background and storytelling traditions as well as of Foote's early work at the Pasadena Playhouse, the American Actors Company, and the King-Smith School. Foote's early attempts to be an actor, his courtship and marriage to Lillian Vallish, and the various interesting careers of his children are chronicled. Seamlessly integrated into Hampton's narrative are revealing correspondence within the Foote family and incisive discussions of many Foote works, especially those for theater and film.

A year later, in 2010, Robert W. Haynes published *The Major Plays of Horton Foote: "The Trip to Bountiful," "The Young Man from Atlanta," and "The Orphans' Home Cycle."* The volume included nine chapters on a variety of Foote subjects, four of them reprints of previously published articles. Haynes studies Foote's interest in family and history but rightly asserts that this interest isn't only a nostalgic record. As Haynes notes, Foote is a high modernist, who uses writing to find order and a sense of place in his own history. Robert Haynes also explains the role of music and religious questions in the major works. But this slim book is most provocative in new subjects he identifies without exhaustive comment. For example, the influence of Leadbelly's blues in *Convicts* suggests the need for more study of folk elements in the plays. Also, despite the lack of rhetorical emphasis, Foote's liberal political position, including his strong support of Lyndon Johnson and the Clintons, informs the social subtext of the work, as Haynes makes clear. Finally, this book suggests that the role of Horton Foote's kind nature and somewhat crafted persona poses a unique dilemma for critics of his work. Foote both shaped much of the conversation about his work and refused to be drawn into highly charged controversies and definitive interpretations.

Three books since serve as celebrations of Foote as a person and writer. In 2011, the DeGolyer Library, at Southern Methodist University in Dallas, Texas, printed *Farewell: Remembering Horton Foote, 1916–2009*, edited by Marion Castleberry and Susan Christensen. As anyone would imagine, this collection holds deeply felt and personal responses to Horton Foote as a warm, generous, and loyal person. The stories in it are riveting and convincing. But probably most unique is the diversity of voices and backgrounds of its contributors. The Foote family and friends are, of course, included. But just as evident are the words of such actors as Robert Duvall, Ellen Burstyn, Matthew Modine, Rochelle Oliver, Carol Goodheart, Lois Smith, Betty Buckley, and Jean Stapleton. And other playwrights, including Edward Albee, John Guare, and Romulus Linney, as well as producers and directors Bruce Beresford, Andre Bishop, Jim Houghton, Calvin Skaggs, and Harris Yulin, share their memories and impressions of Horton. And writers, both for popular and academic readers, are represented. Among them are Ben Brantley, Wilborn Hampton, Marion Castleberry, Laurin Porter, and Jacques Barzun.

In 2012, Mercer University Press published a collection of interviews with Horton Foote titled *The Voice of an American Playwright*, which I coedited with Marion Castleberry. Included in the volume are twenty-four interviews, including previously published ones by David Middleton and Laurin Porter. Among the more popular interviewers are television journalists Peter Roussel and Dan Rather and playwright John Guare. The reprints are taken from a wide variety of sources, including scholarly and popular magazines, newspapers, television, and books. Organized chronologically, each interview is introduced by a description of its significance to the history of Foote criticism. Also included in the volume are an introduction by the editors, a thorough chronology of Foote's life and works, and bibliographies of both Foote's published work and writing about him.

Two years later, in 2014, Marian Burkhart published *Horton Foote's America: A Critical Analysis of His Plays*. Burkhart argues, as she has in other places, that Horton Foote should be considered the most American of our playwrights. While the book doesn't employ notes, it does include a useful list for tracking the characters of *The Orphans' Home Cycle*. Inspired by Laurin Porter's book on the cycle, Burkhart gives two central chapters to a sensitive and insightful discussion of *The Orphans' Home*. In other chapters, she describes the need of Foote's characters to embrace mystery and flexibility in the face of the inevitable injustice and mutability in

---

life, especially in later plays like *The Young Man from Atlanta* and *Laura Dennis*. She also has a nuanced and complex study of home, more as object of a psychological and religious quest than a material one.

That same year, Marion Castleberry published *Blessed Assurance: The Life and Art of Horton Foote*, a fitting revision to Charles Watson's similarly designed literary biography. More than twenty years in coming, this book is more correct in its details and polished in its editing. Organized, like Watson's, chronologically, Castleberry's book weaves telling details and useful insights about the works into the fabric of the author's life. Since Foote lived until 2009, six years after Watson's book was published, Castleberry also had the advantage of knowing the full extent and achievements of Foote's works, including seminal works, like *The Carpetbagger's Children* and the Broadway run of *Dividing the Estate*, as well as the productions of the complete *Orphans' Home* cycle in Hartford, Connecticut, and New York. It is a well-written and heartfelt summary of all Foote's major works and the life that inspired them. It also has a Foote family tree, a chronology of life and works, and a very useful bibliography.

Horton Foote's reputation in the popular press is limited because there was so little in his life for the media and popular audiences to sensationalize. His personal life had tragedies, of course, like the death of his brother in World War II, the drunken uncles who haunt his stories, and the loss of his beloved wife Lillian. But there were no scandals; he loved his parents and had a happy marriage and healthy children. Rather than draw attention to himself by promoting the outrageous, his public persona indicated a warm, benign presence, a person interested in other people's voices and lives as much as his own. He also had the courage to oppose Hollywood, while accepting the loss of money and fame that resulted. Equally limiting have been the misconceptions that because he writes about Texas, he is merely a regional writer, and that because he often writes about the past, his work is nostalgic. Also because his reputation ranges across three genres—the play, the teleplay, and film—few have sufficiently broad knowledge of his achievements to appreciate his artistry in general.

Early writers established that Foote is a Texas writer with a sense of history, family, and southern storytelling. He was identified with William Faulkner, Katherine Anne Porter, and Flannery O'Connor, though it took years for it to become clear that his view of history is much closer to Porter than Faulkner and that his view of choice and freedom distances him from O'Connor's dark Catholicism. Over the years, the rich subtexts of his writing have become better appreciated, as well as his musical designs, the point/counterpoint of his exposition, and the avoidance of closure in his endings. His belief in courage, his search for its sources, and his love of identity and personhood eventually have become clear. But especially for readers and audiences in metropolitan areas like New York, recognition has been slow that Foote, a writer from Wharton, Texas, wrote with a distinctive style about universal issues, patterns, and themes.

Works Cited

Barbera, Jack. "Tomorrow and Tomorrow and *Tomorrow*." *Southern Quarterly* 19 (Spring/Summer 1981): 183–97.

Barr, Terry. "The Ordinary World of Horton Foote." Diss. U of Tennessee, 1987.

Brian, Crystal. "The Roads to Home: Material, Method, and Meditation in Horton Foote's *The Orphans' Home*." Diss. U of California at Los Angeles, 1993.

Briley, Rebecca Luttrell. *You Can Go Home Again: The Focus on Family in the Works of Horton Foote*. New York: Peter Lang, 1993. Also publication of same title, Diss. U of Kentucky, 1990.

Burkhart, Marian. *Horton Foote's America: A Critical Analysis of His Plays*. Foreword by Hallie Foote. Minneapolis: Mill City Press, 2014.

_____. "Horton Foote's Many Roads Home: An American Playwright and his Characters," *Commonweal* 115.4 (26 Feb. 1988): 110–15.

Castleberry, Marion. *Blessed Assurance: The Life and Art of Horton Foote*. Foreword by Hallie Foote. Macon, GA: Mercer UP, 2014.

_____, ed. *Genesis of an American Playwright*. Waco, TX: Baylor UP, 2004.

_____. "Voices from Home: Familial Bonds in the Works of Horton Foote." Diss. Louisiana State University, 1993.

Castleberry, Marion & Susan Christensen, eds. *Farewell: Remembering Horton Foote: 1916–2009*. Dallas, TX: DeGolyer Library (Southern Methodist U), 2011.

Christensen, Susan, ed. *The Horton Foote Review*. Vol. 2. Dallas, TX: Southern Methodist UP and the Horton Foote Society, 2009.

Foote, Horton. *Beginnings: A Memoir*. New York: Scribner, 2001.

_____. *Farewell: A Memoir of a Texas Childhood*. New York: Scribner, 1999.

_____. *Genesis of an American Playwright*. Ed. Marion Castleberry. Waco, TX: Baylor UP, 2004.

Freedman, Samuel G. "From the Heart of Texas." *New York Times Magazine* (9 Feb. 1986): 30–1, 50, 61–3, 73. Web. 1 Oct. 2015. <http://www.nytimes.com/1986/02/09/magazine/from-the-heart-of-texas.html>.

Hampton, Wilborn. *Horton Foote: America's Storyteller*. New York: Free Press, 2009.

Haynes, Robert W. *The Major Plays of Horton Foote: "The Trip to Bountiful," "The Young Man from Atlanta," and "The Orphans' Home Cycle."* Foreword Gerald C. Wood. Lewiston, NY: Mellen, 2010.

Lahaie, Scot, ed. *The Horton Foote Review*. Vol. 1. Lincoln, NE: iUniverse, 2005.

Moore, Barbara & David G. Yellin. *Horton Foote's Three Trips to Bountiful*. Dallas: Southern Methodist UP, 1993.

Porter, Laurin. *Orphans' Home: The Voice and Vision of Horton Foote*. Baton Rouge, LA: Louisiana State UP, 2003.

Skaggs, Merrill Maguire. "The Story and Film of *Barn Burning*." *Southern Quarterly* 21 (Winter 1983): 5–15.

Smith, Amanda. "Horton Foote: A Writer's Journey." *Varia* (July–August, 1987): 18–20, 23, 26–27.

Watson, Charles S. *Horton Foote: A Literary Biography*. Austin, TX: U of Texas P, 2003.

Wood, Gerald C. *Horton Foote and the Theater of Intimacy*. Baton Rouge, LA: Louisiana State UP, 1999.

_____, ed. *Horton Foote: A Casebook.* New York: Garland, 1998.

_____, ed. *Selected One-Act Plays of Horton Foote.* Dallas, TX: Southern Methodist UP, 1989.

_____& Marion Castleberry. eds. *The Voice of an American Playwright: Interviews with Horton Foote.* Macon, GA: Mercer UP, 2012.

Wood, Gerald C. & Terry Barr. "'A Certain Kind of Writer:' An Interview with Horton Foote." *Literature/Film Quarterly* 14 (1986): 226–37.

Yellin, David G. & Marie Connors, eds. *Tomorrow and Tomorrow and Tomorrow.* Jackson: UP of Mississippi, 1985.

Between South and West: Placing *The Young Man From Atlanta*

Robert Donahoo

When Horton Foote's *The Young Man From Atlanta* won the Pulitzer Prize for drama in 1995, it must have seemed a crowning, if belated, tribute for one of America's most prolific and successful playwrights. Yet the play was a Tony Award loser to Alfred Uhry's *The Last Night of Ballyhoo* when it finally reached Broadway in 1997, and a CBS proposal for a television film of the play fell through after the network demanded script changes that Foote would not accept—including having the mysterious young man of the title make a physical appearance, something that never happens in Foote's play (Hampton 238, 234). Moreover, reviews of the play in regional productions over the last almost twenty years have been kind, if not consistently laudatory—as if the play is more significant for having won an award than for its artistry.

Literary criticism has added little insight into this work that, set in Houston in 1950, tells the story of Will Kidder and his wife Lily Dale as they deal with the death of their son—a loss of double proportions, since the circumstances of his death suggest suicide and have revealed a hidden, possibly homosexual life. In a 1998 article, Gerald C. Wood offers an existential reading of the play that attempts to justify a positive view of the play's ending—a view undermined by Foote's own account of the outcome of events that inspired the play. Shirley Knight, who played Lily Dale in the Broadway production, has recounted that Foote told her, "within six months his uncle [the Will Kidder character in the play] found work again but died of a heart attack, and his aunt [the Lily Dale character] had to sell their house. For the rest of her life she was very religious, and never accepted the idea that her son had killed himself" (Gussow). Robert Haynes's 2006 article focuses coherently on the theme of disappointment, but it creates a strong sense that the play is message-driven, offering both a wake-up call and a guide for the problem of "finding strength" in the face of "the blindness and prejudice that have caused so much pain" (33).

For all their value, such readings leave much of the play unexplored and fail to do justice to its literary craftsmanship—particularly the play's relationship to southern literature and its use of regional ideas about place. They share a lack that Foote himself attributed to Will and Lily Dale Kidder, the play's two main characters: "They have no perspective," Foote explained to interviewer Jim O'Quinn. "They only know that there are things about their son they didn't know about, and didn't understand. And Will—who probably does know more than Lily Dale knows—doesn't want to know more" (Foote, "Eye" 188). In dwelling largely on themes and characterization, critics and scholars, too, omit the play's connection to an intellectual world beyond its sets. To grasp clearly the full vision of *Young Man*, a vision that stretches beyond existential commentary, requires discovering the drama's complex interaction with place defined both as regions and as specific cities. In particular, it demands a sense of the play's connection to southern literature's changing view of the West as well as the implications of spreading the play over two major cities: the "Atlanta" of its title and the "Houston" of its setting.

This play is hardly the first in which Foote has stressed place-focused tension. His most frequently produced work, *The Trip to Bountiful*, establishes a stark contrast between the entrapping and claustrophobic apartment of Ludie and Jessie Mae in Houston and the open spaces of Bountiful that Carrie Watts reaches in the final scene. Yet in that play, the two locations are geographically only a bus-ride apart, and their meanings are plain: urban vs. rural, present vs. past, reality vs. myth. In focusing on Atlanta and Houston, *The Young Man from Atlanta* creates a stress on two cities and two regions that requires a more nuanced examination of both.

Recent southern literary scholarship by Robert Brinkmeyer provides tools for launching that examination. In *Remapping Southern Literature: Contemporary Southern Writers and the West* (2000), Brinkmeyer explores his sense of post-Renascence[1] southern novelists moving out of the traditional Confederate South for points west of the Mississippi. And though he makes no reference to Foote's work, Brinkmeyer provides three key insights relevant to *Young Man*:

1. Traditional southern literature "tends to celebrate those who do not leave the community but integrate themselves into it ... without being completely subsumed by the community" (4).

2. Though the popular conception of southern literature is one that focuses on a North-South dichotomy, southern writers as early as the 1920s–1940s "shifted from a north-south to an east-west orientation, with the South now aligned as the East, characteristically described as a version of the settled society of premodern Europe, and the North as the West, a manifestation of the forces of rapacious expansion, which was viewed geographically as imperialist exploration and discovery and viewed economically as industrial capitalism" (5).

3. As literary history approaches the current moment, southern writers increasingly imagine the West as "a dream of starting over in a world wiped clean of history, of embracing the joy, wonder, and possibility found in a present unburdened by the past and one's own memories" (18).

These observations do not attempt to define or stake out the exact line where the South ends and the West begins: is it the Louisiana-Texas border or, as James Lee once described it, "an imaginary line that passes between Dallas and Fort Worth, goes to the west of Waco and the east of San Antonio, and enters the Gulf at Matagorda Bay" (46). Rather, Brinkmeyer treats South and West as psychic and ideological spaces, and his argument focuses its attention on the complexity and tension in the relationship between the South and the West—especially in light of Allen Tate's claim that, in the conflict between the values of the South and those of the West, the West "won" (7).

Brinkmeyer's potential relevance to Foote's work arises from Foote's description of his area of Texas as "very Southern" ("On *The Day*" 291) and is underscored by the fact that Foote's career spans the very years that Brinkmeyer examines to define the South-West relationship. Foote's first play, "Wharton Dance," was produced in 1940 (Castleberry 88), launching his career in an era in which Faulkner remained highly active (he produced the three novels of his Snopes trilogy as well as *Go Down, Moses, Intruder in the Dust, Requiem for a Nun,* and *A Fable* between 1940–1960) and in which Tennessee Williams, southern literature's most canonical playwright, rocketed to prominence (*The Glass Menagerie* opened in 1944). It is also a period that Foote shares with fellow Texan Katherine Anne Porter, whom he frequently named as a major influence on his work (see "From the Heart" 36 and "'A Certain'" 41 for two instances where Foote discusses Porter). At the same time, Foote's career continued well after Faulkner's death in 1962, the same year that saw Porter's active career end with the publication of *Ship of Fools* and a year after Williams's last commercial success, *Night of the Iguana.* In contrast to these canonical southern Renascence authors, the 1970s, 80s, and 90s were among Foote's most fruitful years, producing his nine-play *Orphans' Home Cycle* (1974–1977), his Academy Award-winning screenplay *Tender Mercies* (1983), *The Young Man From Atlanta* (1995), and at least a dozen other plays (Castleberry 469–73). If Foote shares his early career with the most academically esteemed of southern writers, his productivity outlasts them and ties him to a later generation.

Still, it is Brinkmeyer's analysis of specific southern authors that provides the most important insights for *Young Man,* beginning with his analysis of Porter's *Old Mortality.* Brinkmeyer argues that Miranda in Porter's work "expresses the dream of the West—a dream of starting over in a world wiped clean of history, of embracing the joy, wonder, and possibility found in a present unburdened by the past and one's own memories" (18). In Foote's play, Will Kidder proclaims a similar dream, one that rejects the past and traditional community. He makes only one reference to his early life, quickly eliding his past to deal with the present: "I want the best," he states in the play's opening scene:

> Since I was a boy. We were dirt-poor after my father died, and I said to myself then, I'm not going to live like this the rest of my life.

> Will Kidder, I said, you are going from now on to always have the best. And I have. I live in the best country in the world. I live in the best city. I have the finest wife a man could have, work for the best wholesale produce Company…(154).

Brinkmeyer notes of Porter's Miranda that the personal future she envisions "expresses not only her arrogance and pride but also her childishness," ultimately leaving her "isolate[d]" and "alienate[d]" (19). Will, too, over the course of Foote's play, reaches a similar destination, undergoing a series of Job-like losses: the death of his son, the loss of his job, the vanishing of his financial savings, his health, and his optimism. In the play's final scene, he tells his wife, "For the first time in my life, I don't know where to turn to or what to do. Here I am in the finest city in the greatest country in the world and I don't know where to turn. I'm whipped. I'm whipped" (202). The echo of his earlier brag remains, but his optimism is gone, replaced by an image with whiffs of the old South in its wake: that of a slave whipped into submission.

Critics determined to see Foote offering a vision of optimism would likely point out that Will's "whipped" speech is not his last words in the play. Indeed, Foote's text goes much further—but not toward optimism. Instead, Will makes his most naked confession of having "failed" his son, of being driven and upended by a life too focused on himself. He tells his wife:

> I tried to be a good father, but I just think now I only wanted him to be like me, I never tried to understand what he was like. I never tried to find out what he would want to do, what he would want to talk about … I was never close to him, Lily Dale. "How was your day?" "Fine, son, how was yours?" And then he was gone. [Pause] I want my son back, Lily Dale. I want him back. (204)

In the face of what is plainly an impossible desire, he can offer his crying wife only platitudes and conditional hopes: "Don't cry, Lily Dale," he says in the play's closing line. "Everything is going to be all right. If I go back to work and you start teaching, everything will be all right" (207).

For Will, the escape of the West's vision of opportunity and hope has been no escape at all. Indeed, it has put him in an unwanted servitude that recalls the antebellum South, left him hoping for a "sweet chariot" that will carry him to the home he desires as the stage lights fade. Through Will, then, Foote is creating a pattern that Brinkmeyer links to the Renascence writers of Foote's early career, writers who script escapes from the South as leading to the discovery of the West as a false haven—writers who encourage a return to traditional community.

Nevertheless, Foote does not retreat into nostalgia as the slavery image suggests. Rather, the play takes a different tack, exploring why the West fails Southerners. Foote's play addresses this issue through its never-seen title character: Randy Carter, the young man from Atlanta who enacts a mysterious, vampire-like role. Initially, the play merely identifies him as the roommate of Bill, Will and Lily Dale's dead son. But in the subtly crafted speech where he is first discussed, much more is implied:

> He was ten years younger than my son. He came here for the funeral and stayed at our house in Bill's old room. He told my wife that our son had become very religious in the year before his death and that every morning you could hear him praying all over their rooming house. I didn't believe it then and I don't believe it now…. During the funeral he got hysterical and cried more than my wife. She was comforting him and he was comforting her. He calls once a week to talk to me. God knows what he wants. Money, I suppose. Although he tells my secretary he just wants to stay in touch with Bill's dad. (157)

Before the play is over, audiences learn that Randy has taken $50,000 from Bill's grieving mother Lily Dale (172) in addition to at least $100,000 he had previously received from Bill (207). In siphoning funds from Lily Dale, he appears to be exploiting her grief—certainly Will believes this (176)—but Lily Dale defends him as truly needy: "I felt sorry for him," she tells Will. "He lost his job because he was so upset over Bill's death, and then his mother got sick and needed a serious operation, and then his sister had three small children and her husband deserted her…. That's the truth. That's what he told me" (176). For my purposes, the truth of Randy's tales is less important than that they represent the need of an exhausted region to draw sustenance from a fresh territory—a colonial relationship of exploiting a New World to sustain an older one. Given Brinkmeyer's stress upon the old South's standing, in the mind of southern writers, as a version of Europe, such a vision makes historical sense—especially given that in the "Spring 1950" (153) setting of the play, Europe was in the middle of the four-year Marshall Plan that sent $13 billion from the United States to rebuild the old world's war-ravaged societies (Mills 3).

However, there is a second, more complex tie to Europe connected to Randy: the homosexuality that *The Advocate* in its review of the play called "the only logical explanation for Bill's relationship with Randy and for his father's efforts to deny it" (Scanlan). Early in the play, Will describes his son in a way that explains setting off *The Advocate*'s "gaydar": "He was a fine young man. One of the best. We weren't anything at all alike, you know…. I'm crazy about sports. He never cared for them. Not that he was artistic like his mother. He wasn't. He had a fine math mind" (155). Later, he reveals that his son "never married. If he even went with a girl, we never knew about it" (156). At the age of thirty-seven, Bill travelled a lot for his work and shared a room with the much younger Randy, a name echoing a term the Oxford English Dictionary notes is of Scottish and English—European—origin and in its adjectival form can mean "lustful; eager for sexual gratification; sexually aroused" ("Randy"). Their relationship is hardly traditional—unless it is the homoerotic tradition of Europe from the Greeks to Oscar Wilde that surfaces also in classic southern works from *Huckleberry Finn* (see Fiedler) to *Cat on a Hot Tin Roof* (see Arrell). Certainly, their relationship works to erect an image of Bill in stark contrast to the phallic and hyper-masculine heroes of westerns, whom Richard Etulain has described as "courageous…, often a cowboy or at least a man on horseback, who combats evil by opposing villainous characters or institutions and who establishes (or reestablishes) order" (26). Bill may well have tried to fulfill this western stereotype, volunteering for the air force during World War II. His father reveals, "He was a bombardier. Came home without a scratch. Made I don't know how many bombing raids and didn't even get a scratch…. When the war was over, I wanted to bring him here in the business, but he would have none of it. He got a job in Atlanta" (155). Foote's text offers no more detail about Bill's war record, creating one of the play's many gaps that reinforce the mystery that is Bill. But given that Bill "volunteered first thing" when "the war came along" (155), it seems plausible that those air raids were over Europe. Such a possibility allows a reading that diagnoses Bill as suffering from a form of survivor's guilt or post-traumatic stress—a condition exasperated by seeing his war actions as an attack on the kind of world that would accept him. Unquestionably, Bill's war experience is linked to his severing ties with Houston—the West—and seeking recovery in a city emblematic of a South that historically saw itself as the heir to European culture and attitudes. Having played the Texas cowboy riding his modern-day horse through the skies over the Continent and helping to destroy it, he refuses to return to the West that Houston represents and opts instead for Atlanta, where he attempts to build a life with Randy away from Western values and demands.

If such a filling of the play's silent gaps is tortured or stretched, it is those very silences that enable it. As Will Kidder points out, Houston and Atlanta both offer business opportunities; yet one beckoned to Bill while the other did not. Absent any revelation from Bill himself, the gap can only be filled with the little actually known about Bill—knowledge dominated by the hints of his homosexuality, his need for a safe place to be with Randy. Moreover, this response to the play's gaps reveals that its action remains true to the tension between the regions: as Tate had observed, in the struggle between the South and the West, the West wins. And as the South vanishes in the face of the West's dominance, so, too, does Bill: drowning beneath the waters of an unnamed lake in Florida (155).

In both these instances—Randy as economic vampire and Randy as a sign of sexual Otherness—the traditional South through the metonymy of "Atlanta" is limned by the play, at least in Will Kidder's mind, as haunting and corruptive. Haunting, it entices southerners away from the raw West; corruptive, it destroys those it touches. It has these effects because they exist invisibly in the play's gaps, remaining undealt with—a fact underscored by the refusal of Foote's characters to come to terms with Randy. Instead, they opt to try to erase him, using a strategy that Brinkmeyer connects to a post-Renascence group of southern writers. In analyzing James Dickey's 1970 novel *Deliverance*, Brinkmeyer notes that its urban Georgian characters deal with their experience by rewriting history, making events "'unhappen'" so they can "rest easy, comfortable with the resecured borders between savagery and civilization that were temporarily dismantled by the 'unauthorized' version of what happened on that weekend canoe trip down the river" (38). Has Bill attempted to erase, make unhappen, his war experience and/or his closeted childhood in Houston by moving to Atlanta? The play is suggestive but finally unclear. However, Will and Lily Dale are clearly evoking such a strategy: Lily Dale by plunging into religion encouraged by Randy's claim that Bill had become very religious—something for which she has no evidence beyond Randy's word—and Will by sheer rejection of knowledge: "whatever the reasons," he tells Lily Dale as the play moves to its end, "I don't want to know. There was a Bill I knew and a Bill you knew and that's the only Bill I care to know about" (207). Here, the aptness of their son's name jumps across the footlights and off the page. For surely the play's closing line—"If I go back to work and you start teaching, everything will be all right" (207)—suggests that the bill to be paid for the heritage of the South and the West is an inescapable one.

Yet Brinkmeyer's most fascinating contribution to understanding this play is the insight that relates to Lily Dale. She comes to this play with her own unique history in Foote's work. Based on Foote's aunt, Lily Dale Coffee (Castleberry 400), the character appears in three plays in Foote's *The Orphans' Home Cycle*, including one that bears her name as its title. Laurin Porter has characterized Lily Dale as "pampered, coddled, and excused from difficult or onerous responsibilities" (63) in these earlier plays, and this basic characterization holds for *Young Man* as well. Actress Shirley Knight, who played Lily Dale in the Broadway production of *Young Man*, calls her "the most naïve character I've ever worked on" and sees a connection to Tennessee Williams's female leads, particularly Amanda Wingfield from *Glass Menagerie* and Blanche DuBois from *Streetcar*: they "fuel Lily Dale in a curious way," Knight has remarked, and they share a "delicacy" (Gussow).

Yet Brinkmeyer's work acts to point up Lily Dale's relationship to much more contemporary southern writing. Brinkmeyer argues that recent southern writing is structured by "a tension between the desire to bolt for freedom, a centrifugal force flying outward, and the desire to settle in a community, a centripetal force pulling inward." He continues:

> If most of these works begin with a straight line heading west, the tension between these two forces characteristically pulls that line back into a circle, the two forces now taut and balanced around a center point of home and community. The completed circle represents not enclosure but balance—balance between freedom and responsibility, conscience and selfishness, remembering and forgetting. And so, as much as these works center on flight and escape, they end up being most fundamentally about settling in and establishing communities. (67)

In Lily Dale that desire to "bolt to freedom," to escape into a metaphoric West, is seen in her turn to religion and the claims of Randy Carter about her son—matters already discussed here— while the turn inward, the turn back toward the South, is seen in an aspect of the play not yet discussed: a quiet but clear racism. In her first appearance in the play, she tells the following story:

> [d]uring the war, you know, Mrs. Roosevelt got all the maids in Houston to join the Disappointment Club.... It was just awful. A maid would say they were going to work for you. You would arrange the hours and the salary and she would be so nice and polite. Then the day she was supposed to start work, she wouldn't show up, and that meant she was a member of the Disappointment Club whose purpose was to disappoint white people. (165)

Robert Haynes argues that her insistence that others accept her view of history "indicates her separation from reality" and lack of judgment (30), but Brinkmeyer's comments push further, revealing this ideological position as evidence of the counter motion to the western escape of religion: a return to racist assumptions that have marked whites in the South. In fact, it is the characteristic approach to life that the play assigns to Lily Dale. As the play reaches a climax with Will's "I failed him" speech, Lily Dale responds with a confession about an event from the early days of her marriage to Will when she and her cousin brought two men to the house while Will was in Chicago. When Will returned unexpectedly, the young men were hustled out of the back door. "That was twenty years ago," she tells Will. "I don't know why I had to tell you that. It has bothered me all these years—not that I would have done anything wrong—" (203). The scene has little apparent relevance to the play's anxiety over the death of Bill or Will's job and health problems, but it is the motion that matters: invite in and then expel; sin and then confess; confess and then claim innocence. Lily Dale is headed in two directions at once, toward two metaphoric regions, seeking the return to balance within the community of her marriage.

Additionally, the fact that most audiences and readers will see both motions as flawed or insufficient serves to define her condition at the end of the play as the one that Brinkmeyer sees marking recent fiction: "being a refugee, …being displaced" (99). Unquestionably, her son's death, her husband's illness, their loss of financial security, and the casting of doubts about Randy Carter's view of her son have pushed Lily Dale out of her comfortable life. In the closing scene, for example, she tells Will that Randy "wished he could have gone down in the water that day with Bill. That's how much he loved him and missed him" (207). Her words suggest that she is expressing her own feelings, especially since the script immediately calls for her to cry, simulating the drowning and its displacement effects so common in literature from "Lycidas" to *The Waste Land*.

Examining the novels of Barbara Kingsolver, Brinkmeyer sees a trend in recent southern fiction to find in displacement what he labels Kingsolver's subject: "the miracles of human community" (99). And in seeking to claim a positive ending for Foote's play, Gerald Wood sees the result of Lily Dale's displacement as one of embracing "life's ineluctable mystery" (186). However, while it is possible to see the embrace of Will and Lily Dale in the stage direction that ends the play—"*He holds her as the lights fade*" (207)—as the forming of a small human community, a true marriage, that image of embrace is counterbalanced by the fading light. Will's insistence on a positive, take-charge western approach to the dissolution of old communities and ties is hardly given a resounding endorsement, while Lily Dale's acquiescence in tears seems more a lament or dirge than a Reveille. For Foote, the man who adapted Flannery O'Connor's "The Displaced Person" for film, such a darker view of displacement certainly makes sense, emphasizing, as O'Connor often did, the awful cost of any form of salvation (see, for instance, O'Connor's *Habit of Being* 354).

Without question, Brinkmeyer's analysis of the South-West relationship provides tools for uncovering a larger, regional conflict in *Young Man* that moves beyond the close readings, which often make his works seem like miniaturist wonders. But if such a reading relies on treating "Atlanta" and "Houston" as metonymies of their regions, their more specific connotations suggest yet other dimensions of Foote's play.

In his study *The Postsouthern Sense of Place in Contemporary Fiction*, Martyn Bone makes the case that, within southern fiction, Atlanta has been largely invisible, ignored by the South's "major fictional works" (142). For Bone, it is a "nonplace" that, due to "its long-established role as the locus classicus of the urban, capitalist 'New South'" has become "a hypercapitalist city that exists in a (cash) nexus between the local and the global, between material geography and abstract monetary flows" (140). Indeed, Bone argues that the one famous literary work to make extensive use of Atlanta, Margaret Mitchell's *Gone with the Wind*, makes Atlanta emblematic of the capitalist New South that thrives by rejecting the traditional southern agrarian way of life and embracing urbanization and modern business. In Bone's words, "it is the profit from Atlanta's urban development that, transferred to Tara, enables Scarlett's ideological fetishization of the antebellum homeplace as an Old South haven" (145).

Bone's analysis of Atlanta via Mitchell's novel has particular relevance, since it is that novel that links *Young Man*'s Texas-born, New York/New Hampshire based playwright to Georgia's metropolis. In 1972, at a time in his career when his finances were precarious, Foote accepted the job of writing the book for a London-based musical version of *Gone with the Wind* (Hampton 173). None of Foote's three major biographers to date offer detail about his work on the project, though Wilborn Hampton terms it "a huge and complex task" that required Foote to be in London away from his family and living on a tight budget (173–74; see also Castleberry 247–48; Hampton 173–76; Watson 112). Yet for all his time and sacrifice in getting Scarlett O'Hara singing on the stage, the show was not a success either in London or in a later revised staging in Los Angeles. According to Marion Castleberry, the entire project left Foote "discouraged and confused" (248). Nevertheless, in line with Bone's ideas about Atlanta's tie to capital and money flow, it managed to pay, providing, if not the hoped for windfall, enough income for Foote's daughter's wedding (Hampton 177).

In *Young Man*, while Will has to ask his son, "Why Atlanta?" (155), one obvious answer is money—the large sum Bill is able to save and give to Randy. For Bill, clearly Atlanta is, in part, about cash. At the same time, drawing on the image of Atlanta from *Gone with the Wind*, it proves to be more, providing a place to build a faux, idealized image in the wake of a war—World War II rather than the Civil War. Almost eight hundred miles from his parents, Bill can be the "fine young man" Will proclaims him to be (155) or he can be deeply religious, loudly saying "the most beautiful prayers," as Lily Dale believes him to be (167). All the while, Bill is an unknown, a nonperson, the ideal resident of a nonplace, and his death in a Florida lake, an unscheduled stop while traveling "for his company" (155), leaves only pain and intangible theories, not facts. In sum, the choice of placing Bill in Atlanta is far from arbitrary. Its history and literary past do the work of explaining Bill, while the play's text maintains a meaningful silence.

The characters in *Young Man* several times contrast Atlanta with Houston, the play's setting and the place Will calls "the finest city in the whole of the world" (155). Yet, as the dialogue between Will and Carson, a relative of Lily Dale's stepfather, suggests, the contrast is thin:

> CARSON: I met a fellow at the YMCA that said [Houston] was going to be the largest city in the South, and I said, "Hold on, mister, I came from Atlanta, and it's going to be the largest city in the South."
> WILL: It is like hell. Houston is the largest city in the South, and I tell you what, I give it ten years, fifteen, twenty, it will be the largest city in America, the largest and the richest. (187)

Other than a possible allusion to Houston's famous heat—it "shares the 30th parallel with the Sahara Desert and is somewhat south of Algiers and Baghdad" (Webb 17)—this exchange suggests the two cities differ only in terms of size, with both seeking bragging rights on that point. This is a view novelist Walker Percy—himself connected to Foote through his friendship with historian Shelby Foote, a third cousin to Horton (Foote, "Horton Foote" 182)—expressed in a 1978 essay: "You drive through Atlanta (or, for that matter, Dallas or Houston) and take a look around, and up, and you wonder, what is this place? Is this a place?" (28). Yet if Houston shares with Atlanta an image of nonplace-ness to passing tourists such as Percy, for Foote it is a more intimately known locale. Marion Castleberry observes that during the 1960s and 1970s, Foote saw "his hometown of Wharton...enveloped by sprawling urban expansion and technological advancement. Almost overnight, Wharton evolved from an insular community of thirty-five hundred people to a suburb of nearby Houston with a population of nearly ten thousand" (245). Not just a nexus for capital flow, Houston for Foote is a force that has grown more ominous in *Young Man* than it was in *The Trip to Bountiful*, where it functioned as a place of humiliation for Carrie Watts and a place "to prepare for her death" (Castleberry 162). Quite clearly in *Young Man*, change is the defining nature of life in Houston, change that can only be managed, according to Will's boss when he fires Will, by "younger men in charge" (162).

Interestingly, Houston has institutionalized and been defined by such change due to, as numerous commentators on the city note, rejecting zoning regulations (see Huxtable 222–23, Kamps 18, and Scardino et al. viii–ix for examples), creating what Bill Arning and Linda Shearer term an "identity as the unruly and lawless 'Wild West'" (9). Yet Donald Barthelme, whom *Literary Houston* calls "Houston's most celebrated writer" (Theis 215), makes a significant adjustment to the cowboy image of Houston:

> A community of largely bogus cowboys, or cowboys who are uneasy in their roles, provides interesting examples of amateur or do-it-yourself schizophrenia. Thus we have the moneyed cowboy whose money proceeds not from cattle but from a nice little plastics plant. To complicate the picture insanely, let us say he is also, in his rough-hewn way, a patron of the arts. Note that the drama here is generated by the delicious incongruity he presents—in his role of the cultured cowboy: "I died with my boots on of boredom in the Art Museum." When we remember that he is in fact not a cowboy at all but a plastics engineer, the multiple level of the charade is revealed, the lostness of the leading character established. (Barthelme 216)

This context of Houston's image clarifies Will's character. Typical of Foote's sparse scripts that leave much to the discretion of the theatrical production, the text offers minimal physical details beyond his being "*a hearty, burly man with lots of vitality*" (*Young Man* 153). His brag about his locale and his wife (154), combined with his faith in his competitive spirit (154), his assurance of his friends (163), and his belief in his ability to withstand misfortune (163) seem to mark him as a cowboy, but the marking is ironic. His job in the wholesale grocery business earns him Barthelme's description as bogus, suffering from "amateur or do-it-yourself schizophrenia"—a disease that only the assaults in the play bring to the surface.

Yet the assaults themselves are predictable from the setting in Houston. In a collection of essays about the city's architecture, aptly titled *Ephemeral City*, Peter Rowe notes an "ever-present and unvarnished capacity for destabilization and shape-shifting that makes Houston unique" and observes "a restlessness, temporary familiarity, espousal of individuality, and lack of concern for preservation" (vii). Steven Strom in a photographic study of Houston's history of building sees the same thing but more darkly, describing his book's primary purpose as "to impart some idea of the loss and disruption that has been inflicted on the residents of Houston, Texas, by the steady and systematic destruction of the city's built environment over the past century" resulting in "an almost spiritual or psychic level of loss" (1). For Strom, the loss of "childhood neighborhoods, schools, restaurants, stores, or churches" leaves Houstonians feeling "emotional isolation and dislocation from the city that they call home" (1).

If Will's brag suggests he is unconscious of such feelings, the play is not. When a former cook for the Kidders arrives in scene five, she ties the issue directly to Will and Lily Dale:

> ETTA DORIS: I went last week to try to find that house you all lived in when I worked for you. It's gone.
> WILL: Yes, it was torn down a while back.
> ETTA DORIS: They're tearing down everything in Houston, seems like to me. (199)

Young Man's Houston is not just another American city, but a wealth of detail that adds to the play's artistry. It is a place to build wondrous things, such as the Sunshine Southern Wholesale Grocery where Will works, or Lily Dale's musical dreams, or a beautiful family. But it is not a place that values the past or sustains it.

In part, this may stem from Houston's gulf coast geography: "low-lying, climatologically challenged, and flood-prone" (Rowe vii). Houston is perennially threatened by the possibility of hurricanes, tropical storms, even heavy rains. But while Foote explored this aspect of coastal Texas in his teleplay *The Night of the Storm* (March 21, 1961), later reworked into *Roots in a Parched Ground* for his *Orphans' Home Cycle* (see Castleberry 208–09 and Hampton 135–36), in *Young Man* the threat from water is pure metaphor, with, on one hand, Houston's storms transformed into the lake that takes Bill's life, and, on the other, Lily Dale's cascade of tears in the closing scene. The Houston setting becomes the plot, and, rather than suggesting the hope of Job-like recovery, Will and

Lily Dale's residing in Houston—not LA, New York, or Peoria—clarifies the patterns of loss and lostness they are doomed to repeat.

As with the application of Brinkmeyer's pattern, the use of the play's two named locations reveals layers of artistry and insight beyond the emotional melodrama of the plot and the fading topicality of homosexual revelation. Rather than suggesting the play is a regional and second-string *Death of a Salesman* or an *Angels in America* for the provinces, focusing on the region reveals in the play a sense of precision and specificity far different from Miller's universalized drama of middle-class despair and dehumanization or Kushner's gay fantasia. Indeed, it roots Foote's work in the American South's storied meditations on place. It sharpens the play's context and sets up dialogues that are ready to blossom if only they are heard and acknowledged.

Note

1.   Also spelled "Renaissance," the Renascence of southern literature refers to the works of William Faulkner, Katherine Anne Porter, Zora Neale Hurston, and Tennessee Williams, among other notable southern writers who emerged in the 1920s and 1930s.

Works Cited

Arrell, Douglas. "Homosexual Panic in *Cat on a Hot Tin Roof*." *Modern Drama* 51.1 (2008): 60–72. *MLA International Bibliography*. Web. 13 Oct. 2015.

Barthelme, Donald. Untitled essay. *Literary Houston*. Ed. David Theis. Fort Worth: Texas Christian UP, 2010. 215–18.

Bone, Martyn. *The Postsouthern Sense of Place in Contemporary Fiction*. Baton Rouge: Louisiana State UP, 2005.

Brinkmeyer, Robert H., Jr. *Remapping Southern Literature: Contemporary Southern Writers and the West*. Athens: U of Georgia P, 2000.

Castleberry, Marion. *Blessed Assurance: The Life and Art of Horton Foote*. Macon: Mercer UP, 2014.

Etulain, Richard W. *Re-Imagining the History of the American West: A Century of Fiction, History and Art*. Tucson: U of Arizona P, 1996.

Fiedler, Leslie. "Come Back To The Raft Ag'in, Huck Honey!" *Partisan Review* 15.6 (1948): 664–71.

Foote, Horton. "'A Certain Kind of Writer': An Interview with Horton Foote." An Interview by Gerald C. Wood and Terry Barr. *Literature/Film Quarterly* 14 (1986): 226–37. Rpt. in *The Voice of an American Playwright: Interviews with Horton Foote*. Ed. Gerald C. Wood & Marion Castleberry. Macon, GA: Mercer UP, 2012. 40–56.

_____. "Eye of the Beholder." An Interview by Jim O'Quinn. *American Theatre* 12 (1995): 22–36. Rpt. in *The Voice of an American Playwright: Interviews with Horton Foote*. Ed. Gerald C. Wood & Marion Castleberry. Macon: Mercer UP, 2012. 185–88.

_____. "From the Heart of Texas." An Interview by Samuel G. Freedman. *The New York Times Magazine* (9 Feb. 1986): 30–31, 50, 61–63, 73. Rpt. in *The Voice of an American Playwright: Interviews with Horton Foote*. Ed. Gerald C. Wood & Marion Castleberry. Macon, GA: Mercer UP, 2012. 28–39.

_____. "Horton Foote and *Tomorrow*." An Interview by Jerry Roberts. *Movie Talk from the Front Lines: Filmmakers Discuss Their Works with the Los Angeles Film Critics Association*. Jefferson, NC: McFarland, 1995. Rpt. in *The Voice of an American Playwright: Interviews with Horton Foote*. Ed. Gerald C. Wood & Marion Castleberry. Macon, GA: Mercer UP, 2012. 169–84.

_____. "On *The Day Emily Married*: An Interview with Horton Foote." An Interview by Robert Donahoo. *The Horton Foote Review* 2 (2009): 77–94. Rpt. in *The Voice of an American Playwright: Interviews with Horton Foote*. Ed. Gerald C. Wood & Marion Castleberry. Macon, GA: Mercer UP 2012. 285–300.

_____. *Three Plays: "Dividing the Estate," "The Trip to Bountiful," and "The Young Man From Atlanta."* Evanston, IL: Northwestern UP, 2008.

Gussow, Mel. "An Actress in Search of a Character Peeks in the Mirror." *New York Times*. The New York Times Company, 24 May 1997. Web. 15 Apr. 2014.

Hampton, Wilborn. *Horton Foote: America's Storyteller*. New York: Free P, 2009.

Haynes, Robert. "The Kidders and the Disappointment Club: A Critical Theme in Horton Foote's *The Young Man from Atlanta*." *Journal of American Drama and Theatre* 18.1 (2006): 24–33.

Huxtable, Ada Louise. "Deep in the Heart of Nowhere." *New York Times* (15 Feb. 1976). Rpt. in *Literary Houston*. Ed. David Theis. Fort Worth, TX: Texas Christian UP, 2010. 219–25.

Kamps, Toby. "No Zoning: Artists Engage Houston." *No Zoning: Artists Engage Houston*. Ed. Toby Kamps & Meredith Goldsmith. Houston, TX: Houston Contemporary Arts Museum, 2009. 17–31.

Lee, James W. "The Old South in Texas Literature." *The Texas Literary Tradition: Fiction, Folklore, History*. Eds. Don Graham, James W. Lee, & William T. Pilkington. Austin: College of Liberal Arts at the U of Texas at Austin and the Texas State Historical Association, 1983. 46–57.

Mills, Nicolaus. *Winning the Peace: The Marshall Plan and America's Coming of Age as a Superpower*. Hoboken, NJ: Wiley, 2008.

O'Connor, Flannery. *The Habit of Being: Letters*. Ed. Sally Fitzgerald. New York: Farrar, 1979.

Percy, Walker. "Going Back to Georgia." *Signposts in a Strange Land*. Ed. Patrick Samway. New York: Farrar, 1991. 26–38.

Porter, Laurin. *Orphans' Home: The Voice and Vision of Horton Foote*. Baton Rouge: Louisiana State UP, 2003.

"Randy, adj. and n.1." Def. 3. *OED Online*. Oxford UP, Sept. 2015. Web. 13 Oct. 2015.

Rowe, Peter G. "Foreward." *Ephemeral City: "Cite" Looks at Houston*. Ed. Barrie Scardino, Williams F. Stern, & Bruce C. Webb. Austin: U of Texas P, 2003. vii–viii.

Scanlan, Dick. "The Morning After." *Advocate* (29 Apr. 1997): 61–62. *Academic Search Complete*. Web. 20 Oct. 2014.

Scardino, Barrie, William F. Stern & Bruce C. Webb. "Preface." *Ephemeral City:"Cite" Looks at Houston*. Ed. Barrie Scardino, Williams F. Stern, & Bruce C. Webb. Austin: U of Texas P, 2003. viii–xi.

Strom, Steven R. *Houston Lost and Unbuilt*. Austin: U of Texas P, 2010.

Theis, David, ed. *Literary Houston*. Fort Worth, TX: Texas Christian UP. 2010.

Watson, Charles S. *Horton Foote: A Literary Biography*. Austin: U of Texas P, 2003.

Webb, Bruce. "The Name Game." *Cite: The Architecture and Design Review of Houston* (1 Sept. 1999): 16–20. Web. 14 Dec. 2015. <http://

---

offcite.org/wp-content/uploads/sites/3/2010/03/TheNameGame_
Webb_Cite46.pdf>.

Wood, Gerald C. "The Nature of Mystery in *The Young Man From
Atlanta.*" *Horton Foote: A Casebook.* Ed. Gerald C. Wood. New
York: Garland, 1998. 179–88.

Two Cultural Paradigms of Endurance: A Comparative Study of Horton Foote's *The Trip to Bountiful* and Lu Xun's "Blessing"_____

Xueying Wang

Endurance, especially the endurance of women, constitutes the essential theme of both Horton Foote's play *The Trip to Bountiful* and Lu Xun's short story "Blessing" (The Chinese title *zhufu*, which literally means blessing, refers to a sacrifice custom in Luzhen. It is also translated under the English title of "New Year's Sacrifice"). Steven Tötösy de Zepetnek regards "studying literature (text and/ or literary system) with and in the context of culture" (2) as an important area of comparative cultural studies, and this approach enables us to parallelize the study of culture instead of focusing solely on literary elements in one culture only. Based on such theoretical ground, this essay provides a comparative cultural analysis of the issue of endurance reflected in Horton Foote's *The Trip to Bountiful* and Lu Xun's "Blessing." Both Horton Foote and Lu Xun concern themselves with family life, the social entrapment of women, and individual resistance against familial or social oppressions. Though set in different temporal and spatial backgrounds, *The Trip to Bountiful* and "Blessing" share many parallel themes, scenes, and structures. Both Mrs. Watts and Xianglin Sao, the protagonists in these two works, live in historical periods of great social change and are confronted with personal, familial, and social struggles. As ordinary women, bearing their respective burdens, physical as well as psychological, they long for a spiritual home. However, *The Trip to Bountiful* and "Blessing" show two different paradigms of endurance: one that may be called a resistance-transcendence-endurance paradigm and another, an endurance-submission-despair paradigm. These categories reflect two types of tragic consciousness.

The Resistance-Transcendence-Endurance Paradigm in *The Trip to Bountiful*

The Trip to Bountiful recounts Carrie Watts' journey back to her girlhood home in Bountiful. On the trip, Mrs. Watts' dialogues with Thelma and the Sheriff are interspersed with recollections of her earlier life. Prevented by her father from marrying the man she loves, Carrie marries another man. Her first two children die at a very young age. Years later, she is forced to leave her rural home and move to Houston. Living in a cramped apartment with Ludie, her son, and Jessie Mae, her daughter-in-law, Mrs. Watts suffers from Jessie Mae's belligerence and harassment. Jessie Mae forbids Mrs. Watts to sing hymns and accuses her of habitual pouting, even though she lives on the three meals Mrs. Watts cooks every day. She also goes to the beauty parlor with Mrs. Watts' pension check. Her father's dominance is one reason for Mrs. Watts' unhappy marital life, and the industrialization and urbanization in the early twentieth-century American South may partly explain why Carrie Watts had to leave her farmland home. The growing popularity of consumer culture, which Jessie Mae represents, threatens to make Mrs. Watts' traditional way of life obsolete; however, Foote focuses more on Mrs. Watts' interior world than on extrinsic factors. The play presents Mrs. Watts' spiritual transformation in Bountiful, which provides her with strength to endure her worldly sufferings.

Mrs. Watts' desire for homecoming originates from her life-long yearning for freedom. In spite of being deprived of the freedom to marry the man she loves, she never abandons her pursuit of love. Even after her husband dies, she sits on the front gallery every day just to nod hello to her girlhood lover when he goes by the house. Such behavior indicates her resistance against patriarchy and loveless marriage. Compared to her Chinese counterparts, Mrs. Watts, a Western woman of individual subjectivity, cares more about her inner feelings than public opinion; whereas Chinese women, fettered by Confucian ethics of *sancongside* (three obediences and four virtues—in Chinese traditional culture, a woman was required to obey her father before marriage, her husband in marital life, and her sons in widowhood, and to cultivate four virtues of fidelity, physical charm, propriety in speech, and proficiency in needlework), have no other choice but to follow the Confucian moral rules. For them, fulfilling familial responsibilities is more important than pondering over what love means. In China, if a married woman loves any man other than her husband, she will be scorned by the community. In ancient China, even if a woman remarried after her former husband died, she could hardly escape the community's negative judgment. By comparison, Carrie Watts enjoys more freedom in a culture that features individualism, and her personal will outweighs public opinion.

As difficult as it is, Mrs. Watts manages to accept the sufferings of loveless marriage and the loss of a husband and two children. But when life becomes endless conflict with the domineering Jesse Mae in a two-room apartment, Mrs. Watts takes action to resist the meaninglessness and emptiness of life. She makes one last promise to herself—to see her home before death comes. Homecoming, as a topic of universal significance, has rich literary and cultural implications. In traditional China, homecoming was closely connected with kinship and familial responsibilities. According to Confucius, when parents are alive, adult children should not leave home but stay to look after their parents; if they do leave, they must work out ways to take care of their parents. Once they succeed outside, they should come back home with pride and honor to attend to parents. Parents live with their children's families, never deliberating ways to escape from home. However, for Mrs. Watts, home is not the city apartment where her remaining relatives live, but her countryside birthplace, her girlhood rural home in Bountiful, the place of order and tranquility in her memory, even though none of her family lives there. Therefore, as Robert W. Haynes points out, Mrs. Watts "decides to break house rules and depart in search of a more tolerable existence" ("Woman Escapes" 45). Homecoming is not just returning to a physical place, but regaining a spiritual space of freedom. Marian Burkhart explains that the trip to Bountiful enables the green land "to give Carrie the bountiful gift of understanding the strength of her roots.... It is an understanding that permits her to be again the woman she thought herself to be—someone large-souled enough to extricate herself from Jessie Mae's power-games" (111). When she arrives in Bountiful, she says with emotion: "It's so quiet. It's so eternally quiet. I had forgotten the peace. The quiet. And it's given me strength once more" (Foote, *Bountiful* 55). On the farm, her old way of life seems to revive, and she hums hymns freely. Thomas R. Cole notes, "Carrie is reconciled. Her soul is rested" (428). The spiritual transformation enables her release from worldly entrapment. When Ludie comes to retrieve her to Houston, and Jessie Mae informs her of the new rules for life in the apartment, Mrs. Watts accepts calmly. In the 1985 film adaptation, Carrie Watts, played by Geraldine Page, even gives Jessie Mae an unscripted kiss at this point.

In the final scene of the play, Mrs. Watts "drops gently on her knees, puts her hands in the dirt. She kneels for a moment holding the dirt, then slowly lets it drift through her fingers back to the ground" (60). Such a ritualistic presentation of a human gaining peace of mind in nature resembles Tao Yuanming's poetic description of returning to farmland. Tao Yuanming (365 CE–427 CE), an ancient Chinese poet, in his poem "Ah, Homeward Bound I Go!" (the Chinese title is *guiqulaixici*) recounts his life on a farm and expresses his enjoyment of working the land after he resigns from office (115–17). The poem reveals his Taoist pursuit of the unity of man and nature; however, what is implied in the poem is his aversion to the wickedness of official life and his grief at failing to fulfill the Confucian ambition of *xiushen qijia zhiguo pingtianxia* (rectifying the mind, taking care of the family, ruling the country, and promoting world peace). By retreating to nature, he escapes from worldly matters.

However, what on earth makes Mrs. Watts a person capable of enduring her previously intolerable life? Mircea Eliade, in his *The Sacred and the Profane: The Nature of Religion*, discusses the issue of religious nostalgia. Eliade argues that ontological nostalgia is rooted in every individual's heart. It indicates man's solicitude for another world, for a world of order and love. Christopher Dawson affirms that "there is in human nature a hunger and a thirst for the transcendent and the divine" (25). As for Mrs. Watts, Bountiful is her hometown in the ontological sense. Her dream of coming to

Bountiful originates in her religious nostalgia for a world of order and freedom. All her worldly sufferings never quench her faith in the existence of God. She loves the hymn "No, Not One" and often hums its chorus to herself, "There's not a friend like the lowly Jesus." She takes her Bible with her on the trip to Bountiful, comforts Thelma with Psalm 91—"He that dwelleth in the secret place of the most high, shall abide under the shadow of the Almighty," and regards the working out of her escape plan as reflective of the Lord's grace. When she arrives in Bountiful, she delights in the freedom of singing hymns on the farm, and, as one critic suggests, "The hymns resonate with memory, music, and the consolation of Mrs. Watts' traditional values" (Haynes, "The Nature of Nature" 27). Her religious nostalgia opens the door to the old religious order and peace, which has existed on the farm. A spiritual transcendence gives her strength to triumph over the once-empty life in the apartment. No matter what circumstances Mrs. Watts will face after she is brought back to Houston, she is ready to accept her fate.

According to Joan Herrington, Horton Foote believes strongly in "the spiritual component of great art and its ability to transcend human limitations" (6). He eulogizes Mrs. Watts' efforts to resist oppression of any kind and to pursue freedom and dignity. Crystal Brian argues that Foote is able to embody the ineffable and evoke the transcendent (181). What Laurin Porter regards as the "death-resurrection archetype" (207) and I call the resistance-transcendence-endurance paradigm, gives evidence that Mrs. Watts will endure what the future brings.

The Endurance-Submission-Despair Paradigm in Lu Xun's "Blessing"

In this section, I will analyze Xianglin Sao's way of endurance as reflected in Lu Xun's short story "Blessing" (1924), comparing it to that of Mrs. Watts and her journey to acceptance. Xianglin Sao, a representative of submissive Chinese women, suffers both at home and at work, yields to Confucian traditions, and never makes her way to acceptance as does Mrs. Watts. If Mrs. Watts' story occurred in China, the ending would be very different. After she gets married,

Mrs. Watts would not grapple with whether she loves her husband or not, but would instead have to fulfill the responsibility of being a wife, which means obeying her parents-in-law, taking care of her husband, and giving birth to children so as to carry on her husband's family name. After her husband dies, it would be inappropriate for her to show any affection to her previous lover. Upon the deaths of her children, with no preachers to turn to, she would probably resign herself to destiny. Living together with her son and daughter-in-law, she would never struggle to escape from home to a place where no relatives survive. To put it in a nutshell, she would submit herself to *li*, the Confucian norms of ritual propriety, just as Xianglin Sao does in Lu Xun's "Blessing."

Lu Xun (1881–1936), the father of modern Chinese literature and an important figure of the New Culture Movement (May 4, 1919), maintains in his fiction that the feudal moral code, in essence, is life-destroying and that the Chinese people, lacking in subjective consciousness, assume physical roles of servility. He claims that throughout Chinese history, all eras fall into two types—one is the time when man is capable of gaining his stable position of being a slave, and the other is when man strives to become a slave but cannot. Quite a few scholars criticize the evils of the Confucian ethical code revealed in "Blessing" and claim that Xianglin Sao is reduced to a sacrifice for feudal theocracy, clan authority, and patriarchy. What needs to be pointed out is that Xianglin Sao, lacking in individual consciousness, does not realize that it is Confucian moral principle that oppresses her to the edge of death, nor does she know how to fight against such a powerful moral system. Even though she does attempt to resist, she resists only by halves, only to submit herself at last to the feudal moral codes. Therefore, she is doomed to die a pathetic death.

Xianglin Sao shares common life experiences with Mrs. Watts. Both of them are married to men they do not love, both suffer from the loss of husband and children, and both hunger for a spiritual home. However, the endings of their stories differ tremendously. One reason lies in that they live in heterogeneous social communities. Unlike Mrs. Watts, who lives in an individualistic society featuring neighborly love, and receives help, support, and encouragement from the Sheriff and Thelma, as well as preachers, Xianglin Sao lives in a collectivistic society, which features strict hierarchy: she is teased by the villagers, and her story is received with contempt. Si Shu (the narrator's fourth uncle), an old student of the imperial college and guardian of Confucian rites, views Xianglin Sao as a morally degenerate woman because she marries twice. He forbids her to prepare the sacrifice for the ancestor worship ritual. Liu Ma, a superstitious woman, blames Xianglin Sao for marrying again and threatens her that the King of Hell will cut her into two halves for her two husbands. Even the young scholar, the narrator of the story, whom Xianglin Sao reveres, does not show any support or encouragement to Xianglin Sao but observes her sufferings from a distance.

The major reason for Xianglin Sao's tragedy lies in the fact that she lacks subjective consciousness. She does not even know that it is the Confucian moral code that causes her tragedy, let alone how to resist it. At a young age, she is married to a man ten years older than she. Though Lu Xun does not make it clear whether it is an arranged marriage, it is probably so, for in traditional Chinese society, a girl does not have the freedom to choose a husband by herself and can only follow her parents' arrangement. When Xianglin Sao's first husband dies, she does take action to resist familial oppression by escaping from her mother-in-law's house and finding a laborious job as a maidservant at Si Shu's house in Luzhen. Xianglin Sao's pursuit of economic independence fails when her mother-in-law grabs her wages, takes her back home by force, and marries her to another man simply for money. To protect her chastity, she resists marrying again and, on the first night of her second marriage, throws herself against a corner of a table, injuring her head. However, she gradually compromises, acts as an obedient wife, and gives birth to a son. The issue of loveless marriage, which disturbs Carrie Watts, never bothers Xianglin Sao. After her second husband dies of typhoid fever, and her son is eaten by a wolf in the forest, Xianglin Sao is driven out of her home by her husband's brother. She has no alternative but to work at Si Shu's again and endure the villagers' judgment against her loss of chastity. Following Liu Ma's advice, in order to atone for her sins, Xianglin Sao buys a threshold at the Tutelary God's Temple to be her substitute so that people can trample on it. To her disillusion, after she buys the threshold, Si Shen (Si Shu's wife) still considers her an unclean woman and prohibits her from preparing the sacrifice for the ancestor worship ritual, shattering her dream of self-salvation. Devoid of individual subjectivity, Xianglin Sao takes Si Shen's judgment as authoritative and becomes what Guimei Li calls the passive occupant and victim of the traditional ethical code (24).

The structure of "Blessing" is similar to that of *The Trip to Bountiful*. On the trip to Bountiful, Mrs. Watts recalls her personal story of earlier years. In "Blessing," the first-person narrator recounts Xianglin Sao's tragic story during his short stay at home for celebrating the blessing ritual at the end of the year. Homecoming has different meanings for Mrs. Watts, Xianglin Sao, and the narrator of "Blessing." Mrs. Watts' return to Bountiful is, as Laurin Porter puts it, "redemptive, restoring to her a sense of integrity and wholeness" (203). The spiritual transformation gives Mrs. Watts power to transcend worldly concerns. Xianglin Sao, however, is forced to return to her first husband's home to be married off to a stranger in exchange for the bride price, which is used to get her brother-in-law a wife. Having undergone the loss of two husbands and one only son, and having been driven out of her second husband's home and her master Si Shu's house, Xianglin Sao asks the narrator whether those who die will meet their families in hell. She still longs for a home, but the ambiguities concerning the existence of families in hell drive her to despair. As for the narrator, to return to the native place is simply to follow the social etiquette of returning home for the blessing ritual, which is a great event in Luzhen at the end of each year when people pay tribute, such as chicken and pork, to their ancestors and seek good fortune for the coming year. Accustomed to the ways of life and trend of thoughts in the city, he finds the short stay in Luzhen depressing and tries to escape from the old house, the miniature of the traditional society of life-destruction, as soon as possible. However, not knowing the way out of the Confucian dilemma, he falls into the trap of nihilism.

By recounting Xianglin Sao's tragic story, Lu Xun attacks Confucian gender hierarchies. Xianglin Sao does not even have a name, for Xianglin is her first husband's name, and Xianglin Sao means Xianglin's wife. In her society, it is women who prepare the sacrifice for the blessing ritual; however, they are excluded from participating in the worship ritual. Unlike so many female characters in Foote's plays who embody the dignity of being human, Lu Xun's female characters seem ignorant of the origin of their suffering. While the former may suffer from domineering parents, irresponsible husbands, and wild children, they endure with courage; the latter suffer from Confucian devaluation of women and surrender their subjectivity to feudal ethics.

Two Cultural Paradigms of Tragic Consciousness

The different modes of endurance presented in *The Trip to Bountiful* and "Blessing" reflect distinctive paradigms of tragic consciousness in western and Chinese cultures. The essence of Western tragedy lies in conflict between the protagonist's interior desire and the obstacle he/she is confronted with. The spirit of tragedy is embodied in the protagonist's high sense of resistance against fate or oppression of any kind. What matters is not the extent of suffering, but the protagonist's attitude towards it when he/she is forced to the edge of life and death. The audience is often shocked by the strength, dignity, and sublimity reflected in the character's struggle. In the Chinese context, however, tragic consciousness is more connected with bitter circumstances and painful consequences, rather than the spirit of resistance. The Chinese classic tragedy is originally categorized as songs of grief (*aiqu*), which focus on the protagonist's miseries instead of inner conflicts. In the words of Yuanyi Xiong, "the tragic characters rarely experience any inner conflict" (60). The conflict the protagonist undergoes is of ethical implication, and it develops between the good and evil forces. The protagonist, as an ethical persona, suffering from traditional ethical norms, fails to take the initiative to fight against mental bondage. Even though some characters do resist, their struggle ends up with compromise, which arouses the audience's feeling of compassion.

Aristotle, in his *Poetics*, regards tragedy as a process of imitating a serious action. It often involves the suffering or death of the protagonist, which arouses the audience's feeling of pity and fear. The tragic plots include suffering, reversal (change of circumstance), and recognition (sudden awareness of the truth). In a sense, *The Trip to Bountiful* can be regarded as a tragedy with a complex plot, which includes suffering, reversal, and recognition. Mrs. Watts, the protagonist, embodies the tragic consciousness of taking the initiative and struggling for freedom. Mrs. Watts' endurance model is resistance-transcendence-endurance, and she finally triumphs over worldly troubles and is willing to endure whatever comes in life, which embodies the Christian notion of endurance. Her struggle to get to Bountiful reflects the spirit of tragedy, i.e., the sense of protest and the sublimity of humanity. In Houston, she suffers from the conflict between a strong desire for spiritual freedom and the realities of apartment life. She tells the Sheriff she wants to understand "Why my life has grown so empty and meaningless. Why I've turned into a hateful, quarrelsome, old woman. And before I leave this earth, I'd like to recover some of the dignity...the peace I used to know... It's my will to die in Bountiful" (Foote, *Bountiful* 48). Patrick McGilligan observes that "Horton Foote writes about people who—though they are scarred by family, society, or harsh experience—remain admirably indomitable" (8), and Carrie Watts is clearly such a character.

By comparison, Xianglin Sao, entrapped by feudal moral demands, grieves at her miserable fate, but lacks the spirit of resistance. Unlike Mrs. Watts, who knows what she pursues and takes action to reach it, Xianglin Sao does not know how to endure the miseries of life. She endures as much as she can, only to recognize that she is powerless to endure any more. Submitting unconsciously to the authority of Confucian theocracy, patriarchy, and clan power, she finds no justification and no strength for living on. Devoid and deprived of any independent, individual consciousness, she feels impotent to deal with the circumstances of life; she has no way out

---

but to die. Her dilemma reflects the tragedy of losing individual consciousness, as well as the tragedy of a culture that does not provide people with the spirit of independence and transcendence, but degrades them to be physical occupants of Confucian ethical roles.

The differences between the paradigms of endurance and tragic consciousness reflected in *The Trip to Bountiful* and "Blessing" are related to the authors' distinctive styles of writing and the cultural resources they draw inspiration from. Horton Foote, always exploring the redemptive possibilities of human fortitude, often ends his plays with the main characters' spiritual regeneration. For example, in his Pulitzer Prize-winning play *The Young Man from Atlanta*, both Lily Dale and Will Kidder, suffering from their homosexual son's suicide, try at first to gain comfort from the lies they create for themselves, whether it is gaining comfort from a deceitful stranger or evading agony by work. However, when forced to face the truth of life—suffering—they face it with courage. Undergoing spiritual regeneration, Lily Dale returns to giving piano lessons, and Will Kidder decides to resume work in the same company he has previously decided to leave. Life is difficult, but they carry on. Foote observes that it is a mystery why some people are able to move on, while others are not. In his works, Foote investigates what Gerald C. Wood, quoting a phrase from Foote, calls "the 'great mystery' about the sources of courage and personhood" (xix). In *The Trip to Bountiful*, Mrs. Watts shows resolute courage to pursue her dream of freedom. Her transcendental experience of reaching Bountiful gives her power to endure worldly sufferings.

Lu Xun is among the first group of Chinese writers in history to criticize Confucian ethics and seek enlightenment and salvation for individuals. He is keenly aware of the Confucian devaluation of women, the Confucian emphasis on following destiny and avoiding conflicts, and the absence of individual subjectivity and transcendental pursuit in Confucian thought. Confucianism, as the prevailing orthodoxy and ethical philosophy in China for over two thousand years, requires people to follow their prescribed roles in a society of strict hierarchy. Women, at the bottom of the hierarchical system, are forced to obey wifely ethical codes. Bound by a whole set of moral rules on how to behave in a collective society, people can hardly develop a sense of individual subjectivity and defiance. The Confucian evasion of topics concerning religion prevents people from cultivating a spiritual pursuit that might transcend the sufferings caused by the feudal ethical code.

When Xianglin Sao asks the narrator questions about the other world, she desires to get help so as to endure her worldly miseries; however, the narrator, not having thought seriously about these topics, cannot provide an answer that may help her to survive. The ambiguities of his answer weigh down her heart with more agonies and drive her to suicide. As for the narrator himself, he is depressed at the news of Xianglin Sao's death. However, restrained by the Confucian philosophy of avoiding conflict, he withdraws from Xianglin Sao's suffering. On the one hand, he criticizes the maladies of the old feudal culture; but, on the other, he is incapable of resisting it effectively, which reflects the dilemma of some scholars of the New Culture Movement, such as Hu Shi (1891–1962). As a representative of the modern Chinese intellectual, Hu Shi advocates freedom of marriage and emancipation of women, but submits to arranged marriage in person, which makes him, the advocator of new culture, an embarrassed follower of the old culture. Unlike Si Shu, who sticks to feudal ethics, Hu Shi criticizes the concepts of Confucianism, but it is beyond his ability to break through the bondage of tradition. In "Blessing," with no idea about the existence of/in the other world, it is beyond the narrator's capability to enlighten Xianglin Sao and save her from the sufferings of this world. Lu Xun criticizes the narrator's compromise with such Confucian codes as avoiding conflicts and evasion of the questions concerning the other world, as well as his coldness towards Xianglin Sao; however, Lu Xun shows deep sympathy towards him. He expects that this young scholar, on his future trip back home, may bring spiritual enlightenment to tragic figures like Xianglin Sao. By recording the tragedies of individuals who are deprived of subjectivity, Lu Xun voices his compassionate concern towards the deficiencies of Chinese culture.

To conclude, through a comparative approach to literature, this essay brings us closer to two great works that concern themselves with the sufferings of mankind, so as to see what is foreign to us in a way that we can understand ourselves better. It helps us to observe the issues of endurance and tragic consciousness in different cultures. With an introspection on Chinese culture, this essay reveals more of this culture's deficiencies than of its strengths. Chinese literature does not pay sufficient attention to presenting the inner conflicts of human beings and their transcendental pursuit in face of the unavoidable pains of life. The eulogy of individual subjectivity and struggle reflected in Horton Foote's *The Trip to Bountiful* contrasts sharply with the oppression of individual consciousness in Confucianism, which is designed to meet the needs of a collectivistic society. The Confucian idea of obeying an ethical code and following destiny, to some degree, cripples Xianglin Sao's subjectivity and causes her tragedy. Therefore, the comparative reading of Foote and Lu Xun helps us to develop a deeper understanding of Foote's transcendental vision of American family life and to sympathize with Lu Xun's concern for the tragic consciousness in the "optimistic" Chinese culture, which centers on conforming to various moral norms of this life, while disregarding the existence of the spiritual world.

Acknowledgments

I am grateful for a travel grant from the DeGolyer Library of Southern Methodist University, which has enabled me to do research in the Horton Foote Archive, making this essay possible. I appreciate the gracious support provided by Dr. Russell Martin, director of the library; Ruth Ann Elmore, assistant director of the Clements Center for Southwest Studies; and Cynthia Franco, librarian in the Horton Foote Archive.

Works Cited

Aristotle. *Poetics*. Trans. Gerald F. Else. Ann Arbor: U of Michigan P, 1967.

Brian, Crystal. "Horton Foote: Mystic of the American Theatre." *The Playwright's Muse*. Ed. Joan Herrington. New York: Routledge, 2002. 181–206.

Burkhart, Marian. "Horton Foote's Many Roads Home." *Commonweal* 4 (1988): 110–115.

Cincotti, Joseph A. "Horton Foote: The Trip from Wharton." *Backstory 3, Interviews with Screenwriters of the 1960s*. Ed. Patrick McGilligan. Berkeley: U of California P, 1996.

Cole, Thomas R. "Aging, Home and Hollywood in the 1980s." *The Gerontologist* 31.3 (1991): 427–30.

Dawson, Christopher. *The Formation of Christendom*. New York: Sheed & Ward, 1967.

Eliade, Mircea. *The Sacred and the Profane: The Nature of Religion*. Trans. Willard R. Trask. New York: Harcourt Brace Jovanovich, 1987.

Foote, Horton. *The Trip to Bountiful. Horton Foote: Collected Plays: Volume II*. Lyme, NH: Smith & Kraus, 1996.

_____. *Selected One-Act Plays of Horton Foote*. Ed. Gerald C. Wood. Dallas: Southern Methodist UP, 1989.

Haynes, Robert W. "The Nature of Nature in *The Trip to Bountiful*." *The Major Plays of Horton Foote: "The Trip to Bountiful," "The Young Man from Atlanta" and "The Orphans' Home Cycle."* Lewiston, NY: Mellen, 2010.

_____. "Woman Escapes: An Ibsenian Theme in Horton Foote's Play *The Trip to Bountiful*." *The Horton Foote Review* 2 (2009): 40–53.

Herrington, Joan. "Introduction." *The Playwright's Muse*. Ed. Joan Herrington. New York: Routledge, 2002.

Li, Guimei. "A Brief Statement on the Family Ethical Spirit of China and Western Nations." *Journal of Social Science of Hunan Normal University* 34 (2005): 20–23.

Lin, Yutang. *The Importance of Living*. Beijing: Foreign Language Teaching and Research Press. 1998.

Lu Xun. "New Year's Sacrifice." *The Real Story of Ah-Q and Other Tales of China: The Complete Fiction of Lu Xun*. Trans. Julia Lovell. New York: Penguin, 2009. 160–177.

McGilligan, Patrick. *Backstory 3: Interviews with Screenwriters of the 60s*. Berkeley: U of California P, 1997. Web. 4 Oct. 2015. <http://ark.cdlib.org/ark:/13030/ft138nb0zm/>.

Porter, Laurin. *Orphans' Home: The Voice and Vision of Horton Foote.* Baton Rouge: Louisiana State UP, 2003.

Tötösy de Zepetnek, Steven. "From Comparative Literature Today toward Comparative Cultural Studies." *CLCWeb: Comparative Literature and Culture* 1.3 (1999). Web. 26 Jun. 2015. <http://dx.doi.org/10.7771/1481-4374.1041>.

Wood, Gerald C., ed. "Introduction." *Selected One-Act Plays of Horton Foote.* Dallas: Southern Methodist UP, 1989.

Xiong, Yuanyi. "The Form of Chinese Tragedy: A Comparative Study of *Peach Blossom Fan* and *Hamlet.*" *Comparative Drama* 7 (1998): 57–62.

CRITICAL
READINGS

Horton Foote: A Not-So Bitter Southerner_____

Terry Barr

Finding Foote

It's getting late on Eastern Standard Time. After nine o'clock, and
I've indulged in too many mugs of generic American beer. I walk
into the rental that I share with my wife's family—refugees from the
Islamic Republic of Iran—and my sister-in-law says,

"You had a phone call."

She's smiling in that knowing way, and it's not the beer that
keeps me from guessing correctly. For who would guess that Horton
Foote had called your rental home on a Monday night, asking you to
call him back even if it's ten o'clock, or eleven?

"At night? This night?" I ask.

"Yes, tonight. He said to call because you're writing a
dissertation on his work."

That is true. A few days earlier, I had called Foote's agent
and left a message saying that while I understood that he must be
extremely busy, if Mr. Foote had any time to spare, I would love to
interview him for my doctoral thesis. I left my number. And in many
ways, left my request in the part of my brain that thinks, "This likely
won't happen."

I call Mr. Foote, Horton, as he quickly urges me to refer to
him, after he answers. He is so pleasant, so welcoming, but owing
to nerves and the beer, I no longer remember what we say exactly,
especially now, thirty years later. What I do remember is that not
only does he welcome my asking questions and writing about his
career, he invites me to New York for a proper interview. A few
months later, my friend Jerry (who's writing a book on Horton), his
son Tim, and I drive from Knoxville to New York, straight through
the night. We pull off at the New Jersey Turnpike's official rest stop
for a couple of hours' sleep, but by ten that morning, we are sitting
in Horton Foote's Horatio Street apartment in the West Village.

I had read all of Horton's collected plays by then and had viewed both *To Kill a Mockingbird* and his PBS *American Short Story* adaptation of "The Displaced Person." I'll have more to read after our meeting because, as one of the gentlemanly benefits of getting to know Horton, he sends me unpublished manuscripts of many plays that I have and have not heard of.

"Who does this?" I wonder. Maybe many writers would have, and maybe many southerners would not have. To me, though, and I'll always believe this, the southerner and writer in Horton Foote encouraged his generous act. I was a twenty-nine-year-old PhD candidate. A nobody. He was the man who made Harper Lee's novel sing on screen. And now he had just released his own screenplay, *Tender Mercies*. Maybe all publicity is good, but in my view, Horton had very little to gain by trusting me with his work. He wasn't the kind to be flattered either.

In Foote's apartment, Jerry, more seasoned than I, asked most of the questions. But one question kept disturbing me, and I wasn't sure how to ask it. My uncertainty was bred by my fear that my question would offend. And yet as Horton answered and elaborated on everything we asked, I decided that we were all men here— excepting, that is, his wife Lillian who kept refilling our coffee cups—and no question I could ask would deflate this writer or our visit.

I looked at my notes before I spoke, getting everything right.

"Horton, at the end of your play *The Traveling Lady*, Georgette turns to Slim, the man driving her out of town, and says 'From Lovelady to Tyler, from Tyler to Harrison, from Harrison to the Valley. Margaret Rose [her daughter], we sure do get around' (qtd. in Barr 106). My question is this: was Georgette modeled after Faulkner's "Lena Grove," who at the end of *Light in August* says, 'My, my. A body does get around. Here we ain't been coming from Alabama but two months, and now it's already Tennessee'?" (qtd. in Barr 106).

In my dissertation, all I cite for a response was that Foote admitted that Faulkner's novel did have some influence on *The Traveling Lady*. I think he smiled at me when he spoke, and then we moved on to other subjects. Even with graduate degrees nearly attached to my name, I think I was quite naïve in that moment. My thought was that Horton Foote had wholesalely "borrowed" the plot and character of Faulkner's work for his play. In my head, I questioned the ethics of such borrowing, and, for a time anyway, Horton Foote and his work were diminished for me.

However, tomorrow and tomorrow and tomorrow have a way of distancing all of us from naivety and from judging people too harshly. Time also affords us a perspective, one that allows us to see that artists struggling to be seen, read, and heard adapt what they can, borrow what they need, and seek themes that speak to them of their own experience, the stuff of life.

Later, I learn that Foote always admired Faulkner and had read him enthusiastically ever since the 1940s, as any southern writer who would test himself might (Castleberry 194). And, as is true with Faulkner, there are certain southern themes that Foote pays homage to, that he expands, and that he creates anew for his work. The themes he chose or harkened toward, in my view, have announced him not just as a writer, but a southern writer completely in the grain of the masters he read or was contemporary to. These themes—a focus on place, a portrait of a strong individual who defies those around him or her and pursues a dream of a social ideal—were sharpened in Foote by his adaptation of crucial southern tales. Foote never admitted this to me, but I believe that had he not adapted Faulkner's "Tomorrow," "Old Man," and "Barn Burning," O'Connor's "The Displaced Person," and Lee's *Mockingbird*, Foote's central and best films in the 1980s—especially *Tender Mercies*—would not have been as strong, would not have so subtly and richly drawn characters who embody these southern themes. These characters don't exactly win and maybe aren't even admired except by those who more completely know their story. Yet they are characters that, because of their dreams and shortcomings, stir us to consider the ongoing realities of our region and our continuing southern literary Renaissance.

The Character of Southern Giants

When one considers the giant works of the southern literary canon, characters such as Quentin Compson, Thomas Sutpen, Joe Christmas, Hazel Motes, and Atticus Finch come most easily to mind. These characters' absorption of place, propriety, dynasty, justice, and racial and religious lineage serves to guide, limit, doom, and sometimes exalt them, as such ideas have seemingly always marked the southern mind. Among the many great problems with such characters and their environment is that so few others in their company understand them, or even try to. It's difficult to make sense of a man or a woman's actions if the person's background story, deepest outrage, or view of the world is largely unknown. In Faulkner's work, Quentin Compson is depressed to the point of suicide when he understands that one day he'll quit caring about his sister Caddy's wanton behavior. Thomas Sutpen can never compensate for the poor mountain boy who was ordered to the back door by a Negro servant. Joe Christmas has been "watched" by ol' Doc Hines and led to believe that he is something he might not be. And Flannery O'Connor's Hazel Motes? Well, some actions and views are forever a mystery, though we know that religion and sex are often morphed into one entity.

The commonality in these characters is a deep flaw, not so much of their own nature as one that arises because they are born into a place and time that offer severe judgment: an era when justice itself was compromised by Jim Crow, fundamentalist Protestantism, and a social hierarchy that not only determined, but required a mindset that dictated who was better than whom. Individuals who could meet this flaw, conquer it, or even hold their own against it, seem to have been few. But these are the few that Horton Foote was drawn to in his writing: the ones who surely appealed to him most in his choice of adaptations—adaptations, again, which sharpened his own original creations.

Many of Foote's biographers and critics have pointed out that Foote's work, including his adaptations, place him squarely in the "Southern Author" sub-genre of fiction/drama (Briley 49–50 and Castleberry 194, 198). The most crucial of these southern themes for

Foote, as Rebecca Briley correctly asserts, is his focus on "…family issues, father-child relationships in particular." In his adaptations of works by Faulkner, Lee, and O'Connor, she argues, "Foote deals compassionately with the borrowed characters, suspending the plot to linger on their development and sometimes offering them a more healthy society than they had in the original" (50). His earliest adaptations—of Faulkner's "Old Man" and "Tomorrow"—illustrate Briley's point clearly. The male protagonists in both plays sacrifice themselves—physically and spiritually—for the rescue and reputation of the helpless, the needy, a woman with a child whom they pity or love. For their efforts, the unnamed protagonist of "Old Man" gets an extended prison sentence for "escaping," and Jackson Fentry of "Tomorrow" refuses to condemn the boy who, for a few years, he raised all alone. No other character in these two stories understands why the men do what they do. They won't reveal their minds and hearts, either, and are thus sentenced to a fate of ridicule, imprisonment, and infamy. While the reader knows the truth, what we do with that truth as we examine these plays against our own world is certainly up to us. In Foote's adaptation of "Old Man," however, the woman the convict rescues will wait for him while his sentence is served. There are two hearts there, beating as one.

Though these Faulkner adaptations earned Foote only mixed reviews, his adaptation of *To Kill a Mockingbird* not only won him an Academy Award for Best Adapted Screenplay, but it was also undertaken at the request of author Harper Lee herself (Castleberry 213). Briley comments that it didn't take Foote long, once he digested the novel, to realize that the southern atmosphere Lee created was akin to his own:

> The shared penchant for detailed storytelling, as well as the concerns for History and place, were there; Foote felt very much at home with her small-town, Depression-era setting, affectionately peopled with a cross-section of Southern "kinfolks" from the educated to the illiterate, the elderly to the eccentric. But the screenwriter most identified with Atticus Finch's family dealing with loss and reconciliation. (57)

Atticus Finch will be the model for many of Horton Foote's primary characters: a good man who, despite the social forces swirling around him, treats those he encounters with dignity and human concern.

Most of us know the story of Atticus Finch, played in the film by Gregory Peck, and his children, Scout and Jem, though we might forget that it portrays a world where cruelty, bigotry, and racial injustice are part of ordinary life. Briley points out that in Foote's adaptation, however, the "coarser" language is toned down, as are descriptions of both Mayella Ewell's rape and the suggestion that her father also sexually abused her (59). Whatever one may think of Foote's decisions to downplay these cruder aspects, he retains two crucial scenes featuring two interrelated themes that not only demonstrate the power of his adaptation of Lee's world, but, more importantly, shape his original work to come.

The first scene focuses on Miss Maudie. A motherly presence for Scout particularly, Miss Maudie, an across-the-street neighbor, has corrected both Scout and Jem in their wonder and doubt about why Atticus is defending Tom Robinson, the black man accused of raping Mayella. Both children have heard their father called names and that he "defends niggers." Why he *must* do so is Miss Maudie's message: "There are some men in this world who were born to do our unpleasant jobs for us. Your father's one of them" (Lee 197). The line is spoken verbatim in the film, and it particularly lifts Jem's spirit by correctly casting Atticus in the role of noble hero. It also singles him out in the town of Maycomb as a liberal do-gooder, a man who puts justice ahead of skin color, a man who believes in the "living reality" of "equal justice before the law."

The problem is that the only white people, other than his children, who see Atticus for the man he is are Miss Maudie and Sheriff Heck Tate. However, the Finch's maid Calpurnia and all the black citizenry Atticus has stood up for have seemingly always seen him in this light. But this is as it should be, as it was, in such a setting: 1930s Alabama. Such racial/social segregation was also the rule in the early 1960s Alabama in which I grew up. In the film, we see Atticus's stature. We believe in him. He is our moral exemplar, and even Foote's shift away from Lee's more focused examination of civil rights can't disguise the fact, or even lessen the tone, that Atticus is also hated, that to too many, he is a "nigger-lover."

This view is borne out, of course, by that other scene, the one where Bob Ewell, Mayella's father, accosts Atticus at Tom Robinson's home and spits in Atticus's eyes for taking a black man's side "against our'n." Jem witnesses his father wipe his glasses and move, ever so slightly, to strike back. But Atticus refrains from lowering himself, quietly returns to his car, and drives back home. Ewell does not deserve Atticus's dignity, but Ewell no doubt acted for many southerners both in the context of the screenplay and in the life reflected by the audiences outside it.

I say "no doubt," because thirteen years passed from the publication of Lee's novel to a scene from my high school days that reflects the work's intimidating power and cultural taboo. I read the novel when I was sixteen, outside of any literature class. For one of our high school assemblies that year, the honor students were allowed to suggest a film for the entire school to view together. Our school housed around sixteen hundred students, approximately half of them black and half of them white. In our meeting, I suggested that we view *To Kill a Mockingbird*, though, at that point, I hadn't seen the film. Our advisor, despite hearing seconds and thirds from other students and despite the novel's being taught in a humanities section that year, vetoed our suggestion. She explained that the film would cause trouble, be too divisive or too advanced for every student to grasp. We accepted her veto and voted to show Sidney Poitier's *To Sir with Love* (1967) instead. The trial scene in *Mockingbird* would have stirred feelings, maybe hard, uncontainable ones. But I've long suspected that it was the deeper message—a white man standing up for a black man accused of raping a white woman—that caused our advisor to prevent our student body collectively from seeing this film.

I show Foote's adaptation to my southern film class regularly. Students of all colors and ethnic origins view it and usually vote it the one southern film that best captures the complexity of the South. It is these two scenes that come up the most and engender the most discussion. It's easy to love Atticus, but, as Foote wisely knew, it was not so easy to display his courage in the twentieth-century South.

A decade passes. Foote keeps working on original plays and adaptations, but his notoriety from *Mockingbird* ebbs. In the late 1970s, he gets involved again in adapting the giants of southern literature. He is asked to write teleplays for Flannery O'Connor's "The Displaced Person" (1977) and Faulkner's "Barn Burning," (1979), both for PBS's *The American Short Story* series.

With O'Connor's story, it's as if no time and a quantum leap have occurred in the same spirit. The good man, Atticus Finch, has morphed into the good woman, the story's protagonist, Mrs. McIntyre. I'll say this again: Mrs. McIntyre is a good woman. She is beset by bills and by a changing world, too. Barely keeping up her farm after her husband, "The Judge," has passed away, she relies on a series of no-'count white families and two Negro hands. Then one day her priest visits with the proposal that she hire a Polish family, the Guizacs, refugees from Hitler's camps. They're foreign, and like the other workers, they're "extra." But before Mrs. McIntyre's eyes, Mr. Guizac, who can operate any piece of farm machinery, gets the place running, and both he and his family thrive on this land. It becomes frighteningly clear that without this displaced family, Mrs. McIntyre's fortunes will be ruined.

Foote faithfully adapts O'Connor's story using much of her original language and dialogue. The story is a problem, however, because this good woman is also a woman of her day, meaning that while she is tolerant, even liberal regarding the relations among the various people of her world, she also holds views that are both racist and class-based. In other words, Mrs. McIntyre is a complex, realistic depiction of a southern American in her time and place.

One must ask: would Atticus Finch have allowed either of his children to marry someone black? Of course, *Go Set a Watchman* clearly answers that question. With Mrs. McIntyre, however, the personal becomes universal.

On her own terms, when times are relatively tranquil, Foote faithfully captures her discussing the past with one of her Negro workers, the older man Astor, and enjoying that reminiscence. They laugh about the "worthless people" (215) who have worked for her, the Garrits, the Collinses, Shortleys, and the Ringfields. "Sweet Lord, them Ringfields!" Astor says. When discussing the Guizacs, however, Astor proclaims, "we ain't never had one before … like what we got now."

Consider here that a black man, roughly the same age as his employer, a white woman, is freely discussing, disparaging, other white people with that woman. They even laugh together. "Times are changing," Mrs. McIntyre says (216), as if she is the liberal beacon to the modern world. Her only critique of Astor at this point is that in talking to the farm's peacock about her previous husbands, he hasn't included the respectful term "Mister."

Foote has remarked that the characters of Faulkner's and O'Connor's world are well-known to him: "…we shared… a common language that kind of Southerner has…. My family came from Alabama and Georgia. It's the same town with a variation on a theme…. With Flannery and with Faulkner, I can hear them…." (Wood & Castleberry 45). I would add that not only can he hear them, but he also knows how they think, their biases as well as their loves. And so he understands Mrs. McIntyre's inherent southern bigotry, the outrage she shows when she learns that Mr. Guizac is bringing his sixteen-year-old cousin to Georgia to marry the younger Negro, Sulk. "She no care, black," the Pole says. "She in camp three year" (223).

This is more than Mrs. McIntyre can bear. Her initial response is to fire Mr. Guizac, to turn his family out. However, readers of the story and viewers of Foote's adaptation know that the story has an even more tragic ending, one Mrs. McIntyre could have prevented. But this sin is one of omission. She doesn't do anything to save Mr. Guizac, which is the point. But a key component of her literary portraiture is presented in her final conversation with Mr. Guizac— where, in O'Connor's story, we see two worldviews colliding: "You would bring this poor innocent child over here and try to marry her to a half-witted thieving black stinking nigger! What kind of monster are you!" (222). Foote's version, while very close, omits the word "stinking" and shifts "black" to in-between "half-witted" and "thieving." A minute later, he uses O'Connor's words verbatim:

> "...that nigger cannot have a white wife from Europe. You can't talk to a nigger that way. You'll excite him.... Maybe it can be done in Poland but it can't be done here.... That nigger don't have a grain of sense... I cannot understand how a man who calls himself a Christian... could bring a poor innocent girl over here and marry her to something like that." (222–3)

Foote says that while he doesn't understand O'Connor's "tough Catholicism," he is "fascinated" by it. He also has confessed to being deeply religious himself (Wood & Castleberry 45, 48). It is clear in his choice both to adapt the story and in what exactly to include from that story that he sees Mrs. McIntyre as emblematic of the hypocrisy of this Bible-obsessed, or as O'Connor has it, this "Christ-haunted" region of the country. But I think it's a mistake to see Mrs. McIntyre as only a hypocrite or a bigot. Foote's screenplay shows her gazing often at the Judge's grave—which some white trash employee has robbed of its naked granite cherub. We see her lamenting her fate to the Judge's photograph: a woman alone trying to maintain her place. She has been so strong, so willing to work, to persevere. Foote claimed to be unsatisfied by his own ending here, where the priest discusses Purgatory with the now catatonic woman. But Purgatory is right. She isn't in Hell because her southern world made her in its image: a good woman overcome by her inborn prejudices. A very familiar figure.

Foote's last major adaptation, of Faulkner's "Barn Burning," depicts the problematic boy Sarty Snopes, who must choose between blood and the moral/legal code. As Rebecca Briley points out, Foote's ending to the story differs from Faulkner's more ambiguous one, in which it is unclear if Sarty's father Abner, the barn burner, actually dies and, if so, whether Sarty accepts responsibility for his father's death. Foote has Sarty choose "responsibility to society over his commitment to his father" (Briley 55). Family relations, one of the southern themes Foote most often champions, are sacrificed by a young boy who cannot tolerate any longer his father's cold evil: his father's meanness to all, including his son.

The realism of these adapted works and Foote's examination and depiction of people trying to exist the best they can—honoring both morality and social convention—reflect our own world of compromise and complexity, hypocrisy and bravery. Even Sarty protests at the time of his abandoning his father that Abner was "brave." Of course, audiences/readers get to make our own choices. But through Foote's understanding of these master characters, he is able to create one of his own that not only holds his place evenly and respectably amongst the Fentrys, Finches, and McIntyres, but who cements Foote's reputation as a heavyweight original southern writer in his own right: *Tender Mercies*' central figure Mac Sledge.

Overcoming the Bitter: Becoming a Southern Man

Horton Foote's original screenplay for *Tender Mercies* won the 1983 Academy Award. While, initially, he wanted to write about a group of country musicians struggling to make it—reminding him of his own early struggles as a writer—as he conceived the work, he became more fascinated with the deeply-troubled older man, Mac Sledge (played in the film by Robert Duvall), a former country writer/singer himself who has finally hit bottom and passed out "somewhere," with no money, no place to be, and no one who wants him (Wood & Castleberry 46)—very much a southern kind of theme. Sledge, however, is both resilient and persevering, and after he asks Rosa Lee, the owner of the motel whose floor he's just slept on, if he can work off his debt, the pair become friends and eventually husband and wife. Rosa Lee changes Mac, or perhaps it's more that Mac wants to be changed. Saved.

Rosa Lee does save him, literally, by accepting him as husband, father to her son "Sonny," and by persuading him to be baptized on the Sunday also planned for Sonny's immersion.

It's easy to see a lot of Atticus Finch and some of Jackson Fentry in Mac Sledge. They all face misery directly, take vicious blows, and carry on. They are survivors in times that many do not survive because they grow too bitter or too cynical, or get too caught up in hate. As I noted years ago, "If *Tender Mercies* had been a Horton Foote work of the 1950s, it would in all likelihood have ended with Sledge successfully pulling himself out of the depths into which his life has plunged and, with a new family, pursuing a slow-paced but fulfilling life" (207–208). However, through the decades, Foote's themes and stories grew darker, more complex. One simply cannot adapt the works of Faulkner, Lee, and O'Connor and not be changed.

As the movie starts, Mac Sledge had already overcome certain blows: twice married before Rosa Lee, he achieved fame with second wife Dixie, but when she got more famous than he was, he resorted to alcohol and to beating her. Thus continued his downward spiral, cast off from her band; divorced; and, most importantly, barred from seeing his and Dixie's daughter, Sue Ann. After rising again through Rosa Lee's love, Mac tries to find Sue Ann by visiting one of Dixie's touring shows. While he fails here and is thrown out by Dixie, Sue Ann gets the message and visits Mac at his and Rosa Lee's home. "Little Sister," he remembers calling her, though she has forgotten that. What she remembers is the song he used to sing to her, "On the Wings of a Dove." Mac claims not to remember that, but, after Sue Ann leaves, we see and hear the confirmation that he certainly does remember. We understand that, while he is pleased to be back in his daughter's life, he won't let her get too close and deprive Dixie of her own status as the parent who didn't leave.

One would think that after this sacrifice and reconciliation, Mac's life would settle into one of comfort, happiness, and peace. He's even recorded one of his old songs with that band mentioned earlier. But as we know, in the South, being born again might save your soul, but it doesn't protect a person against earthly harm. So Sue Ann dies in a car wreck, as she's running away from her mother with the drummer in her mother's band. This leads to the film's most memorable line, Mac's bitter admission to Rosa Lee that he "don't trust happiness." He asks her why these things happen, all the bad things, and even the good ones, such as when she took pity on him and married him.

Rosa Lee can't any more answer Mac's questions than Atticus Finch can explain to his children why a white jury found a black man guilty of a crime that any fool could see he didn't do. Or why that man runs away and is shot in the back. Or why the boy Jackson Fentry takes on and raises becomes a no-'count killer after he returns to his biological kin. Or why Mrs. McIntyre allows Mr. Guizac to be crushed by a tractor.

Yet it is Rosa Lee's tender mercy that allows Mac to go on. He buys Sonny a football, and as the film ends, the two are calmly passing the ball between them in the open field near the motel. When no answers are forthcoming, it is the good man, the good person, who finds a way to go on, living for a purpose despite all the pain. But good people aren't always so. Being good is a struggle. Owning one's past, looking at one's life squarely and reconciling all our mistakes, or as many as we can remember, is our struggle and, possibly, our redemption.

In Mac Sledge, Horton Foote found his literary southern man. A hero, if we understand that every hero has a flaw that, in the end, he or she chooses to overcome. As Foote biographer Marion Castleberry states, *Tender Mercies* "reveals Horton's perceptive understanding of the ephemeral nature of success, his compassion for people beset with personal problems and professional disappointment, and his unwavering belief in the promise of hope and reconciliation. [It is]…a work of poetic transcendence" (333).

Place and Perspective

Horton Foote created many rich and complex characters in his original plays and screenplays. He would rework one such character, Carrie Watts, for his next film, *The Trip to Bountiful* (1985), which won Geraldine Page an Academy Award for Best Actress. Following that came the autobiographical films of *The Orphans' Home Cycle* and then a return to his first love, the stage. Though *To Kill a Mockingbird* first won him widespread critical attention back in 1962, it wasn't until the mid-1980s, relatively late in his life, that Foote began receiving the attention he deserved from both critics and audiences. One now finds his work taught in many college curricula, both in drama and southern literature courses. Seeing him on a syllabus next to the great Faulkner, O'Connor, Williams, and Lee, one is tempted to remark, "It's about time."

But those aren't words, or even a sentiment, that Horton Foote would have uttered about his work. Not that he wasn't proud of the literary world he created, the life he led. He certainly was, and he was also always glad to talk about that world, just as if its characters were members of his beloved family, which, in the ways of art and love, they certainly were.

Works Cited

Briley, Rebecca. "Southern Accents: Horton Foote's Adaptations of William Faulkner, Harper Lee, and Flannery O'Connor." *Horton Foote: A Casebook*. Ed. Gerald C. Wood. New York: Garland, 1997.

The Displaced Person. Writer Horton Foote. Dir. Glenn Jordan. Perf. Irene Worth, Shirley Stoler, Lane Smith, John Houseman. *The American Short Story*. PBS, 1977.

Castleberry, Marion. *Blessed Assurance: The Life and Art of Horton Foote*. Macon, GA: Mercer UP, 2014.

Foote, Horton. *"To Kill a Mockingbird," "Tender Mercies," and "The Trip to Bountiful": Three Screenplays by Horton Foote*. New York: Grove Press, 1989.

Lee, Harper. *To Kill A Mockingbird*. New York: Lippincott, 1960.

O'Connor, Flannery. *The Complete Stories*. New York: Farrar, Straus & Giroux, 1989.

Wood, Gerald C. & Marion Castleberry, eds. *The Voice of an American Playwright: Interviews with Horton Foote*. Macon, GA: Mercer UP, 2012.

"I always wanted a boy the town could be proud of": Issues of Conformity and Community in Horton Foote's Dual Versions of *The Chase*____

Roy J. Gonzáles, Jr.

When Horton Foote's *The Chase* debuted on the stage in 1952, it met with a mixed reception. Despite being a "Western with an ethical point," according to critic Brooks Atkinson, the play failed to evoke much drama, especially under "self-conscious and pretentious" direction (30). In his literary biography of Foote, Charles Watson writes that Atkinson's fellow critics felt much the same way, seeing only a "Western onstage" (66). Watson argues that though *The Chase* was conceived as an "anti-Western" (62), its suspenseful veneer was mistaken for typical melodrama. The failure of *The Chase* contributed to Foote's growing discontent with Broadway culture in New York. In the interest of supporting a growing family, he began pursuing other avenues of work apart from the theater. Laurence Avery writes that Foote produced scripts for film and television during the 1950s and 1960s (388–89). Foote also achieved notable screenwriting successes, the greatest example of which was his Oscar-winning adaptation of Harper Lee's *To Kill a Mockingbird*. He would win a second Academy Award with *Tender Mercies* (1983), and he would eventually accumulate a host of honors for such stage plays as *The Trip to Bountiful* (Pulitzer Prize, 1995) and his remarkable, nine-play *The Orphans' Home Cycle*. Although Foote's effort to break through into dramatic stardom with *The Chase* was a disappointment, his perseverance kept him afloat as it had with the failure of his first Broadway play, *Only the Heart* (1944).

Though *The Chase* was not successful onstage, the play remains a remarkable example of Foote's artistry. In the words of Foote scholar Marion Castleberry, it is "unquestionably the most mature and skillfully written play of Horton Foote's early career" (138). The drama is a social critique first and foremost. Its central thematic concerns are the consequences of a community's attempts to force its citizens into conformity. Those who fail to conform become alienated, destined to remain outcasts at best and criminals at worst. *The Chase* also examines the role of the law in this conflict between the community and the individual. Sheriff Hawes, the protagonist of the play, stands between his community and its criminals, but he is still an outcast in his own way. The ambivalent dichotomy between lawman and criminal is central to *The Chase*. Hawes's nemesis throughout the play is Bubber Reeves, an escaped convict who blames Hawes for his incarceration. On the surface, the two men are antithetical, yet both are alienated by their shared community of Harrison, Texas. As a criminal, Reeves can never be accepted by the townspeople. As sheriff, Hawes is a resented authority figure, who bears the indignation of the community even as he toils to preserve its safety. Worn out by the burden of responsibility he shoulders as sheriff, Hawes is just as much an outcast as Reeves. The two men are broken by the community around them—one driven to a life of crime and the other disillusioned and exhausted by the struggle to maintain dignity in the face of social pressure.

The Chase is also unique among Foote's work in that it spawned two adaptations: a novel in 1956 and a film in 1966. The novel is noteworthy in that it represents one of Foote's rare efforts to write prose fiction. Like the play, however, it failed to draw much attention despite some positive reviews. Anthony Boucher, for instance, referred to it as a "novel of character" that succeeds in "studying the inherent moral and psychological problems of violence." Nonetheless, the novel suffers from issues of style. The prose is awkwardly paced and filled with many odd half-starts and dead-ends. Watson finds that although the novel is "interesting," it is unfortunately "wordy and much of the action is overwritten" (67). The subsequent film adaptation did not fare much better. Called "overheated" by critic Bosley Crowther, the film, starring heavyweights such as Marlon Brando and Robert Redford, defies the spirit of the original play and indulges in sensationalism (12). Screenwriter Lillian Hellman was brought onto the project under the approval of producer Sam Spiegel. According to Castleberry, both Spiegel and Hellman were interested in using *The Chase* as a springboard for a much more pointed and timely social critique than Foote had intended, especially with regard to the assassination of John F. Kennedy (232). This agenda, however, bogged down the film's production. Castleberry writes, "Hellman's screenplay accentuated everything that Horton had restrained in his play and novel. She ... turned drama into melodrama, and touched upon nearly every social disease troubling America during the decade of the 1960s" (233). Even more trouble came to the script when Spiegel turned to English writer Ivan Moffat for further revisions (235). Ultimately, the screenplay and production so disenchanted Foote, Watson writes, that he never again sold the rights to his works to a Hollywood studio (68). Given Foote's exclusion from what turned out to be a chaotic production, the film cannot be said to represent his vision of the source material, regardless of its merits or lack thereof.

Although neither adaptation redeemed the play's disappointing initial performance, the novel version further develops the drama's social critique. By enhancing and supplementing the material already in the play, the novel builds a more complete, comprehensive view of the tensions inherent in conformity and community. The original work serves as a critique against the overbearing nature of most communities. It is a statement of Foote's preference for intimacy and rural solitude over urban social dysfunction. The novel translates this statement into a more fully realized vision by providing deeper portrayals of its characters and exploring the aftermath of the events of the play. The play ends on a bittersweet note, suggesting that the titular chase that torments Hawes and Bubber Reeves may never end. Foote's appended epilogue to the novel, however, finds Hawes making peace with the violence he endured and inflicted. It is the purpose of this paper to explore first the thematic ramifications of the play and then those of the subsequent novel. The aim is to illustrate that, by championing restorative intimacy—a concept developed by Foote scholar Gerald Wood—the novel provides a possible solution to the social ills originally diagnosed in the play.

As mentioned before, much of the conflict in both versions of *The Chase* relates to Hawes's difficulty in serving the people of his town. From the beginning of the original play, Foote makes efforts to establish Hawes as an exceptional man among his community. Despite having been "wild and cussed" in his formative years (70), Hawes has redeemed himself and risen to the respectable position of sheriff. Moreover, he takes his responsibility as sheriff very seriously. He remarks to deputy Rip in the first scene, "A sheriff is a public servant. The public elects him, they pay his salary, an' they have a right to call on him for anything they want, day or night" (65). For Hawes, the position is not about power, but solemn service. Although he may gripe about the relatively petty affairs he is called to address—such as responding to calls about loud music or being asked to participate in parades—he nonetheless approaches them with a sense of duty. Yet he is still only human, and the constant vigilance expected of him as sheriff has brought fatigue, as is evident when he laments about his state of mind to Mr. Douglas:

> I don't see any future in it for me. I would like to make the change. I'm tired of politics. I hate havin' to do whatever people ask me … I don't have any time for Ruby—I haven't had a vacation since I've been in office. My phone rings at two in the mornin', or three, or four. It's gettin' on my nerves… Drunks and whores and dopeheads and thieves and murderers. It's no life to put a child into. I just can't see it. (69)

Hawes is exhausted by the demands of his job, and he is also cognizant of his growing family. To protect the community, he must dirty his hands and spirit, and this taint, having already worn him down, threatens to do the same to his wife and soon-to-be-born child. Hawes is therefore desperate to escape from the community for which he is responsible. He fixates on the isolation of remote nature as a cure to his weariness. Specifically, he wants a farm. "Every man ought to be entitled to his own farm," he says (64), and when he describes the one he has singled out for himself and his family, he dresses it up in romance and beauty: "It's the richest lookin' land I think I ever saw. Good black dirt. Lots of pecan trees. The prettiest half-moon of a lake covered with water irises runnin' right through it" (71). Hawes is enamored of the idea of escape, and this craving has become desperate by the time the play begins.

The farm itself is not necessarily the solution to Hawes's mental and emotional fatigue. In his book *Horton Foote and the Theater of Intimacy*, Gerald C. Wood argues that Foote supports "finding a place" in his writing, though this place does not have to be anywhere physical. Wood writes that Foote's concern with place stems from a desire to escape isolation, what Wood reads as the "absence of intimacy" (17). The isolation to which he refers is spiritual. Whether surrounded by many people or remote from all society, anyone deprived of genuine, intimate relationships with others is isolated. Foote's answer to isolation, Wood says, is "not a return to the land or villages," but rather a "connection to loved ones and a community" (17). Within civilized society, Hawes is beleaguered and spiritually beaten—isolated despite his position of authority—but a new start in the private seclusion of nature may allow him to restore his happiness and mental strength. He says early on in the play, "I want to live in peace now with my wife and baby an' let other people live in peace" (70). His ultimate desire is to shift his attention from the community onto his family. Thus, the true source of restoration for Hawes is not the farm itself, but the opportunity it affords him to bond with his family. By moving away from the artificiality of the community, Hawes enables himself to build nurturing, restorative relationships with his wife and child. Without doing so, Wood says, "genuine contentment" and a "fully human experience" are unattainable (41). If Hawes does not connect with those closest to him, he risks falling into isolation and further spiritual deficit. Furthermore, any relationship he forms within the context of the community would be lacking. So long as he remains sheriff, a remote authority figure, Hawes cannot truly relate to any of the townspeople. As husband and father, however, he can genuinely know and bond with his family. His true place is with them, and it is there where he hopes to find peace.

Unfortunately, Hawes's weary final days as sheriff are interrupted by the reappearance of Bubber Reeves. If Hawes sets a positive example for the community, despite being alienated, then

Reeves does the opposite. Both men grew up as delinquents, but, while Hawes overcame his weaknesses, Reeves collapsed under his own. Even Reeves's marital situation opposes that of Hawes. While Ruby Hawes is the faithful, honest wife, Anna Reeves distances herself from her husband and sleeps with fellow outcast Knub McDermont. Reeves is a corrupt, imperfect Hawes. Had circumstances in either man's life turned out differently, they may have found their roles reversed. In her study *You Can Go Home Again: The Focus on Family in the Works of Horton Foote*, Rebecca Briley refers to Hawes as an example of Foote's "exemplary father-figure," who advocates compassion and reconciliation over the violent and antagonistic behavior of the community (98). For Briley, *The Chase* is largely a drama about family. Reeves is the prodigal son to Hawes's exemplary father. He is rejected by his community for failing to conform to its standards. Both men are also plagued by a powerful existential exhaustion as a result of their common alienation. Reeves reveals this exhaustion when he confronts Knub:

> I'm tired. Oh, my God, I'm tired! When I was in the Pen waitin' to get out I thought I'd never get tired again until I come back here an' get this done. But I only been out a day an' I'm tired, bone tired. I can't rest. I'm tired an' I can't rest.... If I could just kill that devil, I could rest. If I could just kill that devil, I could rest. (96)

Reeves is consumed by his desire for vengeance against Hawes, the authority figure he associates most immediately with his incarceration. Moreover, his exhaustion reflects his own wearied spirit. Like Hawes, he has been damaged by society, turned into a criminal by social forces outside of his control. Foote does not paint Reeves as particularly sympathetic, but he uses Mrs. Reeves, the mother, to analyze the effects of society upon her son. When she appeals to Hawes to spare her son's life, she reveals how badly she treated the boy in trying to make him conform to social convention:

> I did the best I could. I tried whippin' him. I tried to shame him. I kept him home. I dressed him like a girl to keep him home. I never gave him money unless he worked for it. I prayed like the preachers

told me. I did whatever people said would help.... I can't do anything with him. Nothing. You've all turned him into a mad dog. You and Old Sunshine an' the other sheriffs. You've turned my boy into a mad dog an' now there's no savin' him. (83)

In trying to discipline her son and make him conform to the conventions of society, Mrs. Reeves unwittingly amplified his antisocial tendencies. She beat him and shamed him, and the community enabled and even encouraged this behavior. They pushed, and so Bubber Reeves inevitably pushed back. Briley asserts that, in kowtowing to the pressures of her community and abusing her son, Mrs. Reeves failed him. Foote may be sympathetic to her, but he is nonetheless critical of the abrasive upbringing she provided (98–99). Ironically, and tragically, Reeves's hatred finds its target in Hawes, the man least responsible for his corruption and most interested, next to his mother, in saving his life. As representative of the community, Hawes must bear the consequences of the people's indignation and sin. As the father figure in the play, it thus becomes Hawes's responsibility to not only stop Reeves but also save him spiritually. Hawes must act as savior for both Reeves and the community at large.

This same community at fault for eroding Hawes and vilifying Reeves is also self-righteously interested in discrediting and destroying them. Embodied by local braggart and hothead Hawks Damon, the "good people" to whom he repeatedly refers want to take the law into their own hands and kill Reeves. Damon says to Hawes, "We want him killed. We want him killed. Is that clear? I've been with the good people of this town all day and we want him killed. Not caught. Killed!" (89). Damon is the community's mouthpiece, revealing its violent tendencies. Reeves failed to conform, and his presence as a nonconformist threatens social stability. He is thus more conveniently removed than rehabilitated. Hawes recognizes the community's fear and tries to establish himself as the highest authority, but his position as sheriff means little to the frenzied mob. Damon says as much to Hawes later in the play, remarking, "You're gonna do nothin.' Because they'll tear any man to pieces if you try to get in their way. I've never seen people like this, Hawes, so I warn you to stay out of their way. They'll tear you to pieces if you try to get in their way" (102). The mob becomes just as dangerous as Reeves, if not more so. In its paranoid rush to restore the status quo, it threatens to ruin the town entirely. As a lone individual, Hawes cannot placate the mob. Although he is the sheriff, the community's defender and father-figure, as Briley mentions, he exercises no true power over the people. He is as much at their mercy as Reeves, a fact he despondently acknowledges when considering the fate of a local boy in trouble with the law:

> He's twelve. Her boy's twelve and she says she can't control him. She talks just like Mrs. Reeves used to. Another five years, if he keeps on, we'll have to send him to reform school. Another five, hunt him like I'm huntin' Bubber tonight. And the Damons and the Edwins will be after me to kill him and the chase will be on. How does it begin? How does it start? How does it end? (101)

There will always be those unable to conform, Hawes admits, either because they resist the status quo or the community renders them, through pressure or discrimination, unfit to remain within it. Imbalanced social conditions will continually produce more malcontents, and those malcontents will, in turn, threaten to dismantle the society that produced them. Watson refers to Reeves as a "product of a vicious and cruel society" and "hardly responsible for turning out as he has" (65). Reeves is the victim in the play, and his role reveals the community as mob-like and vindictive. According to Watson, it is through Reeves that Foote is able to "attack the harmful behavior of that society with the purpose of reforming it" (63). Although Hawes fails to save Reeves, Foote presents the possibility for redemption at the play's end. Hawes's wife Ruby encourages Hawes not to give up. "This chase didn't start tonight," she says, "It didn't end tonight. Don't run away, Hawes. Keep on livin'. Keep on tryin'" (110–11). Hawes decides to remain sheriff and continue his attempts to help those in trouble with the law. Exceptional men like Hawes can still make a difference, but it will be an uphill battle.

The novel adaptation of *The Chase* expands upon Foote's critique of an impersonal, violent community. Importantly, it also articulates a more developed antidote for the community's negative influence. While the premise of the story remains the same, the novel's ending resonates with a stronger sense of acceptance and optimism than that of the play. The characters of the novel are also more developed compared to their dramatic counterparts. Hawes's fragile mental state is given much more emphasis, painting a man more clearly at his limit. Hawks Damon, mostly a background threat in the play, is able to indulge in more explicit violence, such as when he beats Edwin Stewart. A more prominent Mrs. Reeves, along with a newly featured Mr. Reeves, better establish Bubber Reeves's history and illuminate his motivations. In fact, Reeves is significantly more dimensional, and thus sympathetic, in the novel than in the play. He is far less violent, and his heightened victimhood aligns with Foote's thematic points. An assortment of new characters are also included, such as Miss Mattie and Minnie Damon, which helps color the town and give it more life. Most significant of all is the inclusion of Hawes's son, S.P., a ten-year-old boy in the novel as opposed to an unborn child in the play. The presence of S.P. lends an added urgency to Hawes's desire to protect his family. In the novel, the stakes are much higher. If Hawes cannot cleanse himself of his emotional pollutants, they may infect not only Ruby but also his son.

Although the play ends without addressing the aftermath of Reeves's death, the novel focuses specifically on how Hawes and the Reeveses cope with their failure to protect the escaped convict's life. Hawes quits his station as sheriff and realizes his dream of owning a farm with his family. The farm, however, is far from the idyllic sanctuary he envisions in the play. The land is poor and the work hard, but Hawes and his family persevere and build something substantial through their efforts. Most importantly, they "talked about nothing of the past," focusing their energies solely on the future (145). In order to build the healing "place" to which Gerald Wood refers in *Horton Foote and the Theater of Intimacy*, they must make a clean break from the past. Hawes is aware of the "terrors of the chase and the kill" (153–154) continuing to haunt him, but he is confident of their fading as time goes on. Hawes may be "broken," as Mr. Reeves says (154), but his farm and family offer him the potential for a spiritual and emotional restructuring. His choice to vacate his position as sheriff is also a significant one. Briley writes that "rather than try to make restitution for the failure with Bubber by taking on another juvenile delinquent's case ... Any penance Hawes will do will be with his own son" (103). Rather than trying to reform the larger community and tainting himself in the process, Hawes elects to strengthen his own family. If, according to Briley's reading, "the community suffers when the family fails" (99), Hawes's decision to serve his family first and his community second is the correct choice. In doing so—in creating a place where he, his wife, and his son can grow and heal—he sets the foundation for a more secure community in the future. When individuals remedy the corruption of society via intimacy, people can be nurtured and assimilated into a community built upon compassion. They can avoid being ostracized, and the chase can be prevented altogether.

Similarly, while the Reeveses are too late to save their son, they spend the rest of their days trying to compensate for the misguided upbringing they provided him. They eventually return to Harrison in order to care for Reeves's grave and protect his memory. Mrs. Reeves acknowledges the part she played in her son's downfall and eventual destruction, lamenting to Mr. Reeves, "I always wanted a boy the town could be proud of. I never gave him a chance to be anything for all my fighting them. I always wanted them to like him so, I killed him trying to make him be someone they could be proud of..." (138). Mrs. Reeves reaffirms her culpability, and the culpability of the town as a whole, in alienating and corrupting her son. Reeves is largely absolved of his delinquency as a result. The novel's narrator says of Reeves, "He had heard about his badness all of his life. Bubber Reeves was bad, Bubber Reeves had been born bad and he had he guessed and there was no help for it" (89). His attempts to reform were constantly met with failure, and his "badness" was only reinforced again and again by the community. The inclusion of a deceased younger sister into the familial tragedy is just another means of highlighting how little agency Reeves possessed throughout his life. Had he been treated differently—had his family made themselves his restorative center—it is likely he would have been more responsible and upstanding. By tending to the graves of their children, Mr. and Mrs. Reeves finally create a healing place of their own, but it is, of course, too late. The fate of the Reeveses is one Hawes is interested in avoiding for the sake of his own family. By caring for his son and nurturing him via intimacy, as Wood suggests, he will do right where the Reeveses did wrong.

Even in death, however, Bubber Reeves finds his own personal peace. When Hawes and his family visit the Harrison graveyard, his wife Ruby looks over Reeves's grave and reflects upon the "violence and the bitterness and the hate ending finally here in this quiet, serene place" (151). Reeves finds peace in the graveyard, a place Briley calls Foote's "typical symbol of reconciliation and forgiveness" (102). In the ultimate exile of death, Reeves finally manages to remove himself from the tumultuous life put upon him by the community. The graveyard, like Hawes's farm, is another space outside of society, a space brimming with the potential for rejuvenation and renewal. In death, Reeves returns to the universal mother of nature. He is truly redeemed, even if he disappears from the civilized world. As his fellow exile, Hawes also disappears from society. He undergoes a social death. At the novel's end, Hawes reflects, "They're all back now. Except Bubber and me. All except Bubber and me. Jackson Reeves and Travis Hawes. Farm and graveyard. Exiles" (158). All the other characters that leave Harrison eventually return, but Hawes and Reeves remain permanently outside its bounds. Their respective departures reflect Foote's belief in intimate solitude over communal isolation. It is through removal that they find peace.

While the original dramatic version of *The Chase* ends in bittersweet tragedy—with Reeves dead and Hawes faced with an indefinite struggle ahead of him—the novel reaches a state of grace in its final pages. With the principal action of the story completed, Foote allows the pages to breathe and settle into a distinctive peace. He demonstrates the "healing power of intimacy," as Wood refers to it ("Grace" 376), in how the families of Hawes and Reeves mend themselves after the trauma they endured. Both families unburden themselves of the connections they shared with the larger community and instead focus their energies on the bonds most truly important. They create real, authentic places of healing that thrive on genuine intimacy. Wood writes that Foote's most contented characters "offer and reciprocate a kindness and peace which can be transformative. They are both humble and strong in controlling their own confusion and anxiety in pursuit of sustaining attachments to loved ones, family, work, nature, or their community" (376). This transformative peace is Foote's ultimate weapon against social dysfunction. The impersonal, artificial trappings of society create a sense of alienation that results in ignorance, fear, and hateful prejudice. The restorative, rejuvenating force of intimacy, no matter the origin or context, can break down these barriers. By allowing Hawes to leave his community and foster true intimacy between the members of his family, Foote allows for the potential for redemption not just for Hawes but for the entire town. The chase *can* end, Foote suggests, but only if individuals like Hawes break away from their respective communities and implement new, restorative cycles of behavior. Future generations will emulate those that came before them, and so the precedents built out of isolation and insecurity must be replaced by new ones built from communion and compassion. Hawes's son, appropriately nurtured, will ostensibly prove this to be true—he will pass on the nurturance provided him by his father to his own children and the people he encounters throughout his life. Ironically, the salvation of society can only be found outside of it. In the seclusion of nature, families can rebuild and then reintegrate themselves into their former communities. In doing so, they repair the communal foundation and build towards a more harmonious future. Foote's play and novel, together, demonstrate that only empathy and understanding can transcend cycles of violence and restore the broken links between people. *The Chase*, despite its relative lack of prominence in Foote's legacy, remains a potent show of his optimism and belief in the power of intimacy.

Works Cited

Atkinson, Brooks. "At The Theatre: Horton Foote's Texan Drama, 'The Chase,' Staged at the Playhouse by Ferrer." *New York Times* (16 Apr. 1952): 30. *ProQuest.* Web. 11 May 2015.

Avery, Laurence G. "Horton Foote and the American Theater." *Mississippi Quarterly: The Journal of Southern Cultures* 58.1 (2004): 43–62. *MLA International Bibliography.* Web. 12 Apr. 2015.

Boucher, Anthony. "Very Young, Very Old." *New York Times* (19 Feb. 1956): BR14. *ProQuest.* Web. 27 Apr. 2015.

Briley, Rebecca Luttrell. *You Can Go Home Again: The Focus on Family in the Works of Horton Foote.* New York: Peter Lang, 1993.

Castleberry, Marion. *Blessed Assurance: The Life and Art of Horton Foote.* Macon: Mercer UP, 2014.

Crowther, Bosley. "The Screen: 'The Chase.'" *New York Times* (19 Feb. 1966): 12. *ProQuest.* Web. 27 Apr. 2015.

Foote, Horton. *The Chase. Collected Plays: Volume II.* Lyme: Smith & Kraus, 1996.

_____. *The Chase.* New York: Signet, 1966.

Watson, Charles S. *Horton Foote: A Literary Biography.* Austin: U of Texas P, 2003.

Wood, Gerald C. *Horton Foote and the Theater of Intimacy.* Baton Rouge: Louisiana State UP, 1999.

_____. "Loving Mac, Beth, and John: Grace in the Plays and Films of Horton Foote." *Religion and the Arts* 10.3 (2006): 374–90. *MLA International Bibliography.* Web. 12 Apr. 2015.

The Orphans' Home Cycle and the Intuition of the Soul

Crystal Brian

> All of them are gone. Except for me. And for me… nothing is gone.
> (Horton Foote)

Horton Foote's play *1918* was performed at Quinnipiac University, in Hamden, Connecticut, on April 16–19, 2015. The actors were students, as well as Equity actors (I directed the play, but also acted as Mrs. Vaughn.). For many years, Foote felt that *The Orphans' Home Cycle* plays should include music and poetry, in conjunction with dance, but theatrical directors, unaware of Foote's love of the music of Charles Ives, tended to disregard such elements. In the Quinnipiac production, we featured music, particularly that of Ives. Michael Delgado, one of our sophomore film, video, and interactive video majors and a theater minor, created the music. Throughout the play, a band (professors in English and criminal justice who were guitarists or pianists or worked on the drum) clad in First World War costumes functioned as part of the production. Many of the songs included were those sung by soldiers who came back from the war. A piano accompanied the hymns that provided background.

In the following essay, this 2015 production of a key play from Foote's greatest work, *The Orphans' Home Cycle*, will provide a central point of reference for a theatrically oriented discussion of this playwright based on the personal and professional experience of a scholar who knew him well. Foote passed away in 2009, and his daughter, Hallie Foote—who still acts in his plays—became the primary producer of Foote's work. Hallie's husband, actor Devon Abner, has also appeared in Foote's plays and films.

Hallie Foote and Devon Abner were able to come to the final Quinnipiac dress rehearsal and performances of *1918* on April 14, 15, and 16, 2015. This play is strongly relevant to what is happening in the world today, notably with war and violence and with the threat of infectious disease. For both the audience and the students, it was intriguing that Foote's works have continued to create so much interest.

Horton Foote was, of course, a mystic of the American theater. In my encounters with this gifted man, I have come to understand much about his dramaturgy and his philosophic approach to art and to life. In October of 2000, Horton Foote spoke with me about his work. Here is part of our conversation.

Crystal Brian: What inspired you to write plays as opposed to any other form?

Horton Foote: I went into it because I was an actor. And I wanted to write parts for myself. [Laughs] And I got very interested in it, in the form. And I think, because my inclination is always to tell things through dialogue, that it's the most natural form for me. And, you know, I don't know that one chooses what one writes about or one's form as much as it chooses you. First of all, I was around plays all my life. And though I was a reader and read novels, I just have never been as interested in, let's say, describing the room or the scenery outside the room as I have been in what goes on between people. That's really what interests me as a writer. And I guess that's why I love Beckett so much. At least his plays. I'm not as familiar with his novels. But his plays. And, you know, it's a constant struggle for me to keep focused on the form, and to see its purest aspects, which I feel essentially is language....

CB: What are the greatest challenges or obstacles that you as a playwright have faced?

HF: Well, I think they vary, you know, from time to time. I think sometimes they're external forces. I think the internal forces are pretty constant in all art forms: to struggle to find out what you want to say and how you want to say it. But playwrights increasingly are faced with diminishing audiences and places to have their plays done or to make a living at their craft. And it's not heartening. I mean, I think curiously that the quality of playwriting has increased and that the talent is there. If you're realistic about it, you know the better it is, maybe the more difficult it will become. Because you think of poets. I mean, how many poets even conceive of making a living off of writing poetry? And so maybe that's really not our business. I get concerned for the theatre itself. I've seen many phases and I've remained an optimist about the theatre because I think it will always survive, but—and I guess we're going through probably the most difficult, at least in America, transition that we've ever gone through. So that the big kind of Broadway houses are just becoming moribund. And so more and more you just have musicals filling them up. And it's all the places outside of New York that really are sustaining playwrights. Regional theaters and colleges, wherever....

CB: What particular satisfactions or dissatisfactions come with playwriting?

HF: It's just enormously satisfying. The writing. Now the dissatisfaction often comes when you try to get a production together. And then you wonder, you know, because it's a question of money and the question of budgets. And you wonder if you just were a novelist or a short story writer, would it be easier to get the work done? And then you realize that playwriting is not a solitary thing. It basically has to be a cooperative venture. And you'd better have good actors and you'd better get a good director. And that's the part that then, well, it almost can be very joyful because, you know, you sometimes get those and then it all works well....

CB: Do you regret not being an actor at all?

HF: No. [Laughs] I really don't. I'm so satisfied writing. As you know, I admire and respect and love actors. And depend on them greatly. But no, no.... I've just finished a new play. And I just sometimes don't think I'm alive unless I'm writing. (Brian 207–209)

Following this conversation with the late playwright, it seems appropriate to hear the voices of some of the participants in a recent production of one of his plays. Drew Scott, an actor and one of the professors in theater at Quinnipiac, was Mr. Vaughn in our production of *1918*. He talked about his experience:

In the spring of 2015, I had the good fortune to be offered the role of Mr. Vaughn in Horton Foote's *1918* in a production at Quinnipiac University. It was an opportunity I welcomed, for while I had read Horton Foote's plays and seen Horton Foote's plays, *1918* would be the first time I had ever tackled the challenge of acting in one of Horton Foote's plays....

I soon found that digging into the text and the supplementary materials was like mining a rich vein of gold. The more I dug, the deeper I was drawn into the play and the character, and the deeper I was drawn into the character, the richer I felt. I don't think any actor feels richer than when he can work on a character that is as detailed, nuanced, and full of unforeseen facets as Mr. Vaughn. Or, indeed, as is any character written by Mr. Foote.

To me, this attention to the completeness and authenticity of his characters is the hallmark of a Horton Foote play. He builds his characters from keen observation of human behavior and renders them with unflinching and unfailing honesty... For an actor to be able to play a character constructed with such care, such attention to detail, such richness is...well, let's just say, it doesn't get much better. (Scott)

Aleta Staton was the associate director for *1918*. She had performed in stage and on screen for many years, and was a Professor of Theater at Quinnipiac University. She observed:

Pacing was another element that I seemed constantly aware of as the college actors melted into these charming characters over the rehearsal period. Their dialogue was like music—well rehearsed songs that were just as well paced. Any straying from the character's pace, once acquired, was awkward and they felt it. In time, they adjusted back into the southern melody on their own....

It seemed that Horton Foote was actually with me and I trusted that feeling immensely, especially with Hallie in the room. At a certain point I felt the imbalance of the music—it was almost too much, but it eventually occurred to me that it was inseparable from the air in the room during that time in our history. There was illness, there was death, there were friends, associates and relatives, and they would disappear one or more at a time. And there was the music—always there. (Staton)

Timothy Dansdill, an associate professor of English at Quinnipiac University, is also an actor and did the music and vocals for the band used in *1918*. His costume was one of those from the First World War. He wrote about the play and performance:

> General kudos to all for making the Perennial Magic and Mystery of Theatre as Community in and on the run—endless lightning in a bottle ... would do more of it if I didn't have a full time job!
>
> *1918* as satire is often so subtle it's easy to misperceive its family drama conventions as its primary intention....
>
> My sense of Foote's understated—almost to the point of muting— hatred of war's absurdity and human stupidity in equating it with God's will required that I not only amp that muting with big songs but also—and here's the risk—vamp his drawing room/parade street pieties of what is essentially a devastating sketch of patriotic gore. (Dansdill)

Ryan Devaney, a freshman theater major at Quinnipiac, was the actor Horace Robedaux in *1918*. He said:

> By reading multiple plays in *The Orphans' Home Cycle*, I was able to comprehend every reference and all emotions of the monologue which made the scene very easy to present to the audience.... In my interpretation, Horace kept all of his feelings and opinions to himself if it ever hurt anyone in the process. Reading Horace's inner thoughts and woes made recreating the character so much easier to play. (Devaney)

The voices of these members of the Quinnipiac theater group convey something of the energies of a production Horton Foote would have loved, and, due to my long familiarity with the man and the playwright, I recall his passion for the theater now in ways best not expressed as academic formulas. Foote himself saw style as something to be pondered:

> What creates a writer's style? Other writers' plays, novels, stories, poems, I'm sure... One of the mysteries of the creative process is what makes us choose what we write about and the style we choose to

share it with others. I wonder if the themes and material we are drawn to as writers aren't given to us at a very really age, before we have done much reading of the works of others, or even begun to think of writing.... I wonder, too, if our writing style can be changed in any really profound way, any more than the color of our eyes or our skin. The perfecting of our style, of course, is consciously cultivated all our writing lives. Katherine Anne Porter wrote in a letter to a friend: "Chaos is—we are in it—my business is to give a little shape and meaning to my share of it."

Foote's own memories of childhood, in so far as they are retained in his drama, center upon the sudden death of his grandfather in 1925. My papa, Jack Brian, died of a heart attack when he was only fifty-eight years old. He was a medic in the Marines in New Guinea during the Second World War. Horton talked to me a great deal about what one feels on having a papa or grandfather die in that way. It was September of 1983 when Jack died. In September of 2013, I had a stroke, and for several months, it seemed I would die. But, after six months in the hospital and another six months as an outpatient, I was able to return to work as a professor, and in April of 2015, I was able to direct Horton Foote's *1918*. I was also Mrs. Vaughn in the play. And Hallie and Devon came to the final dress rehearsal and first performance, worked with students/actors, and talked to an audience. It was the only time they had come to Quinnipiac University in Hamden, Connecticut. And they came because they knew, after a year in the hospital, the fact that I was able to go back to teaching, and to theater, was important. In my work on Horton Foote's plays and screenplays, I have always felt the importance of family to this author and have sought to do justice to his constant engagement with this theme; thus my own involvement in 2015 with his key play, *1918*—produced less than a hundred miles from Hartford, where Foote was working on the marathon version of his great cycle's production at the time of his death in 2009—was enriched by the presence of members of his family.

As I worked on this important Foote play in 2015, after knowing him and his work for such a long time, I remembered some of the actors, directors, and playwrights who had been involved with him for many years. When I was doing research on his plays several years before his death, Horton asked me to call these people on the phone and to let them give me information about his plays, performed in theaters all over the country. Here I include a selection of the generally informal remarks made by some of these artists who knew Foote well.

Robert Duvall was a friend of Horton Foote's for many years and was an actor in several of his plays and films. He talked to me on the phone in 1995:

> We first did Foote's version of *Tomorrow* as a play, before he wrote the film version. It was done in the HB Studio Theater in NYC. It was a wonderful experience. One night a seven year old boy in the front row was crying at the end. This was a long, garage-type building, and at the most 85 or 90 people could get into the theater. One night, Dustin Hoffman came. Bobby DeNiro came as well. He was very young at that time. It was a wonderful night in the theater. I remember they yelled 'Bravo' and they pounded their feet... A great evening. And it was nice, having Horton there, working on it... Everyone admired Horton. (Duvall)

I asked Duvall, "Do you think that he particularly writes for the actor, more than other writers that you've worked with?" He replied:

> I think that he does. I don't know if it's a conscious thing, but his sense of place and his sense of the characters within that place ... that Texas thing which is very local, but universal at the same time... I think he does in many ways write for actors, and it's very delicate ... at times it's something you can't push along or force ... you have to ride along with it. Because it's delicately written sometimes. You can't force it.... We did the films *Tender Mercies* and *Convicts*. That was a wonderful project, the filming of Foote's *Orphan's Home Cycle* play, *Convicts*.... With the films of both *Convicts* and *Tender Mercies* ... it's very delicate. You can't force it along. It's really special.... I know that when you read it (the plays) it's just there. It's very seductive in a good way. As an actor, it leads you along.... There's a certain sweetness about it too ... I call it a legitimate saccharine. A

legitimate sweetness.... I just think he's the kind of guy that's always reaching out to get the truth of what he sees. In what he does and in those around him.... And I think he's always looking for the truth in his own way.... I think that's what he goes for.... He's a major American figure.... But he will be remembered for presenting an accurate vision of a regional sense of reality that can also translate to something universal. (Duvall)

Harper Lee published the novel *To Kill A Mockingbird* in 1960, and in 1962, the story was released as a film, which has since become regarded worldwide as a classic. Horton Foote wrote the screenplay, after meeting with Harper Lee, who had asked that he write it. In 1998, she wrote to me, telling me what she remembered of Foote's work. She didn't like talking on a telephone and instead faxed and mailed me a number of letters. Here are some excerpts from her correspondence:

- Your letter of 17 January has just come to light! I have been away from my New York address for months and months; when that happens it plays merry hell with mail sent here. I do hope I'm not too late to help you in any way that I can with your book on Horton Foote. If you could write me a list of questions I'll be glad to answer them as well as I can and fax them back to you. I do not have a fax machine to receive them, so if you could send them priority mail or something, it would probably save two or three days in transit. I know you've not talked to anybody who doesn't love Horton, so anything I have to say will be boringly repetitious; I never knew a finer person. Sincerely, Harper Lee. (6 April 1998)

- When I returned from faxing an answer to your letter of January 17, I found your letter of 2 April in my mailbox! I notice that your present fax number is different from the one of your first letter, so if you did not receive it, my answer is: I shall be delighted to help you in any way that I can with your work on Horton Foote. Please write me your questions and I'll reply by fax. I think that'll be easier for both of us. I'd say let's do it by telephone but I'm hard of hearing and conversations are not always satisfactory. I'll be at my New York address until early July. (7 April 1998)

- Dear Miss Brian; Herewith a muchly cut down version of my comments on Horton Foote and his screenplay. I discovered that I'd gone on far too long and it made boring reading indeed. (That is, I made it boring.) A wise man once told me, "Clarity is all and brevity its eldest child." If this is not satisfactory to you, please call me…. After you've memorized that number, chewn and swallowed it. And please forgive my uncertain typing. I have arthritis in my hands, and they're what the Scots call widdershine. Sincerely, Harper. (30 June 1998)

- Dear Ms. Brian: Thank you for your letter! It was really at 6s & 7s about what I sent you: it was cut from a rambling (I could go on about this forever) piece that I'd done over the weeks/months, then I realized that if I sent it you'd be over a barrel—would you risk insulting Harper Lee by not including every precious word of it, or would you—I hoped—be professional and take only what you needed? At any rate, I had put you in a corner so I tried to project, using the guidelines you gave me, what you would need and probably use. Judging from your letter, I seem to have hit it about right. You are, of course, free to use any or all of it or none of it. I so look forward to reading your book. I am leaving NYC at the end of the month to go home to Alabama for the remainder of the year. If the book comes out before February 1999, I'll be grateful if you'd send it to me…. Sincerely yours, Harper. I'm sorry I didn't type this—it's easier holding a stick of a pen than trying to hit keys—more legible, too! (7 July 1998).

As is well-known, Harper Lee treasured her privacy and defied many attempts to get interviews or commentary from her. As these passages demonstrate, however, her friendship with Horton Foote made her cheerfully cooperative with a scholar seeking to appreciate Foote's contributions.

Horton Foote's *The Orphans' Home Cycle* plays were first done at Herbert Berghof's HB Playhouse on Bank Street in New York City in 1976 and 1977. Matthew Broderick, in his first theatrical role, played Brother. I spoke with him on the phone in 1998, and he reminisced about his early contacts with the playwright:

> I think I met him (Horton Foote) when I was about fourteen or fifteen … something like that. He did several plays at the HB Studio. And the first time I remember knowing Horton was when my dad was doing … I think it was *1918*. I know that my parents had known him before I was born…. I was in high school at the time that I was acting in plays. So Horton invited me to his apartment in New York City to read scenes. Pretty much with the understanding that he wanted me. It didn't really feel like an audition, but we sat on his couch and we read through my whole part…. He said very little in terms of information for me. He just kept saying, "Oh, that's fine, that's fine. [Laughs] That's going to be just fine." And that was it. He just wanted me to do it and he took a chance, basically. So that was my first real job, I guess, as an actor. (Broderick)

Broderick's account of Foote's gentle cordiality and encouraging demeanor matches many other descriptions of the Texas playwright, an individual whose sympathy for others and honest concern with good acting and good writing often impressed those he met. This personal warmth charmed not only theater professionals but even the academic scholars who sought him out to learn about his literary achievement, and he is remembered with gratitude by many of them. Continuing his narrative, Matthew Broderick comments on Foote's benevolent presence:

> At this point I had done films with Neil Simon, and I guess I was more confident. But still, when you work with Horton, it doesn't really matter what you've—it's not who is more powerful. When I had no experience and when I had some experience, I felt equally comfortable and wanted … I mean, he creates this, he seems to like actors, very much. He used to be one. And I think he enjoys being around them. It's just nice to be in the rehearsal room. I don't just mean nice in an offhand kind of way. It's creative too. Because you feel comfortable and valued … I think beyond everything it's to rehearse and have such an intelligent person there. It makes you feel more comfortable because you trust him…. I've been very lucky to

know Horton. And we've had some success together.... I suppose Tennessee Williams, also from the south, has been interesting as a playwright. But I feel Horton has defined a style. He is original and mysterious. A lot of people can read one of his plays and say, "Well, nothing happened, what's the point of that?" But when you do them and you can feel an audience riveted—it's hard to explain. You don't catch him manipulating you, ever. You don't see him working.

In the fall of 1994, from my office at Whittier College in Whittier, California, I was able to speak with Gregory Peck on the phone. He said:

I didn't meet Horton before the picture (*To Kill a Mockingbird*) started. I met Harper Lee, but not Horton. And I think at that time he was dividing his time between Texas and New York.... When I first read the screenplay, it was a *fait accompli*, it was done. It was very well done, too. I didn't meet Horton until later on, sometime during the filming. But I know that Harper was happy with the screenplay. And, you know, novelists are not always happy with screenplays. But Horton captured the spirit of the book, and Harper was pleased that her book hadn't been violated or diminished in some way. It was a kind of serendipitous operation, the whole thing.... The filming seemed to be quite easy and I think that's because it was a very fine screenplay. The scenes played themselves. I wouldn't say that all we had to do was to show up. (Laughs) We had to invest with our emotions and our interpretation of the lines, and our feelings about the character.... I was a kind of co-producer. My company was involved with everything. I had been down to Monroeville, and the streets were not paved in 1931, as they were in 1962. In 1931 there were no neon signs or television aerials. There were in 1962. So it wasn't possible. That's why we built parts of the town in replica on the Universal backlot in Hollywood.... Horton dramatized the novel. You cannot film a novel. You'd have an eight hour film. Horton was a dramatist, so he was able to select the episodes and the scenes that had cohesion, that told the story that Harper wanted to tell. It was necessary to eliminate some sequences, some quite good things in the novel, but to tell the story in the spirit of Harper Lee, and to maintain the integrity of the characters. That's the talent of Horton and the ability as a dramatist. Without Horton, it wouldn't have been the same. (Laughs) Lord knows what it might have been, but it wouldn't have been the same movie. So he performed his function as a dramatist.... I do remember at one point, when I saw the rough draft, as a co-producer, I came in with my yellow legal pad and a pen at the ready, as I usually do, and make notes about the editing. And I remember after ten or fifteen minutes I rather flamboyantly tossed the yellow pad in the air, and the pencil with it. It was playing so well that it didn't need any suggestions from me.... It was necessary that the novel be dramatized, and Horton was able to do it, to our satisfaction ... to Harper's satisfaction. After thirty-six years, to everybody's satisfaction. It's being played in the middle schools constantly.... I know that some students are sitting in a classroom right now, watching the movie made thirty-six years ago, and getting something of value from it.... It was a team, and Horton made an important contribution, an invaluable contribution, to the film.... I have one story about Horton. When I was called up to receive the golden statue for that performance, I proceeded to thank everybody I could think of. Somehow or other, I forgot to thank Horton. I thanked my agent. I thanked the press. I thanked my little daughter, who—when I left the house—gave me a rabbit's foot to put in my pocket. But I forgot Horton. And somebody told me the next day. Well, I started apologizing long-term to Horton. I talked about him for years. I apologized to Horton over that. But there finally did come some occasion—I forget what it was—but Horton and I were together at some function. Something to do with Hollywood, some charity banquet. And I was given another award for Atticus Finch. And I thanked Horton publicly, on television. I finally made up for it.... I was very glad to be able to thank him, again and again. (Laughs) ... He is the American Chekhov. The writing is not overly dramatic. But if you capture the current that runs below the words, if you capture the current of emotion that runs beneath the words, then it becomes extremely dramatic and emotionally involving. That is the characteristic of Horton's plays. I think there's a very good chance that they will be revived for a long period of time. (Peck)

Frank Rich was the theater critic of the *New York Times* for several years, and he did a number of columns on Horton Foote's productions in New York City. When Horton won the Pulitzer Prize, this came in large part because of Rich's feelings about Horton Foote's works. I was able to speak on the phone with Frank Rich in the fall of 1994. Below is some of what he said. His comments on Ralph Waite and Rip Torn refer to two actors who played the key role of Will Kidder in separate versions of Foote's play *The Young Man from Atlanta*. Rich recalls:

> I felt that Ralph Waite was terrific, but I also thought that Rip Torn was terrific. But in every other way, I felt that the second version of the play, done on Broadway, had more improvement than the earlier performances done at the Signature Theater in NYC. I'd say a draw between those two guys, but it was just a much better, much more solid—upscale if you will—performance. The aesthetics and supporting cast in the second production, as well as stronger physical production. Plays begin in small theaters and are blown up and sometimes distorted for Broadway. This was not an example with this play.... I thought the production in New York and at the Goodman Theater in Chicago was a superb set that fit the play because I felt there was a strong element about the 1950s and a certain kind of post-war ethos in America and in Texas that he was tapping into.... Call it absurdism, for lack of a better word. We think of this as absurdism, but with *The Young Man from Atlanta*, we never know who the young man is. We never know what the story is, why the son died.... My feeling is that he was as good ... as anyone I've seen because his plays are so honest. The virtues of them are timeless. But they are not tied in the end to realistic place and time, specific work and due date, in spite of often being mistaken for that by audiences and critics ... because what he's dealing with is the truth of human beings, whenever they lived, wherever they lived, even if he's dealing with one patch of ground.

It is hoped that the passages provided here from my conversations with these artists and this critic will make possible an enhanced perspective on Horton Foote, a unique American writer whose eighty or more plays, teleplays, and screenplays—on most of which relatively little critical commentary has been made—are being increasingly recognized as foundational to American drama. More work needs to be done, of course; more of his plays need to be reviewed and performed, and more careful thoughts must be meditated on this artist's achievement, for his gift to the theater and to literature is not to be underestimated. My understanding of Horton Foote after many years of study and theatrical engagement with his work remains that he is indeed our transcendental playwright—our "mystic of the American theatre."

Works Cited

Brian, Crystal. "Interview with Horton Foote." October 2000. *The Playwright's Muse*. Ed. Joan Herrington. New York: Routledge, 2002. 207–209.

Broderick, Matthew. Telephone interview with Crystal Brian. June 1998.

Dansdill, Timothy. Personal interview with Crystal Brian. 2015.

Devaney, Ryan. Personal interview with Crystal Brian. 2015.

Duvall, Robert. Telephone interview with Crystal Brian. 1995.

Foote, Horton. "Lecture." Spalding University. Louisville, Kentucky. 13 Nov. 1987.

Lee, Harper. Unpublished correspondence with Crystal Brian. April–July 1998.

Peck, Gregory. Telephone interview with Crystal Brian. Fall 1994.

Rich, Frank. Telephone interview with Crystal Brian. Fall 1994.

Scott, Drew. Personal interview with Crystal Brian. 2015.

Staton, Aleta. Personal interview with Crystal Brian. 2015.

A Dramatist's Archive: An Overview of the Horton Foote Papers at DeGolyer Library_____

Cynthia Franco

Horton Foote was a native of Wharton, Texas, whose career as an actor, playwright, and screenwriter spanned over seven decades. He is best known for his Oscar-winning screenplays for *To Kill a Mockingbird* and *Tender Mercies*, but his heart was always in the theater. His play *The Young Man from Atlanta* won the Pulitzer Prize for Drama in 1995. Throughout his body of work, he wrote of a fictionalized Wharton and the drama of ordinary people.

Horton Foote's papers came to DeGolyer Library at Southern Methodist University as both gift and purchase in 1992. DeGolyer Library is a special collections library with a focus on the humanities, the history of the American West, business history, and transportation history. In a 1996 letter to an SMU student newspaper reporter, Foote wrote "I had several universities interested in my work but I chose SMU because of the respect I had for [library director] David Farmer and his tenacity in winning me over. Too, I wanted the papers to be in Texas. I felt that was the most important."[1] From 1992–2011, Horton Foote's family continued to donate his literary drafts and family papers. After Foote passed away in 2009, librarians traveled to Foote's home in Wharton to collect additional documents and manuscripts, as well as to pick up some items on loan for use in a 2011 exhibit celebrating his life.

This collection has been inventoried several times by different people, in a few different ways. It has been a challenge to respect the original order of Foote's papers, while providing an inventory that makes sense to the researcher. The original fifty boxes of Foote's papers were inventoried at the item level by archivist and biographer Penelope Niven McJunkin in 1985. As Penelope Niven, she published biographies of Carl Sandburg, James Earl Jones, Thornton Wilder, and Edward Steichen. Her inventory included page counts for almost every draft in the collection at that time.

Item-level cataloging is not standard for most of the finding aids produced by DeGolyer Library, so this practice was not continued, with the exception of a list of Horton Foote correspondents. McJunkin's original inventory is available to researchers upon request. Additional gifts to the library in the 1990s were added to the collection with minimal description. In 2014, the Horton Foote archive was organized in twelve series containing the following: Duff and Brooks family papers, correspondence, personal papers, essays and lectures, literary works, business records, programs and publicity, manuscripts and publications, photographs, posters, audio-visual materials, and scrapbooks and clippings.

Some of the boxes obtained from Foote's home in 2009 contained his mother's extended family papers from 1838 to the 1960s. The Duff family papers contain nineteenth-century love letters and general Texas correspondence. The Brooks family papers consist mainly of family and business correspondence, photographs, and ephemera from Texas. It is possible that this material provided inspiration for many of his works. This early family history series would also be of interest to scholars of early Texas business and real estate, or World War II correspondence.

The Foote family correspondence series was originally restricted during Foote's lifetime, but restrictions on these letters were lifted by the family after his passing in 2009. Biographers have pored over the seventeen boxes of correspondence between individuals including Foote's parents, Foote himself, his wife Lillian, their four children, and Foote's literary agent, Lucy Kroll. A number of the Foote family letters are from Horton's mother to her son and span the years 1943–1973. Letters from Foote's brothers and some correspondence between his parents also help paint a portrait of a close Texas family and the environment in which Foote was raised. Letters written by Foote range from 1935 until his death in 2009. His correspondence with Lillian Vallish Foote begins with their courtship in 1944, then jumps to the late 1950s when he was writing for television shows, and continues until 1972. Horton and Lillian's correspondence is both personal and professional and provides details about his various television and film relationships, his creative process, and their own close working relationship. Most of his correspondence was arranged chronologically and alphabetically, and this order was maintained. A PDF file is available online that contains each individual name listed in Foote's correspondence. This should help researchers if they are trying to find all correspondence from one person over the span of his career, such as Reynolds Price or Lillian Gish. Notable correspondents include Stark Young, Mary Hunter Wolf, Herbert Berghof, Agnes de Mille, Alan Pakula, Robert Duvall, Craig Slaight, Michael Wilson, and Romulus Linney. Correspondents would frequently send publications and other items with their letters for Foote's consideration. For example, a 1994 letter from Gerald C. Wood includes a syllabus for a college course on Horton Foote's work.

Scholars will find the forty-four years of correspondence between Foote and his agent Lucy Kroll a valuable business resource for the golden age of television, the Hollywood film industry, and American theater. Her correspondence files include royalty receipts, contracts, and reviews of Foote's work. Kroll, an agent and former member of the American Actors Company, signed Horton Foote as her first client. She represented Foote until the 1990s and was succeeded by Barbara Hogenson. Foote and Hogenson's correspondence from 1995–2007 is also located in the second series.

The third series in the collection consists of Foote's personal papers. These seven boxes include Foote's school work, genealogy, calendars, ephemera, and awards. Foote was a Christian Scientist, and his papers contain two boxes of religious materials. One box is full of Christian Science publications, and the other box contains his religious notes and family Bibles. Although there are few calendars from his early career, there are daily logs from 1992–2003, in which his personal assistant, Kelly Kline Vance, kept track of various appointments and administrivia his work demanded. Of note in this series is a friendly letter from New York theater critic, John Simon, laid in a 2006 appointment book. The last items in this series include awards dating from 1963–2010, most of which are certificates. Highlights include Academy of Motion Picture Awards nominations, an American Academy of Arts and Letters certificate, and mayoral proclamations, as well as honorary doctorates from Austin College, Drew University, Spalding University, and Southern Methodist University. The family retained Foote's Oscars, Pulitzer Prize, Independent Spirit Award, Emmy, and other awards.

The next series in the collection contains three boxes of Foote's essays, lectures, and speeches written from 1973–2006. Many of these lectures were delivered at universities. These essays and lectures describe Foote's childhood in Wharton, his early career in New York City theater, the golden age of television, and his writing process. Laurin Porter wrote in her 2000 article "The Horton Foote Collection at the DeGolyer Library" that Foote's essay "On First Dramatizing Faulkner" provides "much useful information on the writer's influence on Foote and on the process of adaptation and its particular challenges."[2] Foote wrote many adaptations for television and film, but not all were produced.

Foote's written works form the largest part of his archive: notes, drafts, a poetry sketch, two novels, stage plays, teleplays, and screenplays. One hundred thirty-two boxes contain his works alphabetized by title from the 1930s–2011, indicating that he wrote almost every day of his life. Foote also changed the titles of some works, such as *Mamie Borden*, which was renamed *Only the Heart*. He continued to revise and update his works, sometimes decades after they were produced. For example, *The Trip to Bountiful* was revised from the 1953 teleplay up to the 1985 film version, which won an Oscar for Geraldine Page. It appears that Foote saved all of his drafts, and scholars should benefit from this extensive archive when studying his writing process. Early in Foote's career, he would handwrite notes or whole drafts of works using a series of stenographic notebooks, and sometimes bound ledgers, before making typescript copies. From the late 1970s through the 2000s, he used spiral notebooks for early handwritten drafts before producing printed copies. Many of his handwritten notes and drafts during his later years are difficult to decipher, but it is interesting to compare his writing style from the 1930s to the 2000s. Foote's first play "Wharton Dance" was written in 1939 or 1940 and included the names of real people from his hometown. It was the first one-act play written and produced by the American Actors Company. Both "Wharton Dance" and Foote's first full-length play, *Texas Town*, were restricted during Foote's lifetime, but they are now available for research. It is important to note that Foote also wrote some reviews for *Dance Observer* in the 1940s, and these can be found near the end of this series. As Laurin Porter wrote in her overview of the collection, "it is unusual to see Foote functioning as theater critic" (72).

After the American Actors Company disbanded, Horton and his wife moved to Washington, DC, where he wrote and directed plays at the King-Smith School. Four years later, the family returned to New York City, where he worked as a television writer for *The Quaker Oats Show* before becoming a regular writer for various television drama programs. Although Foote later achieved critical success writing screenplays for Hollywood (*To Kill a Mockingbird, The Trip to Bountiful, Tender Mercies*), he also experienced disappointment. Scholars should note that some of his drafts were never produced. These works include a biopic of Lyndon Johnson and commissioned scripts that were not used for the films *The Chase, This Property is Condemned, The Stalking Moon, April Morning, The Grass Harp, Little House on the Prairie,* and *The Great Debaters.* His unproduced works continue to draw interest from the television and film industries. In 2015, the cable television film *Bessie,* a biopic of blues singer Bessie Smith, credited Horton Foote with the story, which he wrote from 1974–1992. This production won an Emmy for Outstanding Television Movie in September 2015. Since Foote passed away, four films have been produced using scripts from his archive: *Main Street* (2010), *One Armed Man* (2014, a short film), *The Trip to Bountiful* (2014), and *Bessie* (2015). Foote's research materials and drafts at the DeGolyer demonstrate a fascinating aspect of his writing process. For instance, his personal annotated copies of *To Kill a Mockingbird* and *Of Mice and Men* contain ideas for scenes and dialogue. This fifth series in the collection ends with three boxes of untitled drafts and notes that are mostly handwritten.

Beginning in the 1980s, Foote began working with independent filmmakers and even backing his film projects with his own money.

He formed a production company, Bountiful Films, and the bulk of the sixth series in the collection contains the company's business records, which include payroll, taxes, contracts, log books, receipts, invoices, and checks. Also included in this series are contracts and financial documents from his early career, as well as book royalty records from his two memoirs.

The seventh series contains programs and publicity materials dating from the 1940s to 2011. Playbills are filed alphabetically and include Foote's plays as well as those he attended by other playwrights. Organizations that produced Foote's plays often sent him playbills, so this series includes items from high schools, colleges, and regional theaters. Theater scholars should note that there are early playbills for HB Playhouse, a program for the American Actors Company's first production, and three boxes of mostly Broadway playbills from the 1980s. Foote also saved many of the programs for events he attended, and these are arranged chronologically from 1963 until the end of his life. These events include various film and theater awards, including one from the Fellowship of Southern Writers, the Pulitzer Prize, the National Medal of Arts, and recognitions from university convocations.

Foote saved a number of other publications related to his career. The eighth series contains works about Horton Foote, manuscripts by other writers, and periodicals featuring his interviews or reviews of his work. The series begins with a box containing dissertations and scholarly works about Horton Foote dating from 1987–2003, sometimes with annotations. Dissertations and theses received after 2009 were added to the DeGolyer Library's main stacks and can be searched in the online library catalog or WorldCat online. During his lifetime, Foote also gave the library signed copies of his published plays. Three boxes of manuscripts and publications contain sheet music (including piano rags by his paternal aunt, Lilyan Dale Foote Coffee); photocopies of Texas research materials; a manuscript entitled "Uncle Remus," written by his mother in 1909; a 1939 translation of *The Sea Gull*, by Stark Young; and photocopies of lectures and articles about playwriting and acting.

The prints and photographs in the collection have been heavily used in recent years for biographies and a documentary film. Nine boxes contain images of Horton Foote, his family, various productions and events, and location photographs. In addition to hundreds of photographs of Horton Foote and his family, there are many photographs with his colleagues, friends, and famous people. Included are Dorothy and Lillian Gish, Bruce Beresford, Robert Duvall, Ronald Reagan, Bill Clinton, and Laura Bush. Most of the slides and photographs for various productions are for publicity purposes, but some provide a window onto the process of filmmaking. The photographs taken for continuity purposes on the set of *1918*, *On Valentine's Day*, and *Courtship* are candid shots of the crew and actors on a hot set in Texas. Foote and his production crew scouted many locations for their films, and almost two boxes contain images of various Texas structures in Beaumont, Waxahachie, Forney, Navasota, Glen Flora, Terrell, and Egypt. Posters of Foote's film and theatrical productions are arranged alphabetically in a separate series. This collection of posters may continue to grow as theater companies occasionally send the library publicity materials when they perform Foote's works.

The eleventh series in the collection contains audiovisual materials dating from 1956–2010. Nine boxes of audio contain dialect recordings, production music, interviews, and lectures. Nineteen boxes of videos also include interviews, lectures, movies, some television shows in which Foote's daughter Hallie acted, auditions for the film *Lily Dale*, and productions of Foote's work. The library has copies of Foote's television plays as early as 1953 and previously provided free streaming of *A Young Lady of Property* for Robert Haynes' graduate class on Foote at Texas A&M International University. Upon request, productions recorded on obsolete formats are digitized and made available for scholars to view in the library. The last film in the video series is *Main Street*. Released in 2010, this was the final film in which Foote was personally engaged. As with the poster series, the library will continue to add to the video series as new productions are released. In addition to the video, the library also has film footage in offsite cold storage. This includes raw footage from *1918*, release prints of *Courtship*, and four television plays (*Drug Store, Sunday Noon*; *Mrs. Wiggs*; *Night of the Storm*; and *Traveling Lady*). The television plays have been transferred to other formats and can be viewed in DeGolyer Library. All of the film in offsite storage is restricted due to preservation issues.

Scrapbooks and newspaper clippings form the final series of Horton Foote's papers. Twenty-eight boxes contain Foote family scrapbooks, theater production scrapbooks, photograph albums, and newspaper clippings. The scrapbooks are arranged chronologically, and the newspaper clippings are arranged alphabetically by production title. Early newspaper clippings document life in Wharton, Texas, and almost all of the scrapbooks are filled with Foote's plays and films. Foote also retained newspaper clippings regarding three of his children, a file on the Pulitzer Prize, and published reviews that were important to him. Also included are the family's planning documents and programs for Foote's memorial services at Lincoln Center, Hartford Stage, and Wharton, Texas.

DeGolyer Library's past outreach initiatives for this collection include an exhibit in 2003 featuring *The Trip to Bountiful* and a 2011 exhibit celebrating his life and work. The 2011 exhibit was part of the Horton Foote Festival held in Dallas, Texas, in which various Dallas arts organizations presented plays by Foote. The library also held a viewing of *A Young Lady of Property*; published a memorial volume of tributes from Foote's colleagues and friends, entitled *Remembering Horton Foote: 1916–2009*; and hosted the casts of *Dividing the Estate* and *The Roads to Home* to review primary source materials for their productions. Joel Ferrell, associate artistic director of Dallas Theater Center, described the cast visit to the library: "We were able to get to the 'gooey goodness' of his process: we could see the evolution from a germ of an idea, through the revisions and refinement, to the completed work. For most of the actors, there was an eye-popping moment when they realized where he was going with their characters."[3]

The library continues to promote Foote's archive to scholars worldwide by providing an online collection of images. Items from the collection that have been digitized for publications or marketing have been cataloged and added to our digital collection site, "Horton Foote: Photographs and Manuscripts."[4] Some items that are copyrighted can only be viewed on campus, such as a studio still from the film *To Kill a Mockingbird*. There are currently fewer than a hundred items online, but, as digitization requests continue, the library will continue to grow this online collection.

After Horton Foote's passing in 2009, the library was faced with the daunting task of organizing an extensive writer's archive that had previously been arranged several different ways. Laurin Porter described the initial 144 boxes for potential researchers in 2000. Foote's archive now encompasses approximately 276 linear feet, including the recent additions of his early family papers, literary works, correspondence, and audiovisual materials from his home in Wharton, Texas. Porter identified particular boxes and folders in her article directing researchers to key documents. These box and folder numbers are now obsolete, and the contents have been integrated into the new inventory. After years of arranging and describing the everyday materials from Horton Foote's life, DeGolyer Library has made his collection more accessible to scholars worldwide both in the library reading room and online. A finding aid to the collection was completed in 2014 and published at Texas Archival Resources Online.[5] Researchers can view the complete inventory of the collection online to make informed inquiries about the collection and prepare for their visit to the library reading room.

In order to encourage research using DeGolyer Library collections, the library has partnered with the Clements Center for Southwest Studies at Southern Methodist University to offer research travel grants to qualified applicants. Interested scholars should first contact the library director to determine if the library's collection fits their research interests. When approval is given by the library director, the applicant then provides a project outline, curriculum vitae, and letters of reference. The Clements Center and DeGolyer Library accept applications twice a year for research stays of one to two weeks. The library will strive to preserve this archive and encourage scholarship on this major American dramatist.

Notes

1. Horton Foote letter to Lindsay Feldhaus, 1996, box 17, folder 3, Horton Foote papers, MSS 88, DeGolyer Library.

2. Porter, Laurin. "The Horton Foote Collection at the DeGolyer Library." *Resources for American Literary Study* 26.1 (2000): 69.

3. *Central University Libraries Annual Report.* Southern Methodist University, 17 Jun. 2015. Web. 15 Dec. 2015. <https://sites.smu.edu/cul/publications/annual-report/docs/annual-report-2011.pdf>. Joel Ferrell quote.

4. "Horton Foote photographs and manuscripts." *CUL Digital Collections.* Southern Methodist University, 17 Jun. 2015. Web. 15 Dec. 2015. <http://digitalcollections.smu.edu/all/cul/hor/index.asp>.

5. "Horton Foote papers: a guide." *Texas Archival Resources Online.* The University of Texas at Austin, 17 Jun. 2015. Web. 15 Dec. 2015. <http://www.lib.utexas.edu/taro/smu/00270/smu-00270.html>.

Works Cited

Horton Foote papers. DeGolyer Library. Southern Methodist University, Dallas, Texas.

Porter, Laurin. "The Horton Foote Collection at the DeGolyer Library." *Resources for American Literary Study* 26.1 (2000): 64–74.

Southern Methodist University. "Central University Libraries Annual Report." Accessed June 17, 2015. https://sites.smu.edu/cul/publications/annual-report/docs/annual-report-2011.pdf.

_____. "Horton Foote Photographs and Manuscripts." Accessed June 17, 2015. http://digitalcollections.smu.edu/all/cul/hor/index.asp.

Texas Archival Resources Online. "Horton Foote Papers: A Guide." Accessed June 17, 2015. http://www.lib.utexas.edu/taro/smu/00270/smu-00270.html.

Monuments, Memory, and Self-Location: Biographical Resources in Horton Foote's Drama

Robert W. Haynes

In a 1960 panel discussion held at Wesleyan College and including Katherine Anne Porter, Caroline Gordon, and Flannery O'Connor, the topic turned to symbolism and the southern writer's engagement with it. In one exchange, Porter declares:

> Symbolism happens of its own self and it comes out of something so deep in your own consciousness and your own experience that I don't think most writers are at all conscious of their use of symbols. I never am until I see them. They come of themselves because they belong to me and have meaning to me, but they come of themselves. I have no way of explaining them... (Magee 72–73)

O'Connor immediately responds, "I would second everything Miss Porter says. I really didn't know what a symbol was until I started reading about them." The agreement of these distinguished women, both of whom were greatly admired by Horton Foote, suggests an approach to the Texas playwright's own perspective on his art and the technique he developed from listening, from reading, and from working on and behind the theatrical stage.

In 1960, Horton Foote, who had established himself as a gifted writer of television drama but who had not yet written the Oscar-winning screenplay for *To Kill a Mockingbird*, saw the production on March 7 of his teleplay *Tomorrow* on CBS's *Playhouse 90*. This show was Foote's second adaptation for *Playhouse* of a William Faulkner story, and, like the first, *Old Man* (1958), it received high praise. *Tomorrow* starred Richard Boone and Kim Stanley, and it was reportedly admired even by Faulkner. Foote, a busy man at this time, moved forward with his work, and in May, he saw the broadcast, again on *Playhouse 90*, of *The Shape of the River*, which presented the story of Mark Twain's struggle to overcome bankruptcy and personal grief. Though it is Foote's Academy Award for the *To Kill a Mockingbird* screenplay that overshadows his other achievements during this time, surely his contemporary work on television is itself impressive. After the two *Playhouse* shows in early 1960, he went directly to work on a play that would much later evolve into the first drama of his major work *The Orphans' Home Cycle*, a teleplay he first titled *A Golden String*, then changed to *Roots in a Parched Ground*. When this work was ready to broadcast, its TV sponsor expressed reservations about the title, and Foote accepted the substitution of the title *The Night of the Storm*. The program appeared in March 1961, with Julie Harris and E. G. Marshall in key roles.

Foote's adaptations of Faulkner and his dramatization of Twain's struggle brought him both professional success and a deeper engagement with issues of southern identity and the vocation of the artist. He dealt with his own and his family's past and with a vertiginous shift in social values, and, in his drama, some forms of remembrance naturally took on symbolic meaning. Now in his forties, he recognized a certain inevitability in his region's and his own transformation in matters of historical memory, a recognition that explains the mantra familiar to all who have read any interviews with this writer, a statement that goes something like: "I don't choose these subjects; they choose me." As he approached his involvement with Harper Lee's blockbuster novel, he was beginning to perceive the literary text as itself a monument which challenges the author's identity and his highest aspirations. And as the southern establishment mobilized against efforts to broaden the recognition of civil rights, Foote saw that his home region's devotion to the past was, in many ways, opposed to its prospects for a hopeful future, and he lent his artistic gifts to a commemoration of human nature, which celebrates the instincts that help individuals through confusion, anger, error, and disappointment.

Politics and Memory

One cannot deny that a glib obscurantism often characterizes professional literary discourse, and Horton Foote may well have written as he wrote in part as artistic defiance of the pretensions of academic sophistry. After all, the theater has always resisted those external figures who profess to know its inner secrets. Al Pacino's film *Looking for Richard* (1996) dramatizes that conflict tellingly, with some comic bias against the professors. One of the most devastating portraits of the great Athenian philosopher Socrates is that presented in Aristophanes' *The Clouds*; it is a harsh portrayal, to which Socrates' star student Plato replies in *The Symposium* by having Socrates explicate dramaturgy to the increasingly inebriated Aristophanes and to a promising and apparently gifted young tragedian named Agathon, none of whose works has survived.

Foote had become a Roosevelt Democrat in the 1930s, sharing enthusiasm for FDR with his father, and he remained in the same party on into the twenty-first century. As an artist, however, he resisted ideology, just as he resisted the temptation to commercialize his drama. He learned early in life of the immense diversity of American culture, and though his own views diverged considerably from those of his old neighbors in the cotton culture of his upbringing, he refused to demonize anyone or to break with the tradition that fed energy into his art from the first play he wrote in 1939—a play in which he thoughtlessly used actual names of the folks back home. He experimented with radicalism in his early days in New York, and he never forgot that period in which the plays of Clifford Odets sought to galvanize the working class, but, as he increasingly realized that his Muse was a Texas muse and that his creativity flowed from memory and from tradition, such exercises lost whatever charm they had seemed to possess. And as he wrote, he found old themes returning to him and empowering his vision.

The theme of memory is essential in Horton Foote's work, and a particular manifestation of memory's importance is the monument, the memorial. Without suggesting that the way to understand this playwright is by reducing his art to some kind of formula, it can be observed that Horton Foote's drama functions memorially. If we think about it, we may remember that even in allegorical plays— *Everyman*, for example—the formulaic foundation of the work becomes, during performance, something of an interpretive option, and, in the case of Horton Foote, who vigorously denied having a formulaic approach to his dramaturgy, it should not be difficult to maintain an appropriate vigilance against simplistic interpretation. Yet it sometimes happens that emotional content is taken for sentimentality unless it involves suicide, mayhem, or hysteria, and in such instances, understanding suffers. But no one can escape emotional memory, and it may be that in the famous Aristotelian catharsis of pity and terror, there is evidence that reconciliation to memory is a kind of reinforcement of sanity.

Memory shapes the two opening plays of Foote's nine-play *Orphans' Home Cycle*. The first play is titled *Roots in a Parched Ground*, and the second is titled *Convicts*. These plays are set in the years just after the turn of the twentieth century, the period when Horace Robedaux, the protagonist of the *Cycle*, was a child. Horace's childhood was based on Foote's father's childhood, as understood and imagined after the senior Mr. Foote's death in 1973.

In the first of these plays, a strange mood of disappointment and depression creates an almost hallucinatory unreality as the child at the center of things loses first his father, who dies as a result of heavy drinking, and his mother, who leaves their small town and finds a husband in Houston who insists that Horace be excluded from her life. Hope springs up now and then, but it is always crushed by the negligence, apathy, or self-interest of the boy's relatives or the leading citizens of Harrison. Horace loses his family, including his neurotic sister Lily Dale, his prospects for education, and his faith in the empty assurances that he will be taken care of. He emerges from this sequence of disappointments with only his father's memory to sustain him. His father was not a successful man, but he had achieved an education and had established some skill in the law, and he also had expressed a desire that his son might pursue a legal career as well. Horace, rejected by family and by his father's friends, believes his father was abandoned and will vanish into oblivion if no one is loyal to his memory, and, though no one pays much attention to the lonely and devastated child, Horace himself resolves that he will secure a place in public memory for his father. Though promises are made that a headstone will be bought for his father's grave,

Horace gradually learns what such well-intentioned promises are worth, and, despite his penniless state and his poor prospects for a respectable future, he is already thinking of getting that modest monument to preserve Paul Horace Robedaux's memory.

At the end of *Roots in a Parched Ground*, young Horace seems almost defeated by the false promises and insincerity of those around him, but his character, though childish and naïve, promises a strength and integrity almost entirely absent in the hypocritical community called Harrison. As the following play, *Convicts*, opens, Horace has recovered from the initial impact of the loss of his parents and has found himself working on the Gautier plantation, where he has found friendship with the black workers who live there. His plan for the future is focused upon earning enough to purchase a gravestone for his father, but we soon learn of his strong interest in others and his uninformed curiosity about religion. In this place, where death and tyranny are almost normal features of life, Horace lives quietly, but with growing anxiety about whether the drunken and partly senile plantation owner Soll Gautier is going to pay him the small amount he is owed for his months of work in the plantation store.

In the first play of the *Cycle*, Horace lives in a world in which the black population is, for dramatic purposes, invisible and in which the white community is cold and dishonest. In this second play, the plantation is largely populated by the black employees and convicts, and the few whites who enter this realm, aside from Horace himself, are such characters as the alcoholic Vaughn couple; the brutal sheriff, who only stays long enough to kill the black convict Leroy Kendricks; and old Soll Gautier himself, a decrepit but still fearsome relic from the frontier past, a Confederate veteran who takes pride in having killed convicts and having enjoyed the black women who live on his family place. Soll owes Horace a small sum for working in the store, but the old man is constitutionally averse to paying, and, though Horace is gently persistent, he gets nothing but promises, some of them full of drunken extravagance, until Soll finally dies holding the boy's arm in a grip that must at last be broken forcibly by Horace's black friend Ben. Before his death, however, Soll has learned that Horace plans to spend his salary on a gravestone for his father, and this sign of filial devotion touches a kind of crazed sympathy in the old man's chaotic mind. Soll is something of an expert on graves, having been the reason for quite a few of them in his life, but his expertise has become intermixed with hallucination and with the Texas tendency to tell elaborate lies. He still admires his own father, who fell dead in the cotton fields at eighty-four while driving the convicts (*Convicts* 157), and he tells Horace: "You know what my daddy said to me just before he died?...'Soll,' he said, 'watch out for that sonofabitch Tyre. He'll steal you blind. He's a rattlesnake and he has venom in his fangs'" (131). Tyre, Soll's brother, is the father of Asa Vaughn, who inherits the plantation at the end of the play and refuses to pay Horace or even to provide a tombstone for Soll's grave.

In his isolation and paranoia, Soll fears that if he dies, his body will be devoured by wild animals, and he develops a sudden sympathy for Horace, the only other white person on the place other than the overseer and two guards who never appear onstage. Soll asks Horace to promise to guard his body after he dies, until it can be put in a coffin, and Horace does so. Despite the dysfunctional familial relations that characterize the violent old man, Soll begins to treat Horace kindly, as though the boy were his own kin, and, shortly after his Lazarus-like emergence from the coffin in which he was thought to have died, he tells Horace, "I never married. I never had no children I know about anyways. You got a daddy?" This question suggests that Soll may be thinking at this point that Horace is as close to being his child as anyone will ever be, but previously, there has been a suggestion that the convict named Tucker—who had hid in the closet hoping to kill Soll and had been killed himself— may have been the child of Sarah Tucker, one of the women the old man has repeatedly asked about and, probably, one of his favorite mistresses. For Soll to have killed his own son would not be entirely out of accord with his relationship with his niece Asa Vaughn, who, at one point, viciously kicks the old man as he lies drunk on the floor. Yet he realizes that he has nothing to fear from Horace, and he appears to understand that there is something noble in the boy's resolution to honor his father. Here is an exchange between the two:

Soll: ...What kind of tombstone did you have in mind for your daddy?
Horace: Just a small one.
Soll: What the hell do you want a small one for? Did you see the one I put on my daddy's grave? It's the biggest goddamned tombstone ever made. It's got angels all over it and two women crying. (135)

Of course, Soll is deteriorating fast by now, seeing things that are not there, imagining things he never did, and firing shots at invisible convicts he accuses of stealing tombstones. Those familiar with Foote's 1985 play "The Prisoner's Song" may notice the similarity between Soll's father's imaginary tombstone and the remarkable monument Mae Murray visits in that play. Mae describes that edifice to her husband:

> ...we drove out to the cemetery to see Mary Martha's tombstone and... I wasn't prepared for it.... Why, it is huge! On the top, you remember, is this marble bust of Mary Martha ... but I didn't think it was like her at all, because Mary Martha was sweet, but she wasn't pretty, not a bit, and this lady on the top of that tombstone is ravishingly beautiful. And you remember on every side of that tombstone they have marble benches and that's a good thing because you can sit while you read all they have written on the tombstone; they practically have the whole Bible up there plus the words to "The Prisoner's Song," which...was Mary Martha's favorite song. (Foote, *Selected One-Act Plays* 407)

Earlier, Mae has mentioned that her son had been born dead and was never named. Instead, his tombstone bore the words "Baby Murray" (403).

Soll boasts that he spent five thousand dollars on his father's tombstone (151) and tells Horace he will buy a stone for Paul Horace's grave: "I'm gonna buy the biggest god-damned tombstone in Texas," he says. "I'm gonna have angels on it and two Confederate veterans.... I'll put "Rest in Peace" on it, and three verses from the Bible" (140). Horace soon learns that Soll's father's grave is plain marble (166) and that his descriptions of graves are not to be trusted. Soll has said that he had put an accusation of murder on his brother

Melvin's gravestone, and he goes on later to claim that he has buried his money in one of the convicts' graves, although he has forgotten which one.

He certainly had a variety of graves to choose from, as there are three separate graveyards on the place: one for Soll's family, another for the black employees, and another still for the convicts who have died while assigned to work on the Gautier plantation. The graves of the white family all have headstones, but in the other graveyards the residents make do with whatever modest documentation of their unmoneyed existence was possible at the times of their deaths. Horace longs to assure his father a place among the remembered, for he himself has been generally forgotten, and the stories he has heard of his family's former status have given him some hope of restoring his family to a respectable status. Yet his heart does not seek a distinction grounded in pretension or false ambition, for as he learns of the deaths of the desperate convicts on the plantation, he seeks to memorialize them in his own way, by reciting prayers over their graves or by at least learning and remembering their names. He rejects both the hypocrisy of Harrison and the mindless force that has kept the plantation system working, and, though his friends wonder at his concern for the violent convicts who are after all strangers to him, his sympathy does not diminish.

Once Old Soll finally gives up the ghost, his funeral is in accord with the madness of his life. No white person except the thirteen-year-old Horace attends, and the few words that are said reach out beyond the old scoundrel's preoccupations to commemorate the permanent processes of natural mutability. Just before Jackson Hall sings his version of "Golden Slippers," Ben declares a vision of life's transience that focuses upon the vanity of human wishes and reminds all present that the ceremonies of human death and its records yield inevitably to disintegration. He says:

> Six months from now you won't know where anybody's buried out here. Not my people, not the convicts, not Mr. Soll. The trees and the weeds, and the cane, will take everything. "Cane land" they called it once, cane land it will be again. The house will go, the store will go, the graves will go, those with tombstones and those without. (166)

Like the graves obliterated in Soll's account of the tidal wave driven ashore by a hurricane (155), the graves on the plantation, ordered now and organized to suit the prejudices of the day, will one day lose all identity.

If we read Horton Foote's *The Orphans' Home Cycle* as a literary version of a monument to the father whose generosity and sympathy made Foote's dramatic art possible, the first two plays show us an artistic modesty that informs a profound vision of history. This thematic preoccupation runs through Foote's career and characterizes a spiritual dimension in the background of such works as *The Trip to Bountiful*, in which Carrie Watts revisits the old farm where she buried her children; *Tender Mercies*, in which Sonny and his mother go to the grave site of Sonny's dead father; and elsewhere in the *Cycle* itself, for when Horace grows up, he is able to accept that, possibly, the gravestone he has placed on his father's grave should be on the grave next to it, the grave of Horace's uncle. He understands that the fitting and proper thing has been done with the right intentions and that this is, at last, enough.

Private Records and Family Drama

In the 1961 teleplay that Foote titled *Roots in a Parched Ground*, a drama on which the first play of *The Orphans' Home Cycle* is roughly based, Horace Robedaux, Sr., who becomes Paul Horace Robedaux in the later version, dies while his son is absent, detained in a hurricane, and his body is taken to Galveston for burial.[1] Foote must have given some attention to the alteration of this detail for the *Cycle*. It is also noted in this 1961 version that Horace Senior was, as Mr. Ritter says, quoting Horace's mother, "Born during a storm and died during a storm" (36). This latter detail is the strongest indication given in either play, aside from references to his drinking, that Horace Robedaux's father's temperament might have included problematic qualities. However, there is some external evidence that Horton Foote's grandfather Albert Harrison Foote was not always a man of quiet disposition. Here is a brief story published in the *Galveston Daily News* in 1886 under the headline "Wharton. A Singular Accident:"

Wharton, October 9.—Rather a singular accident occurred here last night. Mr. A. H. Foote, of Peach Creek, this county, came to town to attend a ball, and after it was over went to the house of his mother, who lives here. Preparing to leave for Peach Creek about 1 o'clock, he went to the bed in which his younger brother and a young companion were sleeping, and proceeded to get his pistol, which had been left under the pillow. In drawing it out he dropped it on the floor, when it exploded. The ball passed through the bed slat, two mattresses and the fleshy part of the thigh of young Stephen Foote, inflicting a painful, but not dangerous wound. ("Wharton" 9)

This story presents only the basic information about this incident, but the mishandling of a pistol at 1:00 am, after a ball, indicates that Foote's future grandfather may have been somewhat less tame than the playwright's portrait of Paul Horace Robedaux would suggest. The light-hearted tone of the news story may mean that the Foote family's misadventures were well within the tolerance zone of the community, but no doubt some attention was subsequently given to A. H. Foote's domestic firearm management. The Stephen Foote wounded in this fiasco was later to become a doctor, and his son, Stephen A. Foote, Jr., MD, would, many years later, sign the death certificate of another man with a fictional counterpart in the *Cycle*, William B. Coffee, on whom Foote would base the character of Will Kidder, husband of Horace's younger sister Lily Dale Robedaux.

Though the dramatized Paul Horace is quietly acknowledged to be a drinker, there is no hint in the plays that he carries a pistol or is so clumsy in doing so as to endanger the lives of family members. Yet it seems very likely that the historical Albert Harrison Foote justly acquired something of a reputation not only as drinker, but also as a man who was capable of mishandling weapons when drunk. His grandson presents him as remembered by his father (who was, during Albert Harrison Foote's life, a loving son), as a gentle spirit unable to bear life's great burdens, and a man whose lack of a formal monument seemed intolerable. Thus Horton Foote chooses to honor his own father's tolerant devotion. Given the importance of Horace's status as virtual orphan in this dramatic cycle, it is of some value for us to know what circumstances led the playwright to develop that status as he did.

The odd story of Albert Harrison Foote's midnight pistol accident adds to our understanding of the background of young Horace Robedaux's predicament. It is also interesting to speculate about what the boy faced after losing his father. The dramatic sequence of the early narrative line of *The Orphans' Home Cycle* is established in the first three plays. In the first play, *Roots in a Parched Ground*, the death of Paul Horace Robedaux occurs, and we see the break-up of the emotional support structure on which Horace has depended. In the second play, *Convicts*, Horace has been abandoned by family and friends and has been sent to work on a rural plantation run by a crazed old tyrant whose antebellum racial attitudes are accompanied by drunken hallucinations and sociopathic violence. When the old man dies, Horace learns that the man's promises were meaningless. In the third play, *Lily Dale*, Horace, years older, travels to Houston to visit his mother, hoping she will help him get the education and training he needs to fulfill his father's wish that he become a lawyer. He soon discovers, however, that his mother's household is very much under the authority of her husband Pete Davenport, whose attitude toward Horace is hostile. Horace's mother is completely intimidated by her husband, and Horace's younger sister, Lily Dale, has conquered her stepfather's affections by charming him with sycophantic deference. Lily Dale, nervous and insecure herself, is quick to betray her brother and to maintain her ingratiating manipulation of Mr. Davenport, while Corrie, her mother, plays the domestic doormat for the bullying railroad man.

Here again, it is helpful to review the relevant biographical material on which Horton Foote drew in composing this play.[2] Corrie Thornton Davenport, formerly Corrie Thornton Robedaux, is based on Horton Foote's grandmother Corella ("Corrie") Horton Cleveland, formerly Corrie Horton Foote. Her husband, Pete Davenport, is based on Corrie Horton's second husband, Peter Cleveland, a native of Elberton, Georgia, who moved to Texas as an employee of the railroad. In the play, we see in the dynamics of the Davenport marriage the hard-working Pete's domination of the household supported by Corrie's diligent compliance and complicated—to Pete's evident satisfaction and Corrie's silent discomfort—by Lily Dale's flirtatious role as daddy's girl. Looking at the biographical background, we learn that Corella Davenport's counterpart Corella Cleveland (the playwright's grandmother, 1869–1940), married to Peter Earl Cleveland (1877–1960), was some eight years older than her husband, who was himself only fourteen years older than his stepdaughter Lilyan Dale Foote (1891–1975) and thirteen years older than his rejected stepson Albert Horton Foote. These ages suggest familial dynamics unspecified in the plays, though the plays themselves reveal that the relationships involved are uneasy. The 1996 film version of *Lily Dale* suggests an amorous tension between Pete (played by Sam Shepard) and Lily Dale (Mary Stuart Masterson), which is only alleviated when Lily Dale persuades Pete to allow Will Kidder to court her. It seems likely that the Cleveland home would have harbored some anxious emotional competition, especially when young Albert was present.

The role of Corella Davenport in the *Cycle* is that of a well-meaning but ignorant woman whose distinguished family background has contributed little or nothing to her life. She first married an educated young man of excellent family whose drinking and illness drew her into a nightmare of poverty and humiliation from which she escaped to labor in Houston as a shirt-maker. There, she met Pete Cleveland, whose devotion to work made him a major improvement upon her previous husband, and perhaps she was flattered by his attention, as she was several years older than he. Pete's personal contempt for education and his uninterrupted work history both made sense to her, and she may have had some sympathetic understanding of Pete's aversion to her son, whose presence was a constant reminder of his improvident father. In fact, the bond between Pete and Corella is a strong one, and, in a later play, Pete, whose character has previously seemed cruel and selfish, announces that he is prepared to sell his house if necessary to meet Corella's medical expenses. Though the connections between these dramatic characters and their real-life antecedents involve counterpoint and variation, it should be noted that Foote's composition of the *Cycle* was an artistic response to his parents' deaths in 1973–1974 and that his aunt Lily Coffee (the original of Lily Dale) died in 1975. Foote's father's relationship to his own mother was permanently damaged by her abandonment of him, and his sister's self-centered competitiveness also did much to establish a distance between them. It is these relationships and their effect upon Albert Horton Foote, Senior, that engaged the playwright in his exploration of his father's struggle to achieve a good life.

Though the imaginative process of dramaturgy must ultimately retain much of its mystery, the fact is that Horton Foote was intrigued by his family's history and especially by his father's life. An affectionate and respectful son, he also realized that his identity as artist was an achievement he owed to his father's generosity and sacrifice. For a poor, small-town southern clothes merchant to have sent a son to a California acting school in the heart of the Depression was a tremendously imprudent-seeming thing to do, and, as Foote realized, his own work was the result of that loving investment by his father. Thus his art was a fusion of his own vision and his father's hopeful, self-sacrificing dream. In *The Orphans' Home Cycle*, Horton Foote sought to complete the work of his father and to emulate him by leaving a monument of filial gratitude and responsibility.

It was difficult for Foote to deal with the final years of his parents' lives, for he himself was busy writing to meet the expenses of his family as his children, all born in the 1950s, grew up and pursued their own activities. Foote's father's mental stability deteriorated in alarming ways, and an effort to have the elder Footes live in the North with Horton and his family became impracticable. Foote's parents, more content in Wharton where they had lived all their lives, returned home to live out their remaining days. Though the 1963 Oscar he received for his screenplay for *To Kill a Mockingbird* had established Horton among the elite of screenwriters, subsequent film projects had brought frustration, and his effort to bring his parents into his own household was doomed by the unexpected developments in their condition. Horton's father died in 1973, and his mother followed a year later. It was the subsequent years he spent during the 1970s that brought him to a reconciliation with both his parents' loss and his own status as something like the "sixty-year-old smiling public man" (8) of William Butler Yeats's poem "Among School Children." Foote turned sixty in 1976 while working on *The Orphans' Home Cycle* and reflecting deeply upon his father's childhood and, no doubt, the passing of his own children into maturity. This major artistic effort of his life occupied much of a decade in which social changes that had erupted in the 1960s continued to alter both the fabric of society and the character of the theater. Foote, however, had led a life of change as he went from being small-town southern schoolboy to apprentice actor in California and New York to "promising playwright" (a phrase he came to detest) and temporarily angry young dramatist in the great city. A substantial figure in early television writing, he had also made a major contribution to civil rights with his successful screenplay for *To Kill a Mockingbird*, a work which was revolutionary in a time when voting rights for blacks were still restricted and public schools and colleges in the South were still racially segregated. He knew change was normal in life, and sentimentality had no attraction for him, though at times he was naturally appalled by destructive insensitivity to the value of the past and often expressed an aversion to the thoughtless cutting of old trees, the demolition of historic buildings, and the selfishness and egotism that always rate profit above values measurable only in terms of the human spirit. The passing of his beloved parents and the chaos that characterized their last decade in the South affected him as a loving and grateful son, but this experience also proved the inspiration for his greatest achievement, the nine-play cycle he titled *The Orphans' Home*.

Though Foote hoped that somehow his *Cycle* would be staged, as individual productions if nothing more, he was an experienced man of the theater and knew the odds were very much against a dramatic project of such magnitude. He went on to see four of the plays done in film versions (the 1961 teleplay of *Roots in a Parched Ground* was quite different from the play of the same name included in the *Cycle*), but, though a PBS television adaptation of three of the plays appeared in 1987, it was only in the next century that a stage version of the *Cycle* became a reality.[3] Foote, always a reflective artist, decided years later to revisit some of the characters of the *Cycle*, and he picked up the threads of their lives in a new drama.

As a final problem in the dramaturgical exercise of biography, Foote's 1995 play *The Young Man from Atlanta*, a play whose power remains widely underestimated, centers upon the marriage of Republican Houston businessman Will Kidder and his somewhat foolish wife Lily Dale. The Kidders' crisis is that their only son has died, probably by suicide, and they are left with stupendous loss, guilt, and confusion. The son's final act of rejection, devastating as it is, is especially hard to deal with because he appears to have been homosexual and possibly to have been blackmailed or otherwise defrauded by an associate. His mother, who passionately seeks to persuade herself that he was very religious and thus could not have taken his own life, refuses to entertain any such explanations and, without telling her more realistic husband, gives large sums of money to a young man who says he was her son's best friend and who plies Lily Dale with hard-luck stories. The main conflict of this complex, but simple-seeming play is that between recognition and false hope, for Lily Dale's feeble religious comfort is forced, by appalling truth, to evaporate, and Will's conviction of his strength as competitor gives way before his realization that he has betrayed the person he loved most. The play ends with Will and Lily Dale embracing as the husband comforts his wife, but Will's health is failing, and Lily Dale's grasp of the situation does not appear very firm.

In writing this play, Horton Foote returned to some characters he had included in his *Orphans' Home Cycle* some twenty years earlier. Lily Dale Robedaux, the sister of Horace Robedaux, protagonist of the *Cycle*, appeared at various points of Horace's life, most notably in the play titled *Lily Dale*, in which she distinguished herself as an insecure, self-centered, and vain girl who had already learned how to manipulate her stepfather and who seemed to resent her brother as much as she loved him. Horace loved his father Paul Horace Robedaux, but his sister, who had not known her father well, had become devoted to her mother's second husband Pete Davenport. Lily Dale's early relationship with Will Kidder, who worked with her stepfather, is portrayed in that play, and she later married the hard-working and energetic Will.

These characters, like others, are based on people Foote knew, in this case, as relatives. Lily Dale is based on Lilyan Dale Foote Coffee (1891–1975), Foote's father's younger sister, a woman whose musical compositions (rags) achieved a modest circulation in her lifetime. Will Kidder's character is derived from that of Lilyan Dale's husband William B. Coffee, Sr. (1886–1958). Mr. Coffee rose from poverty to wealth in Houston business and proudly displayed his status to his wife's relatives whenever possible. The Coffees' one child, William B., Jr., was a year younger than his cousin Horton Foote.

In 2002, commenting upon the origin of this play, Foote told Marion Castleberry the story behind the drama:

> The play is based on a true story. I had an uncle, not a blood uncle, but an uncle by marriage who was a kind of—well, he was the first one I knew in my family to become a Republican, which horrified them. He was what you would call a go-getter. [270] Everything was about the American Dream and then they had a son who was my age, maybe a little younger, who was very bright and had none of his father's ambitions…
>
> Then a curious thing happened: when the Second World War broke out, he volunteered and went into the Air Corps. I don't think he flew, but he was an operator or something, and he lived through the war, and then he came back home. He couldn't swim and one day he was in a bar and for whatever reason—you can't prove it one way or the other—he went down to the beach, walked into the water, and he never came out. He drowned. He was involved, my father told me, with a young man. And my father and the friends of his family thought this young man was out to blackmail them; not overtly, but in other ways. So that was the basis of the story. (Wood & Castleberry 269–270)

Though Foote is relating a much-abbreviated version of this catastrophe, it is useful to compare this version, which appears to encapsulate the family's anecdotal tradition, with some external material. In Foote's play, one significant factor is that Bill Kidder,

Will and Lily Dale's son, has left his parents' beloved Houston to live in Atlanta, a city commercially competing with Houston. Bill's death, as his father tells an office colleague, occurred in Florida when Bill, who couldn't swim, went to a lake and walked out of sight and disappeared (Foote, *Young Man* 5). Will also tells his associate that Bill had been a combat veteran. He says, referring to his son: "Volunteered for the Air Force. He was a bombardier. Came home without a scratch. Made I don't know how many bombing raids and didn't even get a scratch. I thought, my boy has a charmed life for sure" (5). Will ends his narration, "He was thirty-seven— thirty-seven. Drowned. Our only child" (6).

The story of the fictional Bill Kidder departs from that of William B. Coffee, Jr., in specific respects, as can be noted by a consideration of the Certificate of Death on file for the latter at the Florida State Board of Health, Bureau of Vital Statistics. In that document, William Coffee's date of birth is listed as June 17, 1917, and his date of death is June 16, 1947. His death thus occurred the day before his thirtieth birthday, which suggests an aversion to growing old. However, the cause of death is listed as "Drowning (not from a boat)," and, in response to the item reading "If death was due to external causes, fill in the following: (a) (Probably) Accident, suicide, homicide (specify)," the word "Accident" is written in the blank space. The location is noted as Egypt Lake, Hillsborough County, Florida, and the hour as 3:03 pm. Also noted on the form is that Coffee was a veteran of World War II and that he was a salesman. The address listed for him is the same as the Houston address of his father, who signed the form.

Thus we contemplate three versions of a story, one fictionalized into drama, one an anecdotal account by a relative, and one the official report of a death. The official document and the family anecdote do not disagree, but their differences are interesting, for Foote's account does not mention that his cousin died on the day before his thirtieth birthday, a fact surely known to the family, and the state certificate makes no suggestion that the death could have been anything more than an accident. It is the story as presented in the play that departs from what Foote tells us about William Coffee, Jr., and from the factual information on the death report, for, as playwright, Foote adds eight years to the age reached by his cousin and also adds a heroic dimension to his absent character. Will tells Tom Jackson of his son's extensive combat experience, whereas Foote says his cousin was an "operator," who did not fly. No doubt Foote, who was famously sensitive about publishing material that might hurt anyone's feelings, reflected carefully upon his play's use of actual events, yet since neither the Kidders nor the Coffees had children other than the one who died young, and since Pete Davenport— whose counterpart Peter Cleveland was eventually buried near his original home in Georgia, leaving no descendants—was long dead, it does not seem as though the playwright would have changed Bill's age and military history simply to spare the feelings of the living.

Bill Kidder is an important figure in the play, but, of course, he never appears onstage, except in conversation. His picture, on his father's desk, is noted, and his words are repeated, but he is a ghost, and the memories of him—which haunt his father, his mother, and the aged maid (who recalls him as a sweet and loving child)—evoke the sense of Bill as a lonely figure out of touch with his parents and their expectations. The toughness and heroic qualities he showed in combat, additions to Foote's memory of a cousin a year younger than himself, might seem to counter the despair suggested in the play by the apparent suicide of a middle-aging, destitute, and unappreciated man. However, the disturbing suicide rate of American combat veterans in the twenty-first century suggests that the effects of war on soldiers are not so easy to calculate. Though William Coffee, Jr., seems to have felt the weight of his years much as Shelley did (the poet also died at twenty-nine), Foote makes his Bill Kidder live on till his money has run out, thus grimly bearing out his father's once-complacent proverb, "You get what you pay for." Having left his father's beloved Houston, possibly to gain privacy to live as he wished, Bill reaches a state of mind resembling that of the aviator in the Yeats poem "An Irish Airman Foresees His Death." The airman of the poem, separated spiritually from kin and nation, explains why he faces the death he knows awaits him:

I balanced all, brought all to mind:
The years to come seemed waste of breath,
A waste of breath the years behind,
In balance with this life, this death. (13–16)

When Will Kidder describes what he was told of his son's last moments before drowning, he tells Tom Jackson that as Bill walked toward the lake, he waved at the lake's owner, who was watching him. Though one can read too much into a gesture, this casual farewell suggests an attitude like that of the flier in the Yeats poem. Instead of enunciating the pain of his expiring youth as a Shelley might, Bill exits life with authority and composure, facing death with the fortitude that sustained him in air combat as bombardier, a role in which it is likely that he was responsible for much death and devastation. The gesture's suggestion is made with a light, but masterful touch, and thus Bill's death takes on a touch of the heroic quality. If this is so, it may explain, to some extent, Foote's alteration of a story familiar to him, for it introduces a suggestion of hidden nobility into the character of a man whose secret conduct would have made him a disgrace in many realms of conventional life in the year 1950.

This hidden nobility is not limited to Bill, however, for in the crushing blows that strike the Kidder household, we see Will and Lily Dale in a new light. They are not particularly intelligent individuals, and they remain conventional in almost every way. Yet the devastation they undergo allows the audience to see into them, into their biased racial attitudes and their simplistic pieties about religion and business. As a result, the Kidders and their flaws become familiar and familial and subject to a kind of sympathetic redemption, and their unwise prejudices seem no more than that: errors of the kind that distort us all and interfere with our becoming what we hope to be.

Gerald C. Wood's essay on this play proposes that the drama sets forth a perspective that leads to mystery. He explains,

> when Lily Dale and Will decide to remember a different Bill than the one represented by the bank receipts, they are not delusional. They are participating in the invention of their world. By choosing to look and talk no further, the parents embrace life's ineluctable mystery.

After a long and painful pursuit of the truth, they are hungry for myth, in this case the myth of goodness. (Wood, "Nature" 186)

Wood's perception is a valuable one, yet I would add that those hungry for goodness are generally well on their way in the right direction, and if it is mythical to disregard a loved one's faults, that is a good thing, at least according to the New Testament's mythology. The incidental pretensions of Will's embrace of convention and Lily Dale's self-indulgent efforts to make unspeakable facts fit into a comforting ideology are burned away, at least largely, by the hellfire of catastrophe, and it seems that for a moment, wounded and enfeebled as they are, we see in them the source of a courage much like that which enabled their son to function in the nightmare of air combat, a nightmare that had ended the life of Horton's younger brother in 1944. The Kidders became stereotypes in Foote's *The Orphans' Home Cycle*, and they continue on such a path in this play, but here the playwright's powerful sympathetic vision allows us at last to see also their concealed humanity come to light as their illusions dissolve and they find themselves confronting the issue of what finally means most to them.[4]

Acknowledgments

My work on Foote owes much to research grants awarded by Graduate Dean Jeffrey Brown and the University Research Councilat Texas A&M International University. Two additional grants from the Clements Center for the Study of the Southwest and the DeGolyer Library at Southern Methodist University provided additional support. I am grateful to Director Russell Martin and Librarian Cynthia Franco of the DeGolyer for valuable assistance, and I am also happy to acknowledge the kind contributions of Elizabeth Garver and Cristina Meisner of the Harry Ransom Center of the University of Texas, Matthew J. Boylan of the New York Public Library, and the learned and helpful staff at the Manuscript Reading Room at the Library of Congress.

Notes

1. *Roots in a Parched Ground*, page 35. Marion Castleberry notes that Foote's title was replaced with "The Night of the Storm" due to objections from the sponsor of the *DuPont Show of the Month*, on which the episode was shown (208).

2. Biographical data employed here derive from a variety of online resources, including federal census records, state records, and genealogical databases, such as *Family Search*. The author has sought to verify such data where possible and provides the material given here with reasonable confidence of its validity.

3. Wood notes that the PBS plays were *Courtship*, *On Valentine's Day*, and *1918* (*A Casebook* 210).

Works Cited

Castleberry, Marion. *Blessed Assurance: The Life and Art of Horton Foote.* Macon, GA: Mercer UP, 2014.

Death Certificate for William B. Coffee, September 17, 1958. State File No. 51097. Texas Department of Health, Bureau of Vital Statistics. *FamilySearch.org.* 7 Oct. 2015.

Death Certificate for William B. Coffee, Jr., June 16, 1947. State File No. 12347, Registrar's No. 1164. Florida State Board of Health. Certified copy in possession of author.

Foote, Horton. *Convicts. The Orphans' Home Cycle.* New York: Grove Press, 1989.

_____. *Lily Dale. The Orphans' Home Cycle.* New York: Grove Press, 1989.

_____. *The Orphans' Home Cycle.* New York: Grove Press, 1989.

_____. *The Prisoner's Song. Selected One-Act Plays.* Ed. Gerald C. Wood. 391–413.

_____. *Roots in a Parched Ground.* Foreword by Stark Young. New York: Dramatists Play Service, 1962.

_____. *Roots in a Parched Ground. The Orphans' Home Cycle.* New York: Grove Press, 1989.

_____. *Selected One-Act Plays of Horton Foote.* Ed. Gerald C. Wood. Dallas: Southern Methodist UP, 1989.

_____. *"To Kill a Mockingbird," "Tender Mercies," and "The Trip to Bountiful": Three Screenplays by Horton Foote.* New York: Grove Press, 1989.

_____. *The Trip to Bountiful. Horton Foote's Three Trips to Bountiful.* Ed. Barbara Moore & David G. Yellin. Dallas: Southern Methodist UP, 1993.

_____. *The Young Man from Atlanta.* New York: Dutton, 1995.

Lily Dale. Screenplay by Horton Foote. Dir. Peter Masterson. Perf. Sam Shepard, Mary Stuart Masterson, Stockard Channing, and Tim Guinee. Hallmark, 1996.

Looking for Richard. Dir. Al Pacino. Perf. Al Pacino. Twentieth Century Fox, 1996.

Magee, Rosemary M. *Conversations with Flannery O'Connor.* Jackson: UP of Mississippi, 1987. Literary Conversations Ser.

Moore, Barbara & David G. Yellin, eds. *Horton Foote's Three Trips to Bountiful.* Dallas: Southern Methodist UP, 1993.

Wood, Gerald C., ed. *Horton Foote: A Casebook.* New York: Garland, 1998.

_____. *Horton Foote and the Theater of Intimacy.* Baton Rouge: Louisiana State UP, 1999.

_____. "The Nature of Mystery in *The Young Man from Atlanta.*" *Horton Foote: A Casebook.* Ed. Gerald C. Wood. New York: Garland, 1998. 179–188.

_____ & Marion Castleberry, eds. *The Voice of an American Playwright: Interviews with Horton Foote.* Macon, GA: Mercer UP, 2012.

"Wharton. A Singular Accident—The Condition of the Cotton Crop." *Galveston Daily News.* (10 Oct. 1886): 9. *NewspaperARCHIVE.com.* Killam Library, Texas A&M International University. 1 Dec. 2013.

Yeats, William Butler. *Collected Poems.* New York: Macmillan, 1946.

"And a Little Child Shall Lead Them": Scout and Jem Finch from Novel to Film_____

Jan Whitt

Whether in the novel *To Kill a Mockingbird* or the film based upon it, Jean Louise Finch and Jeremy Atticus Finch remain two of the best-known and most beloved characters in twentieth-century American literature. Horton Foote's screenplay adaptation of the novel is a memory play in which a mature narrator remembers life in 1930s Maycomb, Alabama. The novel itself is a mockingbird's song—innocent, melodic, resplendent.

The "tired old town" (Lee 5) of Monroeville, Alabama, upon which Maycomb is based, was home to Nelle Harper Lee. The success of the novel and film dramatically enlarged her literary and social sphere, and an international audience joined her on a nostalgic journey into another time and place. The Great Depression and racial and gender inequality unsettled the Deep South financially and socially, although white residents in the novel and film appear content to live in a town where only the Radleys lock their doors. The black experience, represented by Tom Robinson and Calpurnia, was decidedly different.

The title of this chapter, "'And a Little Child Shall Lead Them': Scout and Jem Finch from Novel to Film," is drawn from Isaiah 11:6, which reads, "The wolf also shall dwell with the lamb, and the leopard shall lie down with the kid; and the calf and the young lion and the fatling together; and a little child shall lead them" (KJV). The well-known verse is important for at least two reasons: first, it highlights the roles that Scout and Jem Finch play in the novel, screenplay, and film; second, it addresses the central theme of all three texts—the significance of moving from innocence to experience (and, as much as possible, back again). Charles Baker (Dill) Harris's amusing and incisive declaration—"I'm little but I'm old" (Lee 10)—both points to childhood as the central theme and suggests the inherent wisdom of the young. At the end of the novel, Scout, too, acknowledges weariness far beyond her years: "As I made my way home, I felt very old" (322). The world of children dominates the film musically, thematically, and visually; for example, in the introductory montage of crayons and children's toys—overlaid with the sounds of a child humming—lies the promise of uncorrupted, unscripted insight.

When Horton Foote transformed Lee's coming-of-age novel into an award-winning screenplay, he necessarily omitted certain characters and scenes. Not only does adaptation demand focus—often making it necessary to abbreviate the narrative and/or eliminate or combine characters—but in the case of *To Kill a Mockingbird* (1960), which is more than three hundred pages long, Foote's task was to produce not only a screenplay that was less than one-third of Lee's Pulitzer Prize-winning book, but also one that preserved the dramatic intensity and suspense of the original. His success is evident in the fact that—nominated for eight Academy Awards—the 1962 film won for "Best Screenplay Based on Material from Another Medium." It also won for "Best Actor" with Gregory Peck as Atticus Finch and "Best Art Direction and Set Decoration." The film itself lost to "Lawrence of Arabia."

However, in addition to omitting certain characters and events, Foote added a few scenes to provide cohesiveness and dramatic power, and he altered the chronology. Noticeable differences between the novel and screenplay include modifying the timeline; amplifying, changing, or omitting the roles of Alexandra Finch Hancock, Jem, Scout, and Dill; altering the first-person point of view; abbreviating trial scenes; and adding references to Atticus's wife and Tom Robinson's children and father. In all of his alterations, Foote remained focused upon the role of the children and longed for his screenplay to help "discover the evil and hypocrisy in this small southern pastoral town along with and through the eyes of the children" (*Three Screenplays* xiii).

Although Lee applauded Foote's work, not all critics or viewers were as enthusiastic. As Charles J. Shields explains, Robert Mulligan, the director, was concerned that Atticus Finch overshadowed the children in the screenplay. Discussing his concerns with producer Alan J. Pakula, Mulligan said: "You know what your problem is ...

too often you lose the point of view of the children" (Shields 206). At the heart of Bosley Crowther's notable 1963 *New York Times* review is a concern about what he considers the loss of the child's perspective in the screenplay, which led to a film that Crowther considered only partially "rewarding." Crowther writes:

> And for a fair spell it looks as though maybe we are going to be squeezed inside the skin of Scott [sic] and Jem as they go racing and tumbling around the neighborhood, shrieking with childish defiance at crusty old Mrs. Dubose, skirting with awe around the dark house where the mysterious Boo Radley lives....
>
> It is when the drama develops along the conventional lines of a social crisis in the community—the charging of a Negro with the rape of a white woman—that the children are switched to the roles of lookers-on....
>
> While this still permits vivid melodrama and some touching observations of the children, especially in their relations with their father, which is the crucial relationship in the film, it leaves the viewer wondering precisely how the children feel. How have they really reacted to the things that affect our grown-up minds?

This study addresses Crowther's concerns at some length and explores the artistic journey from novel to screenplay to film, noting especially Lee's enthusiasm for the Horton Foote masterpiece. It explores the coming-of-age narratives, the place of didacticism and point of view in the novel and film, and other literary techniques. It focuses upon the film as a memory play and upon the children's emerging consciousness, which takes them from the trivial events of the everyday—such as wondering whether or not Atticus will play football for the Methodists—to an expansive awareness of social justice.

The children's evolving consciousness culminates in a loss of innocence, as Scout, Jem, and Dill pay the price for living in a world both miraculous and violent, both bathed in soft morning light and haunted by shadows. Of course, Lee, who is writing a largely autobiographical tale, understands clearly the cost of the trio's newfound awareness; however, she also wants for them to remain open and childlike (as "harmless as doves") as they move into adulthood, where, according to Matthew 10:16, they soon enough will have to be as "wise as serpents" (KJV). Lee's desire to hold innocence and experience in balance is evident even in the epigraph: "Lawyers, I suppose, were children once." What follows Charles Lamb's statement are questions: "Is the world all grown up? Is childhood dead? Or is there not in the bosoms of the wisest and the best some of the child's heart left, to respond to its earliest enchantments?" (Lamb 93). Both Lee and Foote emphasize the "child's heart," although Foote chooses to compress the timeline— which provides a smaller window into the children's development— and to let Atticus take center stage.

Adaptation of *To Kill a Mockingbird*
Offered the opportunity to write the screenplay for her novel, Harper Lee declined. Pakula then selected Horton Foote, a southerner whose own plays, such as *The Chase* and *The Trip to Bountiful*, are character-based. Foote loved and, more importantly, understood life and relationships in a small town because of his own involvement and family history in Wharton, Texas. He was perhaps the perfect screenwriter to adapt a novel he appreciated by a fellow southerner whom he respected. In the foreword to *Three Screenplays*, Foote writes about his affinity for all things southern and his respect for particular writers of the Deep South:

> For me to have any chance of successfully dramatizing the work of another writer, I have to choose material that I respect and that I am in sympathy with, that deals with people and a world I understand. Whenever I've done that with Faulkner, Flannery O'Connor, or Harper Lee, I have felt a real satisfaction in the work; when I haven't, I've felt lost and confused. I felt I understood the world of Harper Lee's novel and its people. The town of the novel was not unlike the town I was born and brought up in, and the time of the novel, the depression era of the 1930s, was a period I had lived through. (xii)

However, his affection for the novel and its creator is precisely the reason he delayed accepting Pakula's offer, fearing he might like the novel too much to recreate it effectively. According to Charles Kiselyak's documentary film *Fearful Symmetry: The Making of "To Kill a Mockingbird,"* Foote met Lee for the first time at his home in Nyack, New York. "It was love at first sight on my part," said Foote. "And I just somehow felt that we were members of the same family." Alice Lee ("Boaty") Boatwright, who cast the children in the film, said Foote was the "perfect person" to adapt the novel. Lee and Foote "became the closest and the best of friends and stayed totally, completely in touch" until Foote died in 2009. Of his ability to transform the novel set in Monroeville, Boatright said, "He was a poet, and he understood those people" (55).

After Foote agreed to take on the project, Pakula suggested that Foote write a screenplay that compressed the action into a year instead of three and that he consider the similarities between Scout Finch's experiences and those of Huckleberry Finn and Tom Sawyer. When Foote complied, Scout joined the legendary company of children in celebrated American novels. In the Kiselyak documentary, Pakula notes that Foote wanted to "honor the book and be true to the book," and he concludes that Foote achieved that goal. Foote and Pakula collaborated easily because Pakula, too, is known to favor character-oriented adaptations, as shown in his later films *All the President's Men* (1976) and *Sophie's Choice* (1982).

The novel *To Kill a Mockingbird* and the film provide both the sense of a mature narrator looking back on her life and a child experiencing for the first time the adult world (with all of its conflicts, inequalities, and mysteries). However, less is explicit in the film, in part because children cannot fully understand the events that affect their family and community and in part because Foote expects the viewer to understand that what is portrayed on screen is no more potent and metaphorical than what remains in the shadows. For example, the audience does not need for Mayella Ewell's rape to be reenacted; the horror of her life and her father's assault are perhaps even more disturbing if her abuse occurs off screen. Foote, who had written for television for over a decade, had considerable experience in presenting the child's point of view in anxious situations in his teleplays, notably in "The Tears of My Sister" (1956, in which a young girl *is* the camera). He had completed, in 1961, a teleplay titled *Roots in a Parched Ground* (broadcast that year as *The Night of the Storm*), portraying a traumatic episode in his own father's childhood.

Casting in *Mockingbird* contributed mightily to its reception and to Foote's success. In an essay about the impact of the film, actress and media celebrity Oprah Winfrey praises both the novel and the film, especially the actors:

> I loved it from the beginning, and like a lot of people, I get the lines blurred between the movie and the book. The movie is very distinct for me because the reading experience comes alive for me in a way that my imagination cannot. In the history of filmmaking I have never seen a book really live its essence through film like this one, and that is because of the casting of Scout and Atticus, and all of them, really. (Murphy 201–202)

When Mary Badham left her fellow students in her fourth-grade classroom in Birmingham, Alabama, to audition for the role of Scout Finch, she could never have imagined the unparalleled success that she and the film would achieve. Little did she know that she would be nominated for an Academy Award in what would become an American film classic. In fact, the film mirrors some of Badham's life, making the child actor even more determined to bring Scout Finch to life. For example, two black women, Beddie Harris and Frankie McCall, helped to raise Badham, and she rebelled against sitting away from them in the front of the bus when one of them accompanied her around town. "I would love to have included the parts of the book that talked of our relationship with Calpurnia, for it was so close to my relationship with the ladies who raised me," Badham said (Murphy 46). Ten years old when the film was released, Badham had developed a close and sustaining relationship with Gregory Peck, who played Atticus Finch, and she remained in contact with him until his death in 2003. In an online interview with Sandra McElwaine, Badham said, "He was my other daddy," she said. "He really was Atticus: fine, firm, and gentle."

Other relationships developed from the experiences on the set of the film and facilitated the adaptation and the film that followed it. Lee and Peck liked one another immensely, and many years later, Peck's daughter would name her own daughter "Harper" (McElwaine). Lee and Foote, too, liked and respected one another. "If the integrity of a film adaptation is measured by the degree to which the novelist's intent is preserved, Mr. Foote's screenplay should be studied as a classic" (Shields 206), Lee said. Later, she observed: "I can only say that I am a happy author. They have made my story into a beautiful and moving motion picture. I am very proud and grateful" (Sherrod).

In *Fearful Symmetry*, Pakula said he believes the "triumph" of the film is that it captures the "soul" of the novel. However, although what adaptation scholars call "fidelity" is one of the ways of assessing the film's success, it is far from the only one. Furthermore, some scholars of adaptation history and practice now diminish the importance of faithfulness to the original text in order to highlight other methods of analysis. In the introduction to *Now a Major Motion Picture: Film Adaptations of Literature and Drama,* Christine Geraghty encourages film critics to focus on more than fidelity and suggests that other approaches employed in film criticism might be similarly shallow. She challenges several common assumptions:

> So, it is ruled that, among other things, novels are verbal and use words while films are visual and rely on images; novels can express internal knowledge of a character, but screen adaptations have to imply feelings or motivations from a character's actions since the camera is best suited to the objective recording of physical appearances; films can only use the present tense; voice-overs are noncinematic; and cinema and television rely on realism while literature requires the reader's imagination. (Geraghty 1–2)

Geraghty also opposes what she calls the prevailing "hierarchy of judgment" because it "privileges literature, reading, and authorship over screen, viewing, and mass production" (2). Because "texts develop from a network of sources that have no single author," Geraghty celebrates what she calls a "plurality of meanings," which

---

depend in part on the "textual skills and the contextual positioning of the reader" (2); in other words, much of the success of Foote's screenplay and other texts depends upon the connection that readers and viewers make individually with the text.

Furthermore, Geraghty argues that scholars should analyze the film or television adaptation itself—separate and apart from its original source—taking into account the transformative impact of "genre, editing, and acting" (5) or, as she later suggests, "space and landscapes" (7). For example, Peck's portrayal of Atticus Finch is his own. He creates a character that readers might or might not have imagined as they immersed themselves in Lee's novel. The fact that Lee often said she appreciated Peck's talent and that he reminded her of her father is, in some ways, irrelevant. An actor's performance may be distinct from what the author imagined and may be either better or worse than the character depicted in the original source.

Also, as the editors of *The Pedagogy of Adaptation* suggest, if a film and the novel upon which it is based are "indistinguishable" (Cutchins et al. xii), then viewers have lost the opportunity to interact with two texts, which, although they are intimately connected, are by definition free-standing and culturally and historically distinct. Reinforcing this viewpoint, Suzanne Diamond writes:

> Various contemporary psychological and epistemological findings establish that our notions of the world we inhabit—indeed, our most basic ideas about who we *are*—come to us by way of the story lines our cultures make possible and the work we do with these story lines. We are, in other words, constant and inveterate adapters. (96)

Consequently, Diamond disagrees with critics who want to diminish the importance of fidelity because the original text is a good place to begin a conversation about the multiple adaptations readers and viewers might discover for themselves: "And the serial nature of the adaptation process produces far more complex discourses, rather than simply stating that 'the book was better,' even if that's where the discussion begins," she maintains (101).

Specifically, discussing "how a given adaptation sustains or departs from *any* remembered 'source text'" is itself a fruitful exercise that can lead to a conversation about "who we collectively *are,* how we recall, and what we continue to find important" (105), Diamond argues. Analysis of the original and adapted texts makes possible what Diamond calls "social memory work" (98), and social memory derives from a study of culture, history, politics, psychology, and the "function of remembering within all of these."

Unfortunately, one can argue that Foote diminished Lee's novel when he drastically reduced the parts that Mrs. Henry Lafayette Dubose and Charles Baker Harris play. In the screenplay, Jem does not visit Mrs. Dubose, who cures herself of an addiction to painkillers, wanting to be free of them even though she has been diagnosed with terminal cancer. In the novel, foreshadowing his own loss in the Tom Robinson case, Atticus tells his son what Mrs. Dubose represents:

> I wanted you to see something about her—I wanted you to see what real courage is, instead of getting the idea that courage is a man with a gun in his hand. It's when you know you're licked before you begin but you begin anyway and you see it through no matter what.... She was the bravest person I ever knew. (128)

Similarly, in the screenplay, Dill, who is based on Lee's lifelong friend Truman Capote, no longer functions as a social conscience in the community, nor does he interact with Adolphus Raymond, who is (thankfully) not what he appears to be. In the novel, Dill provides extensive social documentary and is a deeply sympathetic figure, especially during his encounter with Raymond; in the film, however, he is ancillary to most of the central action. In the novel, Dill's compassion for the black community is profound and based, perhaps, on his own isolation and sense of rejection. He tells Scout that he left home because his mother, as he says, "just wasn't interested in me" (162), and when she asks him why Boo Radley never fled the town, Dill replies, "Maybe he doesn't have anywhere to run off to" (164).

It is Dill's identification with the plight of blacks in Maycomb that constitutes the greatest loss in the transition from novel to film. Brokenhearted about the jury's cowardice and the prosecutor's

---

Critical Insights

racism during Tom Robinson's trial, Dill "started crying and couldn't stop," and others in the courthouse began to notice him. Jem asks Scout to take him outside. In a tribute to the child's perspective in the novel, Lee lets Scout try to figure out why her friend is distressed. "I guessed he hadn't fully recovered from running away," she thinks, followed closely by another speculation, "Heat got you, I expect" (226). When Dill explains how devastated he is by a black man being called "boy," Scout replies, "Well, Dill, after all he's just a Negro," and Dill says, "It ain't right, somehow it ain't right to do 'em that way. Hasn't anybody got any business talkin' like that—it just makes me sick" (227). Raymond, who eavesdrops on the children, compliments Dill:

> Things haven't caught up with that one's instinct yet. Let him get a little older and he won't get sick and cry.... Cry about the simple hell people give other people—without even thinking. Cry about the hell white people give colored folks, without even stopping to think that they're people, too. (229)

In short, Dill is the child who leads them, the voice Scout hears, the voice that affects her, the voice as yet uncorrupted by the world in which he lives. Because Dill's role in the screenplay is minor, it falls to Jem and Scout to provide his perspective.

Childhood in Novel and Film

Mary McDonagh Murphy argues that Foote's screenplay became "what many consider to be one of the greatest screen adaptations of all time" (31). One reason may be that Foote's screenplay remains true to the culture, history, politics, and psychology of *To Kill a Mockingbird* and relies upon memory to provide narrative cohesion. Foote also is faithful to the themes Lee develops, especially what Pakula calls in *Fearful Symmetry* the "mysterious" and "secret world of childhood."

The producer especially praised the beginning of the film, where a marble hits another marble and the music begins. That moment, Pakula said in the documentary, is "magical." In fact, childhood and its mysteries and challenges are at the heart of the novel and the screenplay. In his foreword to *Scout, Atticus & Boo: A Celebration of Fifty Years of "To Kill a Mockingbird,"* Wally Lamb compares Mark Twain's *Adventures of Huckleberry Finn* and J. D. Salinger's *The Catcher in the Rye* to *To Kill a Mockingbird*: "All three novels, each a product of its era, give voice to outsider American kids trying to negotiate an adult world full of hypocrites" (x).

In addition to its other themes, *To Kill a Mockingbird* addresses social expectations in a small town, where residents delight in dissecting their neighbors. Yet even this theme is tied inextricably to childhood. As Mark Childress writes, even little children such as Scout and Dill are not safe from the scrutiny and criticism of their elders: "The two of them, they were both odd birds in their town" (80), Childress writes, both reinforcing Wally Lamb's reference to "outsider American kids" and highlighting the cruelty of gossip and character assassination. The novel focuses upon the criticism that members of the community heap upon the heads of Atticus Finch, Boo Radley, Adolphus Raymond, and others; the pressure Aunt Alexandra puts on Scout to meet the expectations of southern womanhood; and even the anger Jem turns on his sister. The film, too, portrays the proper ways of doing things in the Deep South and the price paid by those who flout the expectations of others.

Because film is a visual medium, Foote modified the first-person point of view of the novel *To Kill a Mockingbird.* To say that he abandoned it, as Crowther appears to suggest, is simply not accurate; however, there is no doubt that Scout Finch no longer controls what the reader, or in the case of the film, the viewer, sees and understands. In the screenplay and film, Jem Finch, who is older and, because of his gender, inherits more than his father's pocket watch, often becomes the focal point of the film in a patriarchal community. In one scene, he refuses his father's request that he go home; in another, he asks if he can accompany his father, is told "no," and announces that he's going with him anyway.

Much redeemed at the end of the novel, Aunt Alexandra disappears entirely from the screenplay, perhaps because Foote believed Scout's struggle to adapt to southern womanhood could be addressed adequately by particular vignettes (wearing a dress on the first day of school, fighting Walter Cunningham and Cecil Jacobs, happily accepting the promise of her mother's jewelry, being berated by her brother for behaving more and more "like a girl," etc.). Jem criticizes his sister at least twice in the novel, saying, "I swear, Scout, sometimes you act so much like a girl it's mortifyin'" (42) and "I declare to the Lord you're gettin' more like a girl every day!" (58), but it is Aunt Alexandra who wants to mold Scout into a southern belle. In the screenplay, Jem says: "Then go home if you're scared. I swear, Scout, you act more like a girl all the time" (Foote, *Three Screenplays* 24). In the screenplay, Aunt Alexandra is absent, and it is Calpurnia who loves and guides Scout.

In spite of Foote's editorial changes, the film preserves a decidedly childlike perspective—from the credits that scroll across the screen during the first few moments to Scout's voice-over at the end of the film: "I was to think of these days many times; of Jem, and Dill, and Boo Radley, and Tom Robinson ... and Atticus. He would be in Jem's room all night. And he would be there when Jem waked up in the morning" (*Three Screenplays* 80). Lee Smith states that the novel is "dead-on about childhood" and adds that "it evokes childhood so beautifully" (178). Foote does not wander far from the novel as he creates a little girl in overalls, a boy who walks like an Egyptian, and a visitor from Meridian, Mississippi, who tries to hide his sadness by inventing a father.

Elmer Bernstein's score, too, reinforces a child's view of the world, as he suggests in *Fearful Symmetry*. The single notes—that imitate the way a child might play a piano—and the cardboard box filled with toys and treasures converge. The viewer hears a ticking watch and the humming of a child. Objects such as crayons, marbles, and a whistle contribute to a viewer's nostalgia for the familiar things of childhood. Allan Gurganus underscores the importance of the opening sequence when he suggests that the "toys and images of the precious things saved" work to let viewers know they're part of a "child's vision" (97).

Nonetheless, Crowther mourns the ways in which the child's perspective is diluted in the screenplay. He suggests that when the viewer is dropped "serenely in the comfort of a grubby Southern

---

town" and the audience encounters a "thoroughly beguiling tomboy" and her father—"clearly the kindest man in town"—the film is nothing short of "bewitching." Crowther appreciates the relationship between the children and their father, writing that it alone is "worth all the footage of the film." The primary issue Crowther has with the film appears in the first paragraph of the review, where he suggests that Foote does not maintain the child's point of view, although he does not clarify how Foote might have done so. He writes:

> There is so much feeling for children in the film that has been made from Harper Lees [sic] best-selling novel, "To Kill a Mockingbird"... so much delightful observation of their spirit, energy and charm as depicted by two superb discoveries, Mary Badham and Phillip Alford—that it comes as a bit of a letdown at the end to realize that, for all the picture's feeling for children, it doesn't tell us very much of how they feel. (Crowther)

Rather than debating Crowther's perspective again, it might be helpful to suggest a representative scene in which the film undercuts Crowther's claim that the viewer cannot surmise what Jem, Scout, and Dill are thinking. For example, Jem is devastated by the verdict in the Tom Robinson trial, and his agony—not conveyed in a soliloquy, of course—is nonetheless made clear as he sits in the rocking chair on the porch. Although his father tells Jem he cannot protect him from the horrors of the world around him and although Calpurnia gazes at him compassionately, Jem is alone, revealing by his expression and his posture exactly what he feels. Wrestling with demons too terrifying for a child his age, he sits silently and in disbelief.

Although the film amplifies the role that Jem plays (he babysits for his sister, he accompanies his father, he finds Boo's gifts in the tree, etc.), he is a formidable figure in the novel as well; in fact, as he moves into adolescence, Lee is careful to highlight Jem's moodiness, his desire for privacy, and other aspects of his relationship with Scout. Because the novel spans three years and the film compresses the children's experiences into one, any perceived amplification of Jem's role in the film can, in part, be explained by

---

the altered timeline and the demands of adapting a full-length novel. Nonetheless, Crowther is correct about the dilution of the child's perspective in the film, although, to some extent, Jem's voice simply replaces Scout's.

Other changes between the novel and the screenplay occur as well, and a few affect the development of the child's viewpoint in the film, although some of them are incidental to it. Stephanie Crawford becomes Dill's aunt in the film, and Scout fights Cecil Jacobs instead of Francis Hancock. Scout and Jem are not shown inside the school. Jem doesn't read to Mrs. Dubose, nor does he learn why she is Atticus Finch's definition of courage. Maudie Atkinson's house does not burn. The children do not attend Calpurnia's church. None of these editorial decisions diminishes the themes Foote develops, although it is impossible to suggest that they are superfluous in the novel: to a greater or lesser extent, each event serves to enrich the reader's understanding of the plot and makes characters more complex. One of the significant differences between the novel and the film is Foote's insertion of a conversation between Jem and Scout about their mother. The moment when the siblings discuss their memory of her is even more poignant because their father overhears them as he sits on the porch swing:

> Scout: "How old was I when Mama died?"
> Jem: "Two."
> Scout: "And how old were you?"
> Jem: "Six."
> Scout: "Old as I am now?"
> Jem: "Uh huh."
> Scout: "Was Mama pretty?"
> Jem: "Uh huh."
> Scout: "Was Mama nice?"
> Jem: "Uh huh."
> Scout: "Did you love her?"
> Jem: "Yes."
> Scout: "Did I love her?"
> Jem: "Yes." (*Three Screenplays* 17)

Lessons in Social Justice

However, although Scout is, as Crowther notes, "beguiling," her innocence is shattered by events in her community, and she struggles to maintain hope in a world that is coming apart. She encounters haunted houses, rabid dogs, stories about witches, and, most terrifyingly, a murderous stalker in the woods. Although readers and viewers understand that the mockingbirds at the heart of the novel and the screenplay represent the children, there are other wounded people, including Mayella Ewell, Atticus Finch, Arthur (Boo) Radley, and Tom Robinson. Atticus tells the children that "it's a sin to kill a mockingbird" (Lee 103), and Miss Maudie explains why: "Mockingbirds don't do one thing but make music for us to enjoy."

Mayella is hardly a sympathetic figure; however, as Atticus Finch states in the film, he has "nothing but pity" for her, although he says promptly, "My pity does not extend so far as to her putting a man's life at stake, which she has done in an effort to get rid of her own guilt" (*Three Screenplays* 66). Interestingly, in the novel, Scout is the first person to express concern for Mayella: "As Tom Robinson gave his testimony, it came to me that Mayella Ewell must have been the loneliest person in the world.... She was as sad, I thought, as what Jem called a mixed child.... Tom Robinson was probably the only person who was ever decent to her" (Lee 219).

Other mockingbirds exist as well. Atticus frequently is the object of derision and ridicule, criticized in the novel even by his sister. During Atticus's vigil outside the locked jail, Lee and Foote describe his fear. Scout sees a "flash of plain fear" (Lee 173) on her father's face, and in the screenplay, she notices the "look of fear on his face" (*Three Screenplays* 51). Of course, this description undercuts Atticus's role as an attorney who never loses his composure. Because of his fragility when confronted by the mob and his desire to protect his children, Atticus is a person with whom the reader and the viewer can identify. Boo Radley is the town's shadowy recluse who is also heroic. Importantly, he remains always a child. When he asks Scout to walk him home at the end of the novel, Lee writes, "He almost whispered it, in the voice of a child afraid of the dark" (320). Throughout the novel, Lee emphasizes

Boo's isolation by comparing him to the Radley house itself: "The old house was the same, droopy and sick, but as we stared down the street we thought we saw an inside shutter move. Flick. A tiny, almost invisible movement, and the house was still" (16). Finally, although he pays with his life, Tom is guilty only of caring about a poverty-stricken, uneducated white woman who lives with her tormentor because she has nowhere else to go.

To shoot Tom, to exclude Boo, to ignore Mayella, and to force Atticus—as Miss Maudie said—to do what others refuse to do is, in effect, to kill a mockingbird. "I simply want to tell you that there are some men in this world who were born to do our unpleasant jobs for us," she tells the children. "Your father's one of them" (Lee 246–47). Later, she adds: "We're so rarely called on to be Christians, but when we are, we've got men like Atticus to go for us."

In spite of its portrayal of a loving father and his children, *To Kill a Mockingbird* is far from a celebration of childhood. Robert E. Lee (Bob) Ewell spits on Scout's father and tries to murder Scout and Jem in the dark woods. Boo Radley is trapped in a ramshackle house. A jury of twelve white men finds someone guilty of a crime he could not possibly have committed. Mayella Ewell is lost in ignorance and poverty, motherless, and the sole caretaker of her siblings. Calpurnia—who tells the children she has no birthday, which evokes no surprise on their parts— cannot interact freely with the whites in Maycomb. The Great Depression has made agrarian life even more difficult for the Cunninghams and others like them than it had been before.

In fact, as Claudia Durst Johnson notes, the novel introduces the reader to Scout and Jem, who "encounter the strange, sometimes evil reality outside the slow, Edenic existence of their own house" (32). Rooted in what Johnson calls the "persistent past" (35), Maycomb, for all its neighborliness and system of manners, "has been shaped irrevocably by a plantation system, the Civil War, and a cotton-based economy" (35). In a novel in which the "chief defining symbols" (38) are children and mockingbirds, Johnson mourns the treatment of Boo Radley and every black resident, all of whom are relegated to the edges of a dangerous and segregated community.

Originally entitled *Atticus*, the novel *To Kill a Mockingbird* outgrew its initial title. Although Atticus Finch features prominently in the lives of his children and defends Tom Robinson in one of the most famous courtroom dramas in literature, the novel is more expansive than the story of any one character. Telling the story through a child's eyes creates an identification and empathy the book might not otherwise possess. The innocence of tire swings and treehouses dissipates, replaced by attempted murder, an unfounded charge of rape, an outcast imprisoned in his own house, the widespread effects of ignorance and poverty, and a little boy who lies about having a father who is a train conductor and a pilot because he is afraid and—except for his visits to Maycomb—alone.

At the beginning of the screenplay, Scout is six years old, Jem ten. When Foote introduces them and their friend Dill Harris, he does not patronize them; in fact, Foote's respect for the wisdom of children is apparent even in some of the director's notes. For example, when Dill first appears, Foote describes him as having a "solemn, owlish face, a knowledge and imagination too old for his years" (9).

By the end of the screenplay, the children are only a year older, but Jem and Scout have taken their "longest journey together" (Lee 290; *Three Screenplays* 72), a phrase that denotes far more than their harrowing confrontation with Bob Ewell. They have learned that their father is "civilized in his heart" (Lee 112), and they want to follow his example. It is perhaps Dill who best embodies the conflicting forces in the hearts of the children. In a lavish description of her friend Truman Capote, Lee juxtaposes the magical qualities Dill embodies and reintroduces Boo as a reminder that all is not well in Maycomb:

> Dill was off again. Beautiful things floated around in his dreamy head. He could read two books to my one, but he preferred the magic of his own inventions. He could add and subtract faster than lightning, but he preferred his own twilight world, a world where babies slept, waiting to be gathered like morning lilies. He was slowly talking himself to sleep and taking me with him, but in the quietness of his

foggy island there rose the faded image of a gray house with sad brown doors. (164)

To Kill a Mockingbird and the screenplay and film that followed it highlight issues of social justice and portray a time and place that are perhaps not so different from our own. It is with respect and wonder that Atticus remembers the three children who saved him from the mob at the jail: "So it took an eight-year-old child to bring 'em to their senses, didn't it?... Hmp, maybe we need a police force of children" (Lee 180), he says. And when Jem asks his father how the jury could have made the decision they made, Atticus Finch again invokes the wisdom of the children: "I don't know, but they did it. They've done it before and they did it tonight and they'll do it again and when they do it—seems that only children weep" (244). These words allude to literature that celebrates the wisdom of children as yet untainted by discriminatory social constructs. They also invoke the Old Testament, where "a child shall lead them."

Works Cited

Boatright, Alice Lee ("Boaty"). Interview. *Scout, Atticus & Boo: A Celebration of Fifty Years of "To Kill a Mockingbird."* Ed. Mary McDonagh Murphy. New York: HarperCollins, 2010. 51–56.

Childress, Mark. Interview. *Scout, Atticus & Boo: A Celebration of Fifty Years of "To Kill a Mockingbird."* Ed. Mary McDonagh Murphy. New York: HarperCollins, 2010. 76–84.

Crowther, Bosley. *"To Kill a Mockingbird*: One Adult Omission in a Fine Film." *New York Times.* The New York Times Company, 15 Feb. 1963. Web. 1 Jun. 2015. <http://www.nytimes.com/movie/review?r es=9D06EED143CEF3BBC4D52DFB4668388679EDE>.

Cutchins, Dennis, Laurence Raw, & James M. Welsh, eds. *The Pedagogy of Adaptation.* Lanham, MD: Scarecrow Press, 2010.

_____, eds. *Redefining Adaptation Studies.* Lanham, MD.: Scarecrow Press, 2010.

Diamond, Suzanne. "Whose Life *Is* It, Anyway?: Adaptation, Collective Memory, and (Auto)Biographical Processes." *Redefining Adaptation Studies.* Ed. Dennis Cutchins, Laurence Raw, & James M. Welsh. Lanham, MD: Scarecrow Press, 2010. 95-110.

Fearful Symmetry: The Making of "To Kill a Mockingbird." Dir. Charles Kiselyak. Universal Studios Home Video, 1998. Included on *To Kill a Mockingbird* 50th Anniversary Edition DVD, Universal Studios, 2012.

Foote, Horton. *Roots in a Parched Ground.* Foreword by Stark Young. New York: Dramatists Play Service, 1962.

_____. "The Tears of My Sister." *Selected One-Act Plays of Horton Foote.* Ed. Gerald C. Wood. Southern Methodist UP, 1989. 149–165.

_____. *"To Kill a Mockingbird," "Tender Mercies," and "The Trip to Bountiful": Three Screenplays by Horton Foote.* New York: Grove Press, 1989.

Geraghty, Christine. *Now a Major Motion Picture: Film Adaptations of Literature and Drama.* Lanham, MD: Rowman & Littlefield, 2008.

Gurganus, Allan. Interview. *Scout, Atticus & Boo: A Celebration of Fifty Years of "To Kill a Mockingbird."* Ed. Mary McDonagh Murphy. New York: HarperCollins, 2010. 95–103.

Johnson, Claudia Durst. *"To Kill a Mockingbird": Threatening Boundaries.* New York: Twayne, 1994.

Keats, Amanda. "Amanda's Adaptations: *To Kill a Mockingbird,* Book vs. Film." *The Hollywood News.* The Hollywood News, 25 Jul. 2014. Web. 1 Jun. 2015. <http://www.thehollywoodnews.com/2014/07/25/amandas-adaptations-to-kill-a-mockingbird-book-vs-film/>.

Lamb, Charles. *Essays of Elia.* Paris: Baudry's European Library, 1835.

Lamb, Wally. "Foreword: A Mockingbird Mosaic." *Scout, Atticus & Boo: A Celebration of Fifty Years of "To Kill a Mockingbird."* Ed. Mary McDonagh Murphy. New York: HarperCollins, 2010. ix–xiv.

Lee, Harper. *To Kill a Mockingbird.* 1960. New York: HarperCollins, 1999.

McElwaine, Sandra. "'To Kill a Mockingbird' Makes Its Mark, 50 Years After the Film's Release." *The Daily Beast.* The Daily Beast Company LLC, 31 Jan. 2012. Web. 26 Sept. 2015. <http://www.thedailybeast.com/articles/2012/01/31/to-kill-a-mockingbird-makes-its-mark-50-years-after-the-film-s-release.html>.

Murphy, Mary McDonagh. *Scout, Atticus & Boo: A Celebration of Fifty Years of "To Kill a Mockingbird."* New York: HarperCollins, 2010.

Sherrod, Kerryn. "To Kill a Mockingbird." *Turner Classic Movies.* Turner Entertainment Networks, Inc., 2015. Web. 1 Jun. 2015. <http://www.

tcm.com/this-month/article/35384%7C0/To-Kill-a-Mockingbird. html>.

Shields, Charles J. *Mockingbird: A Portrait of Harper Lee.* New York: Henry Holt, 2006.

Smith, Lee. Interview. *Scout, Atticus & Boo: A Celebration of Fifty Years of "To Kill a Mockingbird."* Ed. Mary McDonagh Murphy. New York: HarperCollins, 2010. 176–80.

Horton Foote, the Evolution of a Film Script, and the Art of Collaboration in *Tender Mercies*_____

Gerald C. Wood

In the late 1970s Horton Foote was deeply committed to his nine-play cycle *The Orphans' Home*, which was being developed and produced by Herbert Berghof and the HB Theater in New York. But the process had become time-consuming and expensive. The writer needed other income to, in his words, put some butter on the table. So, as at other times in his career, Foote's screenwriting served his first love—the theater. To support the cycle, he returned to his family history, in this case, his nephew's entry into country and western music—and the ripples that lifestyle caused throughout the family—for inspiration. Foote also drew from memories of his youth as an aspiring actor:

> I had a nephew who had begun in a country and western band. Much to his father's horror, really, although he loved country and western music. And it reminded me of my early days as an actor. I mean, they were traveling great distances, and sometimes there'd be nobody there, and no pay.... [I]t turned out very well ... the band ... was ... [that of] George Strait, who is now a great country star. But they had the usual vicissitudes of getting started.... So, I really began to work on it in the point of view of the young men. (Wood & Barr 230)

Once he had the basic idea, Foote took an unusual step. After a bit of cajoling by his agent, he flew to Hollywood. There he would try to sell his idea to Twentieth Century Fox: "I just said to my agent I was going to do a story about these young men. She said, 'You're foolish. You can get an advance from the Hollywood studio. All you have to do is give a brief synopsis of the idea.' I was very embarrassed; I'd never done that. But finally I said 'O.K.'" (Foote). Although pitching his own work was new territory for the writer, things went surprisingly well in LA. Foote explains that he "told the idea to Boaty Boatwright, who was at Twentieth-Century Fox at the time." He continues:

> And she said, "This is fascinating, and would you tell it to Gareth" (can't think of his name). And, again, I had never done this before, and I was embarrassed, but I mumbled out a few things. And he said, "Well, I like this. And, uh, I have a film we've just finished, and I want you to see it to show you that we can handle young people and their themes . . . *Breaking Away*." So, he said, "Well, have your agent come out. (And he was a partner with Alan Ladd, you know.) And we'll make a deal." And I thought, "Well, why haven't I done this before. This is kind of snazzy." (Wood & Barr 230)

With neither a screenplay nor even a written description, Foote pitched merely a "verbal treatment" of the general subject and a few scenes toward "a very straightforward story about these five young men from very disparate backgrounds, all having to do part-time jobs to keep themselves going. And they're trying to get ahead, and they have tribulations.... And I also had a scene where they ... would pass one of these big buses with a band, a country and western band that had arrived. I really just described kind of the atmosphere of their lives. And I said that it would end up ... with finding a way to succeed" (Foote). Unfortunately, when Foote's agent Lucy Kroll flew to Hollywood to finalize the deal, her luck wasn't as good as Foote's. The day she arrived in Los Angeles, a major shake-up was announced at Fox in which a number of executives, including even Alan Ladd, Jr., were fired. Out in the housecleaning were Foote's connections and, of course, his idea for a movie. Although he had successfully pitched his story to the studio, no money from Fox arrived to support the plays in *The Orphans' Home Cycle*. And the writer didn't have even a written treatment of the story.

Despite the failed negotiations, Horton Foote stayed true to his film idea. Returning to his preferred way of working, he wrote the original notes "on my own.... I didn't have any ... help from a studio" (Wood & Barr 230). This new direction appealed to Ms. Kroll, who believed the absence of studio control offered Horton an opportunity to determine "who was going to direct it, who was going to design it, who was going to act in it, who was going to produce it." In her view, the changes at the top at Twentieth Century Fox might "redefine the role of an independent producer" to include the writer, who would gain "artistic control of his own material" (Kroll). Meanwhile, as Foote started to develop the screenplay from the verbal treatment, he remembered Gareth's suggestion that "there should be an older guy in it somewhere" to contrast with the young band (Foote; Wood & Barr 230). Taking this advice, Horton made the older character the primary subject, drawing on his history with actors and alcoholics. The original notes for this draft, written front and back on lined notebook paper, are (except for the last page) in the author's own handwriting.[1] Though sometimes fragmentary, these pieces reveal Horton Foote writing quickly and mixing dialogue with action. Sometimes scratching out useless ideas, Foote often hurriedly completed dramatic business. Names and details usually appear in the margins, though he also wrote across the page or at angles to either side. This sprawling fifty-one-page draft was first titled "The Singer and the Song," although "Tender Mercies" is listed as an alternative on the first page. Foote named his older singer both "Ed Lowry" and "Mac Davis" before he settled on Mac Sledge. And, at one point, he used the name "Tammy Wynette" until he settled on Dixie as Mac's ex-wife. In "The Singer and the Song," the band members are integral to Mac's story. They help him sober up. He gives them advice on the music business. While love grows between Ed/Mac and Rosa Lee, the young men in the band contribute to his healing as much as she.

The original notes end, as in the treatment, with the success of the group. Interestingly, the personal demons are evenly distributed between the two main female characters. The struggles of Tammy/Dixie are portrayed sympathetically. In flashback, we learn that Ed/Mac has been repeatedly irresponsible, at one point failing to pick up their daughter from school. Despite his failures, she is reluctant to use legal methods in dealing with Ed/Mac. On the other hand, in Foote's first notes, Rosa Lee is divorced (not widowed), responsible for a sick father as well as Sonny, and less self-assured than in the final film.

Most interesting in "The Singer and the Song" are the pieces that survive in *Tender Mercies*, such as, for example, a confrontation between Tammy/Dixie and Ed/Mac and Rosa Lee's jealousy at her husband's attending his ex-wife's concert. As in the film, Sue Anne (first called Sue Ellen Harris) elopes and dies in an automobile accident. A reporter invades the singer's privacy as Mac retreats into a field. Sonny also visits his father's grave, though in the early notes the father was killed in Korea, not Vietnam. Toward the end of the manuscript, Foote has Ed/Mac and Rosa Lee sending the boy off to school.

This became the initial scene in the original screenplay, a 111-page document, written in irregular form, with FIRSTDRAFT appearing on the lower third of the title page's left side. Repeated from "The Singer and the Song" are scenes in which country people complain of the high cost of gas and have trouble finding enough money, Rosa Lee and Sonny visit his father's grave, and the reporter appears at the house. The scene at the auditorium is similar as well. As in the first notes, Dixie and Harry "live together." Cryptic fragments in "The Singer and the Song" about lightning, the Heavenly Mansion, and Jesus freaks are developed in FIRSTDRAFT into a scene where Henry, a band member nearly struck by lightning, quits music to join a religious sect in San Marcos. In the screenplay, Mac, rather than a minor character, describes being in the special forces in Korea. Most striking is the regional and pastoral nature of the first draft of *Tender Mercies*. Where the notes had established a place fifteen miles from Austin, the completed screenplay has "a small south central Texas town" where Rosa Lee was "born and raised." It relies on concrete names, the boy at school says Sonny's father wasn't from "this part of Texas," and the boys in the band mention San Marcos, Waxahachie, Dripping Springs, and Lockhart. Grounded in this specific place, Rosa Lee gardens, and she and Mac sing hymns while they work their land. The last shot even describes geese flying overhead, another place-specific touch.

The first draft is more theatrical than cinematic. As on stage, backstory and relationships are clarified in the dialogue, not visually. For example, Sue Anne is introduced in a conversation between

---

Mac and Sonny. Similarly, the screenplay explains that Sue Anne learned of Mac's whereabouts from a secretary named Margaret. Substituting reporting for action, Foote has Sonny describe his confrontation at school to his parents. On the river, the site of an emotional baptism, Mac and Sonny discuss the boy's father, his school, and the insurance money. More significant is Rosa Lee's assertive, expressive nature. She makes Mac leave the motel for three days because of his drinking, is openly angry about Dixie Scott, frets over money and Mac's intentions, and even cries before the baptism. Also, more talky than in the later version, Rosa Lee declares: "We have to take what the Lord sends," "All humans have troubles it looks like," and "Because we never seem to know what's around the corner ... all we can do is pray we have the strength to bear it if it's bad." She sings, too, including "Wings of a Dove" in the last scene.

Two other scenes, filmed and edited from the film, were central to this version of *Tender Mercies*. The first was a trip to the home of the grandparents, Etta R. and Mr. Wadsworth, who believe in providence, express concern that Mac is good to Rosa Lee and Sonny, and want their grandchild to remember his biological father. Even more remarkable is a gravesite appearance by Dixie, who disobeys her doctor and enters as the service begins, first talking to Harry and then to Mac: "I want him [Mac] to know that I forgive him. In front of my baby's grave I want him to know I forgive him for everything he ever done to me. (Calling) Mac. I forgive you, because my little girl would want me to." This complex blend of Dixie's taste for drama and a genuine yearning for forgiveness didn't survive further revisions and edits.

A number of scenes did survive the final cut. Mac tells the band to "sing it the way you feel it," and he gives a song to Harry, who rejects the offer at the motel. Harry announces Sue Anne's elopement, and Rosa Lee and Mac discuss his first marriage. The scene where Rosa Lee discusses Vietnam and drugs, goes out to the road, looks at the picture, and Mac returns is only changed in small details. And Mac sings "Wings of a Dove," though in the presence of Sonny and Rosa Lee down at the river. The discussion of change after the baptism is already present, as are most of the words over Sonny's father's grave, though they are in the truck after the baptisms. The dialogue after Mac first sings with the band is very similar, and Sonny discusses fathers with a boy at that same dance. Already in FIRSTDRAFT, there is a "trusting happiness" speech, but it is longer and addressed to both Rosa Lee and Sonny on the return from the Dallas airport. In this draft, Rosa Lee also discusses Sonny's father with him in a penultimate scene.

This is the draft Horton Foote shared with his friend and collaborator Robert Duvall, anxious that he risked his relationship with Duvall. But Horton's fears were unfounded, for when Foote read the story to Duvall, the actor immediately said "I want to do it" (Duvall; Wood & Barr 230). In fact, the two artists tried to produce the film themselves as an independent project, along the lines supported by Foote's agent, Lucy Kroll (Kroll). When Foote and Duvall couldn't get financing, they turned to Philip Hobel, who was interested in filming Foote's play *1918*. When Horton said, "I'm not able to do [*1918*] as a film because I'm too interested in [*Tender Mercies*] right now," [Hobel] said, "May I read that?" And Hobel happily "switched allegiance and really helped us get it done" (Wood & Barr 230; Hobel).

Two crucial decisions followed. As the filmmakers began looking for locations, they considered Florida, Oklahoma, and Georgia, particularly the Atlanta area, which offered accessibility and experienced crews. But Duvall and Foote both had strong ties to Texas. The actor's mother came from there, and the writer's plays and most personal films are based on the fictional Harrison in coastal Southeast Texas. The producers finally agreed, recognizing that "in film you have to be true to the place," "something Robert Duvall sensed and needed as an actor" (Hobel). In addition to a setting, the film needed a director. Foote's early favorite was Barbara Loden, who had written and directed the independent feature *Wanda* in 1970. But Loden became ill, dying in September 1980, and many major US directors passed on the film (Foote; Hobel). Nearly desperate, the producers sent the script to Bruce Beresford, the Australian director internationally famous for the just-released *Breaker Morant*

(1980). Beresford not only agreed, but he also brought to the project two other talented artists from his country, director of photography Russell Boyd and editor William Anderson.

In the meantime, after FIRSTDRAFT, Horton Foote initially made some significant (and unrelated) changes in his screenplay. He added the scene in the restaurant where Mac says he doesn't know what he wants and demands the music be turned down, followed by a near accident with his truck. In a long conversation between Mac and the band, Foote dropped Henry as the member who, after being nearly electrocuted, joined the Heavenly Mansion commune of "Jesus freaks." In Mac's meeting with Sue Anne, the writer cut early dialogue about her being named after Mac's mother and her offer of money to Mac. Even more substantial cuts came later, with Foote dropping scenes where Sonny and Rosa Lee wait for Mac's return from the funeral and the three ride back from the airport, the occasion for Mac's "why" speech.

But these revisions were relatively minor compared with those made in the first two weeks of November 1980. By then, Foote knew Beresford felt "the first draft of the script was often repetitive" and even excellent scenes must be cut that "didn't advance the story" (Beresford). To streamline the text, the writer reduced substantially the scenes where Harry announces Sue Anne's elopement, Dixie and her daughter fight, and Harry fires Menefee. Eliminated are references to Sonny's substitute teacher (a friend of Rosa Lee's mother) and Rosa Lee's anxiety about Mac's past. Similar lines of dialogue about Sonny's father and Mac's guilt over serving in the entertainment unit during the Korean War were dropped, as was the business of Sonny being alone as Rosa Lee takes Mac to the airport. But significant additions were also made on the first day of November 1980. Dixie imagines Mac is hiding Sue Anne's whereabouts "out of spite" (sc. 98b), Sue Anne visits Rosa Lee during the elopement, Mac looks for the couple in Austin, and he hears of his daughter's death after the visit by the band (no longer while working in the garden).

On November 11, 1980, Foote revised the scene at Sonny's father's grave to include resonant discussion of those who grieved at that funeral. But Rosa Lee's religious testimony, including her belief in the efficacy of prayer, was omitted. While he cut more explication, Foote refueled the conflicts between Dixie and Sue Anne over Menefee and the daughter's singing career. For the first time, Mac meets the boys on the streets of the town, and the "why" speech (still without "trusting happiness") is shifted from the truck to the back of the motel, though not yet to the garden. By November 14, 1980, the screenwriter (clearly open to new locations and visuals) added road scenes in which the band members find Mac and react to meeting him. While Foote also cut long discussions at the river between Mac and Sonny (dealing with Sonny's father, money for the motel, and Mac's previous fights with Dixie), he retains that location for Mac's singing "Wings of a Dove" and being baptized. At the rehearsal hall, Mac talks with the wives of the boys in the band, and Sonny approves of Mac, while the other boy admits his father is "not so much either" (sc. 112a). For the first time, Mac tells Harry to "stop bugging me," and the screenwriter creates a Central Texas image in the final direction: "the camera pulls back until MAC, ROSA LEE, and SONNY are dots against the TEXAS sky" (sc. 134).

In anticipation of shooting, Horton Foote began in the following fall to fashion a shooting script. Backing away from the pastoral impulse that shaped the opening of FIRSTDRAFT, he returned the story to Mac's first arrival at the motel—showing him in a drunken fight with a male companion—and refocused on the Mac/Rosa Lee/ Sonny triad. On October 6, 1981, Foote shifted back to two country people at the gas pump (from a single woman not identified as "country"). Dropped are Rosa Lee's doubts Mac will stay, leaving only a brief scene where she invites Mac to breakfast and church. While he leaves the church scene intact, the writer drops a family trip to the drive-in, shifting much of that dialogue to the television scene at the house. Omitting much of the action, Foote retains scenes in which Rosa Lee and Sonny see Mac drunk on the streets of the town (scenes 31–11). Later, in scene 73H, Harry and Dixie are discovered in pajamas in a hotel bedroom, making explicit the sexual nature of their relationship.

Two days later—on October 8, 1981—Horton Foote further simplified the story for Bruce Beresford. After the reporter leaves,

Mac and Sonny no longer go off to the fields; Harry doesn't pursue Sue Anne after her fight with Dixie. Changing Menefee's first name from Harris to Lewis in scenes 97 and 107A, Foote retains Sue Anne's interest in singing. Dixie no longer imagines Mac to be interested in Sue Anne's trust fund, and the woman baptized before Sonny and Mac is eliminated. Similarly, Foote and Beresford dropped scenes where Mac pursues Sue Anne and Menefee in Austin motels (other than the Jeff Davis) and a bar, as well as Mac's travels to the Dallas/ Fort Worth Airport and Nashville. For the first time, Mac ends his "why" speech with the abrupt "I don't trust happiness" (sc. 155). Rosa Lee no longer sings "Wings of a Dove" in the final scene, and the geese are dropped, leaving the final instruction "ROSA LEE watches."

Over the next two weeks—until October 20, 1981—the revisions became focused on accuracy and economy. Sonny, not Rosa Lee, invites Mac to supper after his drunken trip to town. Before the television, Mac says his girl is seven or eight, not four or five, years older than Sonny. In the fight between Larue and Sonny, "Vietnam" is identified as the place where Sonny's father was killed. At the grandparents' house, Rosa Lee no longer establishes that Mac was at the motel one year before their marriage; at Dixie's performance, Mac doesn't bother to ask the doorman to find Sue Anne. On the twentieth, Foote continues the replacing of Menefee's first name from Harris to Lewis (in scenes 112, 113, 131 and 133), and Harry's discussion of Sue Anne's elopement and earnest money (though not yet named that) is moved from the filling station to a town garage. And Foote adds to Sue Anne's second trip to the motel her words: "My husband drinks. Most musicians do, you know. He says he'll quit when he gets a job" (sc. 130).

After these clarifications, Horton Foote emphasizes atmosphere on October 28. He adds a scene in which a man asks about a room at the motel, and Rosa Lee explains it costs fourteen dollars and breakfast is four miles down the road. Following this addition, Foote recovers Mac's discussion with Sonny of school and his conviction he would've liked the boy's father. More sense of place is gained by shots of Mac listening to music and playing his guitar in the trailer and Rosa Lee's recounting her history with Sonny's father at his grave. Visual effects are gained when a conversation between Mac and Rosa Lee at the river is exchanged for a wordless meeting between Sonny and Rosa Lee in the field across from the motel. On this day, Foote removes the sexuality between Dixie and Harry by shifting Dixie's "to spite me" speech from a hotel to her dressing room. Added is dialogue about lost fortune and previously dropped dialogue about Mac's travel.

On November 4, 1981, just as shooting began, the writer fine-tuned two scenes. The one with the reporter is revised to include sexual innuendo and Mac's decision to retreat to the house rather than remain outside. Dropped are Mac's words to Rosa Lee about "a damn reporter" (sc. 46). Even more extensive were revisions to the sequence in town with the band members. Foote takes the boys out of their car and has Mac turn into a restaurant (rather than a supermarket) and move on to a feed store. The dialogue is also refocused on the private lives of the boys and the success of the recording. The final revisions before shooting—made on November 16, 1981—all involve the sequence of scenes after Sue Anne's death. In the interest of economy, Foote cuts a few of Dixie's words at the house. More substantial is his omission of the trip to the church and the service there. And, while there is still a scene at the gravesite, where Dixie screams and faints, she no longer tells Harry that she forgives Mac (sc. 153).

As the filming began, the most substantial change made by the filmmakers was a visual shift to a Texas both more western and mythic. Foote's stories tend toward the claustrophobic; they are placed in small towns informed by neighbors, gossip, and communal expectations. *Tender Mercies*, on the other hand, was set, in the words of Art Director Jeannine Oppewall, "in the middle of an utterly flat cotton field. There were no other human structures in sight. It was exactly the kind of place that would make one begin to understand why people like Mac and Rosa Lee would get together— in part because there is simply very little else for one's eye to settle on. The landscape itself was strong and suggested a kind of interior loneliness and demanded of its inhabitants a quiet resignation and self-sufficiency" (Oppewall).

Such emptiness was emphasized by the photographic style. Finding the Texas location "similar to the far west of NSW [New South Wales]," director Beresford and photographer Boyd

> deliberately composed the shots, particularly around the Mariposa Motel, either very low in the frame with a lot of sky, or, the other way around, with the motel high in the frame and a lot of foreground. And that was just to get across a feeling for the very desolate and flat part of Texas that we were shooting in. (Boyd)

For example, in the shot where Mac asks Sonny to stop throwing rocks, in Boyd's words, "we deliberately put the camera up in the air a bit so that the motel and the horizon would actually be above their heads in the frame" (Boyd). Consequently, the fields are more expressive, the distances more haunting than in most Foote tales. This imaginative space is further expanded by the preference of Beresford and Boyd for depth of field, as when Sonny and Mac are placed in the same shot in the opening sequence or Mac is shot in profile with the reporter in the hallway behind him.

In visual contrast to the forbidding, empty landscapes, Jeanine Oppewall built the motel "in the shape of the letter Y, extending itself toward the passerby, open, and inviting him in." She found just as much resonance in naming the motel the Mariposa:

> First of all, it was the right length word for the sign; second it had a Spanish flavor appropriate to the area; and third, I am myself an amateur lepidopterist (butterfly collector) and liked the personal subtext of the word. I knew that "mariposa" is the Spanish word for butterfly. Butterflies have been frequently taken in literature as symbols of the psyche. But it was the idea of metamorphosis that appealed to me most: it was absolutely right of the story of Mac Sledge. (Oppewall)

For the furnishings at the Mariposa, the art designer chose patterns suggesting "continuity with the past" and colored

---

with "greens, yellows, reds, and browns ... traditionally and psychologically associated with growth, flowering, and warmth." The "caterpillar greens" and "yellow ochres" would express Rosa Lee's "life giving and asserting nature." She added "ceramic armadillos" for a Texas flavor and felt "dried butterfly plaques" would accent the mariposa theme. Rosa Lee's religious impulses—her southern Baptist character—were represented by "a ceramic plaque of [Albrecht] D[ü]rer's praying hands" and "family photos and the bird and flower pictures" (Oppewall).

As Russell Boyd explained, for the most part, *Tender Mercies* has a direct, sparse style that evolved "from the restrictions of economy. And, in fact, the way that Bruce placed the people in the frames was probably because he couldn't afford the time to cut away [which] led to a fairly distinctive look." But complementing this restraint in the composition of *Tender Mercies* are brief flourishes of (1) distinctive lighting and (2) subjective camera. As Boyd pointed out, the scene in which Mac sings at the window reveals the preference for soft light in the indoor shots at the motel, a legacy of the photographer's study of impressionism in his Australian period films of the late 1970s. For this effect, the artists pumped "light through and let the windows themselves become the light sources, and have very little else lit in the room. Because there are drapes or sheers on the windows, the quality of light is very soft" (Boyd). More startling is the scene at the back of the house after the reporter leaves. There, as Mac looks out over the tilled field, the camera assumes his point of view. In the film's one purely expressionistic moment, the field becomes a metaphor for Mac's consciousness—prepared for a fertile change as yet unrealized.

Key to Tess Harper's acting in *Tender Mercies* are emotions from her own past. In her words, "raised in a fundamentalist background," she "recognized the better parts of fundamentalism in Rosa Lee—Christian grace" and imagined "a kind of plains Madonna" who, like Mary in the Bible, "watched and kept these things in her heart." According to Harper, Rosa Lee listens without being judgmental; "she's trying to empathize and understand what the people around her are going through, and she kind of absorbs all of this. But she doesn't have the facility to verbalize it." As Tess summarized, "there is real love and respect [between Rosa Lee and Mac], but it's not your passionate, typical movie love story. It's much deeper than that. She ... needs a father for her son and she needs the companionship" (Harper).

Unable to draw as specifically on his past as Harper, Robert Duvall relied on his instincts for Foote's writing. In Duvall's words, Foote's writing is:

> kind of simple, deep stuff that you can't force; you gotta deal with it as it is, you know, without pushing it.... It's not fragile, but if you try to force something else into it, then you're making it fragile. It's there; it's minimum, complete but minimum. So you just have to deal with it in a very relaxed, human way without working at it or pushing it.

As he often does when preparing for a film, Duvall "went down and drove all around East Texas ... to look for accents and different things. It's a kind of a saturation process" in order to imitate specific Texas realities. On the set, as Allan Hubbard explained, the artists would improvise by establishing a general feeling and saying "Just go along with him [Duvall], react to whatever he says, just talk to him." As Duvall has explained, the scenes playing the guitar were "straight improvisation," but the tossing of the stones was "within the form [and] against the written word [but designed] to enhance it" as something Mac Sledge might do in real life (Duvall; Hubbard).

Once the structure of that story was established, William Anderson and Bruce Beresford made the film lean, verging on the elliptical. Most obvious was the cutting of the marriage (and following comic scene) and shots of Sue Anne's car speeding to her death. Congruent with this de-dramatization of *Tender Mercies* was the omission of the visit to the grandparents, arguments between Dixie and Sue Anne, and Harry's firing of Menefee. Sue Anne's singing (and Menefee's plans to have her join the band) became unnecessary as well. Finally, even the funeral and gravesite scenes, though powerfully acted, were redundant—and removed. Mac no longer walks drunkenly through the town. Dixie doesn't make a hysterical phone call to Mac, and he never approaches the doorman at Dixie's concert. Sonny doesn't hear Mac's boots drop as he gets into bed after the night of temptation. Mac and the boy play only football, not baseball, and Mac never talks to the wives of the band members.

During the pre-production, shooting, and editing of *Tender Mercies*, some of Horton Foote's interests were lost, including the "look" of coastal Southeast Texas and its cotton fields, as well as the focus on forgiveness. But the integrity of his vision survived and, in some cases, flourished because, as Tess Harper explained, "the whole magic of *Tender Mercies* is in Horton's writing, and in Beresford's respect for it," as well that of the other artists, including Russell Boyd, who considered the film "wonderfully...written" by "a great American writer" (Harper; Boyd). Even as these artists transformed Horton's work from page to screen by employing their own histories, talents, and beliefs, it remained a Foote story.

No less than Horace Robedaux in Foote's nine-play cycle *The Orphans' Home*, Mac and Sonny are orphans looking for a nourishing, comforting home. Mac's search is exacerbated by the death of his daughter, tempting him to turn inward like Dixie, and the main character in an early Foote teleplay *Ludie Brooks*. Unlike Dixie and Ludie, Mac shares his grief with Rosa Lee. In the process, he becomes aware of his own demon (the failure to trust happiness) and awakens more fully to the reality of his life. His new family, like the one established by Elizabeth and Horace in *The Orphans' Home Cycle*, offers a healing sense of order in the face of the mystery and chaos of human experience. Having found an emotional and spiritual home, Mac summons the courage to control his alcoholism and face life's many vagaries. In the process, he discovers the radically human grace visited by Horton Foote's most fortunate characters.

Note

1. All citations to the various scripts that led to the film are taken from my library, given to me by Horton Foote before he placed his papers at Southern Methodist University (SMU), Dallas, Texas. The most complete collection is held in the DeGolyer Library at SMU.

Works Cited

Beresford, Bruce. Correspondence with author. 6 Feb. 1989.

Boyd, Russell. Telephone interview. 20 Apr. 1994.

Duvall, Robert. Telephone interview. 16 Dec. 1993.

Foote, Horton. Interview at his home in Wharton, Texas. 15 Mar. 1988.

Harper, Tess. Telephone interview. 24 Apr. 1991.

Hobel, Philip & Mary-Ann. Interview at their offices in New York. 27 Sept.1990.

Hubbard, Allan. Interview at his home in Paris, Texas. 31 Mar. 1991.

Kroll, Lucy. Telephone interview from her New York office. 5 Jun. 1990.

Oppewall, Jeanine. Personal correspondence. 2 Oct. 1990.

Wood, Gerald C. & Terry Barr. "'A Certain Kind of Writer': An Interview with Horton Foote." *Literature/Film Quarterly* 14.4 (1986): 226–37.

What the Old Folks Say: Repetition, Circular Thinking, and Magical Thinking in Three Plays by Horton Foote_____

Elizabeth Fifer

Alberta, in *The Last of the Thorntons* (2000); Carrie, in *The Trip to Bountiful* (1953); and Myrtle, in *A Coffin in Egypt* (1996)—three strong women in mental decline—fight back against powerlessness, diminishment, and loss of identity. Horton Foote's sensitivity to how their minds operate, his ability to portray them honestly and lovingly, in the context of family, community, and history, humanizes these aged characters. His interest in women's issues grew naturally from his close relationship with his mother and with Wharton, his hometown, represented as Harrison in the plays. Alberta, a lonely spinster in decline; Carrie, a widow who raised her young son; and Myrtle, a betrayed wife, would have been familiar to him.

From Wharton to Harrison

Foote's plays reflect a rich storehouse of family and town history. Conversations heard on porches and in backyards found their way into his plays as direct references with the names changed or composites of several stories, a crazy quilt of "the scandals, private and public, and the deaths by drowning in the river, the tales of gamblers, and drunks, and murderers, and the ones murdered, of adulterers and adulteresses" (Foote, *Farewell* 206). Everyday life offered him ample opportunity to listen. Next to his father's haberdashery, where he clerked as a young man, stood a dry goods store owned by the Kreitsteins. Mrs. Kreitstein could be counted on to relay "in great detail all the sad and tragic events suffered by various families in town" (186). The melodramas described there provided a fertile ground that he later drew upon. He appreciated the exaggeration in such accounts that reflected an earlier fraught time in history, "when Wharton was often lawless, filled with feuds and outsized characters, some ruthless, some generous" (202).

Cycles, circles, circularity, and repetition lie at the heart of Foote's work. These techniques establish his modernist style. Roads that leave come round to home again (as in *The Roads to Home* trilogy). The *Orphans' Home Cycle* enacts his father and mother's lives. Relatives and people in the community connect in a web of stories. Gerald C. Wood has spoken of Foote's "endless search for connectedness, order, and contentment" (*Selected One-Act Plays* xv). Crystal Brian cites Foote, remarking that his work is "like a collage" of tales (97). Repeated themes and plots intertwine through the years. In "Remembering Wharton, Texas," Marion Castleberry identifies Foote's great subject as the "small-town setting, its fixed values pitted against an ever-changing world, its array of simple but spiritually bankrupt people, and its characters' need for a sense of order and stability in their lives" (27). He quotes Foote in a 1998 interview, discussing "country people and lost people…voices and stories of weather and crops, of illnesses or hard times" (qtd. in Castleberry 21).

Of the three women, Alberta, sixty, seems most affected by early-onset Alzheimer's disease. She cannot form new ideas but is caught in a continual recycling of memories and desires. Carrie, also sixty, forgets and misplaces things in her everyday life, but her memory of the past, particularly Bountiful, remains vivid. Myrtle, ninety, uses her flow of memories as a tool for healing. The characters of Alberta, Carrie, and Myrtle offer unparalleled insight into minds damaged by old age and the pain of experience, inhabiting and vividly conveying their troubling and unpredictable symptoms and behavior.

Alberta's Denial of the Present in *The Last of the Thorntons*

As *The Last of the Thorntons* opens, the year is 1970. Alberta sits in her room, refusing to get dressed. Miss Pearl, the receptionist, complains "We've had to lock her in her room to keep her from walking in the halls naked" (Foote, *Last* 15). Even though only moderately disabled, she is still in danger of losing her place in the nursing home. Nurse Clarabelle is fed up—"Either she starts behaving sensibly or she leaves or I leave" (28). Here, as elsewhere in Foote's plays, the idea of home, often returning to the first home, becomes paramount.

That first home lies further back than Alberta's lost farm or the duplex her cousin Douglas sold in Houston. Alberta believes her family suffers from a century-old curse brought on by slavery. But when she refers to her great-grandfather Colonel Thornton's "hundred and seventy slaves," her visitor Fannie Mae Gosset demurs, saying "I don't know about that" (25). Alberta's obsession links present to past suffering. She wants to make reparation. She begins by asking Clarabelle the nurse to forgive her, which Clarabelle hotly refuses: "You are talking to the wrong woman. I never been nobody's slave" (17). A self-described descendant from the Thornton slaves named Ramsey warns her "punishment's bound to come unless you ask forgiveness [of] … every colored person you meet from now on" (57). She hears the crying outside of shadowy figures, slaves from the past and hippies from the unruly present.

Alberta knows parts of the past but does not understand her present. Geographically unmoored, she expects to return soon to a home that has already been torn down to make way for Houston's newly renovated West University Street. Her mental condition, in-between one home and another, refusing to acknowledge what has happened to her, floats through a transient and unstable reality.

> Alberta: I'm going back, you know. Tomorrow or the next day. I've gotten over my nervousness.
> Douglas: Now, Alberta, you know you can't go back. Be sensible.
> Alberta: I certainly can go back. I left because I was nervous and I'm not nervous anymore.
> Douglas: Now you can't go back, Alberta. Be sensible, this is your home now. (80–81)

Douglas' meaning is clear. Clarabelle explains to Fannie Mae, "They just bring the old here now to be taken care of until they die" (19). Alberta feels robbed of earthly real estate and her final resting place as well. Her position as the carrier of the family name should at least entitle her to lie with them. But the wives of the Thorntons got the family plots, making Alberta's decision to obey her father and stay single, to keep her maiden name, irrelevant. Her only choice is to be buried "as close to them as you can get me" (66).

In many of Foote's plays, chilling tales of deaths serve as touchstones for memory. Prompted by Fannie Mae, seventy-six, and Lewis, eighty-five, the sensational stories Alberta recounts orient her. She tells of her notorious "second cousin once removed," Toddy Hodges, who knifed Huston Faubion over a woman's honor (41). Foote retells this incident in *Cousins*. Annie Gayle Long, now a resident of the home, watched Mr. Sledge, about to lose his plantation after a series of bad harvests, shoot her banker father (59). Foote's mother told him a version of this story (*Farewell* 90) and it also appears in *The Roads to Home*. Alberta keeps a photo of her sister Mabel's husband, who committed suicide during their honeymoon, explaining: "He laughed and said, Mabel, if I thought you didn't love me I'd kill myself, and pulled the trigger and shot himself" (76). At first, Lewis thinks Alberta herself is dead—"Go on. My God, she's changed" (36).

Like the sensational stories from Harrison, magical thinking about Hollywood helps Alberta to bear her considerably reduced life. Her sister Willa compared her to the movie star Bebe Daniels (54). As a girl, Alberta dreamed about Hollywood but only got as far as Culver City. The photos autographed by Rudolph Valentino and Barbara La Marr bring back the excitement of those early years of film. On her photo, La Marr writes "Lest ye forget" (87). A family member from West Texas sends money for Annie Long's upkeep. Her closest relatives are in retirement residences themselves. If Annie repeatedly cries "I want to go home," Clarabelle takes her back to her room (64–65). Alberta says of the residence, "It's not my home" (81).

Alberta doesn't exist in any palpable way. Without agency, unable to decide how she will live or even to know where she is, she can be pushed aside by those with more economic power. Her cousin Douglas interrupts her—too busy to stay for a visit, the same as her nephew, the alcoholic Little Tom. Douglas shows his impatience at listening. "That's all done, Alberta.... Why don't we change the subject, Alberta?" (80). He has only come to the residence to give her those photos of movie stars. He quickly dismisses her queries about her duplex.

> Alberta: But it was to be mine, Willa said, as long as…
> Douglas *(Interrupting)*: It was practical for you to live there then, but it's no longer practical for you to live there now. (81)

When Alberta leaves the room in anger, her actions elicit no sympathy or understanding from him—"Leave her alone. She'll get over it" (84). The monthly check for Alberta's care will come, even if Douglas, now her guardian, does not.

Carrie's Miraculous Migration in *The Trip to Bountiful*

Mrs. Carrie Watts from *The Trip to Bountiful* (1953), sixty like Alberta, echoes these residents' concerns. She is both repetitive in her demands and circular in her behavior. "At least twice a year we have to try and keep her from getting on a train to go back to her home town," her daughter-in-law Jessie Mae complains (*Bountiful* 30). She begs her son, "Ludie, please, I want to go home." "Mama, you know I can't make a living there" he replies (18). While Carrie is not "crazy," as Jessie Mae suggests (32), Mother Watts is forgetful and anxious, her short-term memory unreliable. She has lived in Houston for twenty years, now in a two-room apartment with her son and his wife, who infantilize her as Alberta's caretakers do their patient. Carrie cannot look in Jessie Mae's dresser drawer for a mislaid recipe, but her daughter-in-law can rifle through her purse for the monthly pension check.

If Alberta does not feel happy there, at least inside the residence, she speaks and moves freely. In the tiny apartment, Carrie can't hum hymns or walk too fast. Jessie Mae belittles Carrie both behind her back and to her face. Carrie can't argue because of Ludie. Jessie Mae insults Bountiful, calling it "some old swamp" she hates visiting (32). The past holds no appeal. "The passin's of time makes me sad … you're better off forgetting" (11). With her love of movies, Coca-Cola, and beauty parlors, Foote's Jessie Mae is a modern foil to her backward-gazing mother-in-law. Carrie's visceral memory of Bountiful, where she lived and raised her son, and where she longs to return, occupies the same obsessive place as Alberta's farm and duplex. Carrie is no better living with Ludie than the childless Alberta under the cold guardianship of her cousin Douglas. Carrie cleans the house, cooks three meals a day, and helps with the monthly expenses. Yet Jessie Mae chafes at having her there. She must stay home to babysit Mother Watts. This particular day, Jessie Mae suspects the worst. She declares: "[T]o me it's always a sure sign she's gonna try and run off when she starts actin' silent" (20). When Jessie Mae steps out for a Coca-Cola, Carrie leaves, embarking like a migrating bird on her quixotic journey.

As with Alberta, Carrie's mind drifts to fantasies of freedom. Practicality plays no role in her thinking. At the bus station, she tells the ticket man that "I need money to get me started in Bountiful. I want to hire someone to drive me out there and look at my house and get a few groceries. Try to find a cot to sleep on," to which he replies dryly "I'm sorry, lady. You're not going to Bountiful.... That's how it is" (46–47). The time she hopes to spend shrinks as her hope shifts from moving there permanently to the more humble desire "just to see it." Negotiating desperately, she tells the ticket man: "I'll settle for less now. Much, much less. An hour. A half hour. Fifteen minutes" (47). Disastrous crop failures, as with Alberta's family farm, caused the sell-off of all the acreage and forced Carrie and Ludie's move to Houston when he was seven. A "sinking spell" in the morning from Carrie's worsening heart gives this return a special urgency.

Both Alberta and Carrie sense the end. Carrie muses, "When you've lived longer than your house or your family, maybe you've lived too long" (50). The body does not necessarily die with the death of the self. Alberta blames a curse. Carrie speaks more broadly, about a loveless marriage and her enduring attachment to another man, Ray John Murray. Like Alberta, she obeyed her father and lost her chance for happiness. As Barbara Moore and David G. Yellin explain, "Foote heard the story of a young man and woman who were deeply in love but were not allowed to marry each other. They married other people, but he continued to walk by her house on his way to work every day just to see her" (1). That woman became the dramatic character Carrie Watts, who finds she needs to retrieve the happier self of Bountiful to replace her "hateful, quarrelsome" self (48).

Repetition provides comic business for Carrie's journey. News of the death two days before of her close friend Callie Davis both jars her and calls forth the places and names of an earlier generation. This list of names adds unwitting black humor to her exchange with the ticket man.

> Mrs. Watts: Do they still have dances in Borden's Opera House?
> Ticket Man: No, ma'm. It's torn down. They condemned it, you know. *(He starts on. He pauses.)* Did you ever know anybody in Harrison?
> Mrs. Watts: I knew a few people when I was a girl. Priscilla Nytelle. Did you know her?
> Ticket Man: No, ma'm.
> Mrs. Watts: Nancy Lee Goodhue?
> Ticket Man: No, ma'm.
> Mrs. Watts: The Fay girls?
> Ticket Man: No, ma'm.
> Mrs. Watts: I used to trade in Mr. Ewing's store…
> Ticket Man: Which Ewing was that?
> Mrs. Watts: George White Ewing.
> Ticket Man: He's dead. (44)

The repetition of Jessie Mae's rules for Carrie to live by creates another opportunity for humor:

> Jessie Mae: Number one. There will be no more running away…
> Jessie Mae: Number two. No more hymn singing, when I'm in the apartment…
> Jessie Mae: Number three.
> Ludie: *(Interrupting)* Jessie Mae, can't this wait till we get home? (57)

Each person Carrie meets offers her another opportunity to recount a piece of her history. Thelma hears about Jessie Mae, the ticket man about Harrison, and the sheriff about land: "Three hundred and seventy-five acres.… I sold off all but the house and the yard" (51). She weaves connections, blindly repeating the name of her destination. Thelma accompanies her on the bus, and the sheriff drives her to her decaying house on an overgrown lot (46). The ritual of reentering reconciles Carrie to her two rooms in Houston. Fueled by the sight of the actual place, Carrie's new-found dignity convinces Jessie Mae to give her more autonomy. The repressed mother-in-law has demanded her rights. As she tells the ticket man, "But I'm going... This is a free country" (47). Her old home holds answers to her "empty and meaningless" life (48). Owning and keeping up a house or farm confers a personhood that even ranks above family. Carrie sadly tells the Sheriff, "Maybe the need to belong to a house, and a family and a town has gone from the rest of the world" (51). Her friend Callie, who had made her farm sustainable, rode her tractor the day before she died.

> Mrs. Watts: Callie Davis kept her farm going.
> Sheriff: ...Lonely death she had. All by herself in that big house.
> Mrs. Watts: There are worse things. (51)

Nothing changes after she reaches her destination—in fact, she leaves her purse behind—but she reinvents herself. "I'm home. I'm home. Thank you. I thank you. I thank you. I thank you," she says to the sheriff (49). As she goes she tells Ludie, "We can never lose what it has given us" (56). Returning home has retrieved her life.

Personal and Regional Decline

Foote creates Carrie and Alberta not just as "Alzheimer's patients," but as complex women with cultural, geographical, and historical identities. Both grew up in Harrison with networks of family and friends. Alberta worked at the gas company, and the sale of her house supports her. Carrie farmed and now receives a pension check from the government. Yet their current mental confusion allows predatory behavior from caretakers and family. After the death of her sister Willa, her nephew stalked Alberta to get his share of the inheritance. "Little Tom kept coming around every day asking how much she had left me," [saying] "her share of the duplex should now be his" (*Last* 56). Carrie mothers both her son and daughter-in-law, yet Jessie Mae still considers her a burden, telling Thelma, "I hope you're lucky enough not to have to fool with any in-laws" (*Bountiful* 30).

Alberta and Carrie's thoughts take them from the nineteenth and early twentieth century's agrarian life of Harrison to Houston's crowded city streets. The slave Elizabeth Ramsay's family letters seize Alberta's attention and provide an explanation for her otherwise inexplicable losses. The sight of Bountiful rouses a passion in Carrie to possess land once again.

> Mrs. Watts: Ludie. Ludie. What's happened to us? Why have we come to this?
> Ludie: I don't know, Mama.
> Mrs. Watts: To have stayed and fought the land would have been better than this. (55)

Alberta and Carrie's mental decline follows a decline in the autonomy of farming and the closeness of family connection. The distance between Houston and Harrison constitutes a profound abyss for women in fixed spaces. When minds are wandering, as Alberta's is, a person "can't stay alone anymore" (*Last* 47). The receptionist Miss Pearl says brightly to Douglas "We're all having a good time here talking. Just one big happy family" (71). Alberta's tenuous hold on truth appears as shards of a broken past that scatter as soon as they are spoken. Slaves morph into hippies, great-grandfather Colonel Thornton into father Arthur Thornton, who owned a pool hall and only looked aristocratic. On one level, she knows the house she describes has been demolished, but she insists "I have a home, I'm happy to say. It's a duplex in Houston" (65). Although her rebellion, her refusal to recognize harsh reality, marks her descent into dementia, it also makes her character strangely admirable.

As a close observer of the way the old were treated and how they felt about it, Foote skillfully displays the fraught interaction between these women and their families. He recalls, "Since our houses were so close, I spent as much time with my grandparents as with my mother and father" (*Farewell* 92). The characters of Alberta Thornton and Carrie Watts have much to teach about the difficulty of providing care for people with Alzheimer's and advanced dementia who have lost memory and even identity. Since interaction depends on a shared store of knowledge now eroded by disease, their conflicts with their environment occur during mind slips and erasures. Their minds cannot distinguish between fantasy and reality. At the time Foote wrote *The Trip to Bountiful*, and even by the time of *The Last of the Thorntons*, the causes of diseases of the aging mind were not well understood, even though their effects were clear enough in personality changes, depression, and combativeness. Alberta was once a cheerleader, "Miss Personality," the "pet of the town" (*Last* 14). Her life parallels Foote's aunt's story about "the life and times of Miss Minnie May, a prototype of all such tales about the mystery of the town beauty becoming the town eccentric" (*Farewell* 53).

Foote lets these plays speak the characters' rage against their changed environments, the foiled attempts to control their lives. Jerry Tallmer cites Foote as remarking, "The thing that is relevant for all time … is the subject of grief" (*Four New Plays* ix). Rather than a medical description of symptoms, we are given these characters' thoughts and actions to portray their situations. Alberta's mind roams freely from present to past, lucid and disoriented by turns. Carrie runs away. They grapple with misunderstanding. Referring to Alberta, Clarabelle speaks succinctly. "I can't tell her nothing" (*Last* 17). Jessie Mae is more vehement about Carrie: "Oh, she's so stubborn. I could just wring her neck" (Foote, *Bountiful* 31). Financial considerations outweigh spiritual connections. Both living and dead women have a price. Alberta's duplex goes to fund her care. The pragmatic Jessie Mae fears Carrie will "get to Bountiful and die from the excitement and then we'll have all kinds of expenses bringing her body back here" (33).

Myrtle's Monologues as Medicine in *A Coffin in Egypt*
Foote's multiple narratives enclose stories within stories that ripple outward from individual works to the larger society. Resistance to change and the stubborn desire to control their own lives define many of his women characters, like Myrtle Bledsoe of *A Coffin in Egypt* (1996), a ninety-year-old widow with two deceased daughters. In the

rambling monologue to her companion Jessie Lydell, Myrtle's use of recurring images and motifs places her mental clarity somewhere between that of Alberta and that of Carrie. Her wealth allowed her to escape an adulterous husband and take her children abroad. When she had to return to Hunter's house, she felt, as she tells Jessie, "This wasn't my home.... This is Hunter's home" (Foote, *Coffin* 115). The repetition of "It was him or me" at the end of the play applies to her own situation as much as to Hunter's feud with Lovell Davis— "What else? Hunter and me" (135). While he lived, she tried "not to bring up unpleasant subjects" (123). But at times, Myrtle found herself shouting: "God damn you Hunter, I hate you!" (124). After his death, she must cleanse herself of the past. "I began to scream out again all my old grievances I held against him.... Poisoned by the memories of him" (124).

While adding and embroidering on her monologue she asks, "Anyway, where was I?" She realizes "I've told you that" (120–121). Hunter preyed on the black, the poor, and the young, including Iris Davis. When Myrtle tried to take a lover, the difference in sexual freedom for men and women became apparent. Speaking of her flirtation with Captain Lawson, "I wanted badly to slip away somewhere and meet him.... I got mad at Hunter and I told him what I wanted to do. That I thought it was unfair because he could openly go across the tracks and out to the cabins to his Negro woman" (120). Myrtle fought back by wounding his vanity. "You mean to tell me you're fool enough to believe a seventeen-year-old girl loves a sixty-eight-year-old man?" At the same time, she could scare her cowardly husband—"What if they kill you for killing [Iris' father Lovell Davis]...? You won't have many years to spend in peace then" (125).

Her companion Jessie supports Myrtle's version of the past and her vision of herself as an aging southern belle by telling her, "You're still beautiful. Very beautiful. A queen … a princess..." (115). Myrtle's memory of other men's admiration is a salve to her grief. Her tales of suitors and even promises of stardom change the mood. While she was in Africa, a Sheik in Algiers asked for her hand in marriage (114), and, closer to home, her Captain Lawson, "a wonderful dancer," swept her off her feet (120). She recalls a "Mr. Daniel Frohman," who "begged me to go on the stage when he met me... 'your beauty should not be wasted, it belongs to the world'" (127). This echoes Alberta's memory of resembling Bebe Daniels and reveals the magical thinking about glittering possibilities that enables these women, if only for a few moments, to escape their limited horizons and their litany of loss.

Myrtle hated Hunter's hypocrisy. He loved a black woman but at the same time shared his father's opinion that black people should only know how "to farm and work" (116). Myrtle wonders what will be needed to break the cycle of black poverty:

> They're still poor you know... I don't know how most of them live... Maybe education will help. Think it will? I thought Hunter would die the day they let them go to school with the white children. You, of all people, I thought to myself, objecting to something like that. (123)

As a poet and artist, Myrtle changes reality to match her vision. Painting allows her to immerse herself in a different world. She says of her portrayal of trees, "I paint how they look to me" (122). With the same attitude, she narrates her past. To tell the stark truth heals. Her anger reaches beyond the grave. Hunter's misdeeds were also those of a generation of men who wasted their lives and fortunes on women, cards, and drink. As Foote explains, "There was no work for a young man to do in Wharton in those days ... the young men of these families were often indolent, and arrogant, and many of them became compulsive gamblers" (*Farewell* 160–161). Her own daughter Lois "found out about husbands ... long before she died" (*Coffin* 119). In death, Hunter cannot give Myrtle reparation for the suffering he caused her in life, yet she tells her companion, "That's where I'll end too, of course, next to Hunter and my two daughters in a coffin in Egypt" (128).

Repetition and Circularity

These are women in the last part of their lives, the last of their line, or the last ones who remember the past well enough to tell its story.

Critical Insights

Foote himself was thirty-seven when he published *The Trip to Bountiful*, eighty when *A Coffin in Egypt* appeared, and eighty-four when he produced *The Last of the Thorntons*. That gives his accounts of old age, especially in the last two plays, a searing veracity. He knew he would be the last to hear and pass on his treasure house of family stories. He layers the unexpected with the mundane to produce original characters. Alberta challenges others to refute her assertions about corruption and evil in her family and in society. Carrie's behavior shows her family she values tradition. Myrtle bares the most intimate details of the kind of marriage suffered by many women of her generation.

His style of writing reflects the spoken word—its unexpected twists, its rising and falling rhythms, its musicality, the meandering and yet purposeful structure. His innovative and frank expression makes these plays refreshing. Repetition defines his modernism and connects him to such avant-garde playwrights of the twentieth century as Gertrude Stein. Circles within circles, pauses, ellipses, and emphases mirror the style of Samuel Beckett. As with Beckett, Foote's geriatric black humor appears throughout, a relief from the heaviness of sorrow. Alberta leaves the audience with a mélange of memories and images she has recycled from earlier monologues: "If only I hadn't gotten nervous, but I heard what I thought were slaves but they turned out to be hippies, and Willa and Mabel were dead then, and I'm the last of the Thorntons" (Foote, *Last* 90). The stage directions read "*She is quiet now.*" Foote adds silence to the run-on lament. Both comedy and pathos lie in the familiarity of the words. This is what she knows. Carrie's exaggerated gratitude to the sheriff that opens Act Three undercuts the sentimentality of her arrival at Bountiful: "I'm home. I'm home. Thank you. I thank you. I thank you. I thank you" (*Bountiful* 49). Her use of direct repetition and repetition with difference has a powerful and moving effect. Myrtle repeats her stories with greater or less detail but also uses direct repetition for emphasis. The words "It was him or me" appear seven times during her retelling of Lovell's death; the words finally come to represent her own victimization and determination to fight back (124–5).

Foote doubles the effect of repetition by employing it both as a symptom and a stylistic technique. Natural speech contains a high level of repetition. In these plays, that level increases to mimic the limited resources of the aging mind. According to their context, repeated words take on different shades of meaning. The word *duplex* frequently appears in Alberta's monologues. It represents Houston, ownership, the idea of family, somewhere to return to, money, a material object that can be destroyed, something precious lost. The word *land* provides the refrain for Carrie's journey. She waxes lyrical about its power to the sheriff—her father's land, then "our land," then "on this land" where her father was born (*Bountiful* 50). Her strength flows more from it than from houses or people (55). Myrtle obsesses over beauty—"I was a beauty" she tells Jessie who murmurs that she is "still beautiful … very beautiful." Only the beauty of nature compares (*Coffin* 115).

Alberta is locked in, Carrie runs away, and Myrtle comes home to bear witness. They have an incomplete status, in a hinterland of the mind. Few dramatists have presented characters at this stage of life. Instead of a fragmentary style, such as that used by Arthur Kopit in *Wings* (1978) to approximate the sound of stroke and language disorder, Foote blends life history, personal anecdotes, and family dynamics into characters who speak from a place of deep existential despair. They repeat because no one listens. They ruminate to focus their anxiety. On the surface, they live inside a safe structure, whether an institution, an apartment, or a lavish home. Yet these structures cannot begin to contain the intensity of their desires.

Works Cited

Brian, Crystal. "'To Be Quiet and Listen,' *The Orphans' Home Cycle* and the Music of Charles Ives." *Horton Foote: A Casebook*. Ed. Gerald C. Wood. New York: Garland, 1998. 89–108.

Castleberry, Marion. "Remembering Wharton Texas." *Horton Foote: A Casebook*. Ed. Gerald C. Wood. New York: Garland, 1998. 13–47.

Foote, Horton. *Collected Plays: Volume II* [*The Trip to Bountiful, The Chase, The Traveling Lady, The Roads to Home*]. Intr. Robert Ellerman. Lyme, NH: Smith & Kraus, 1996.

_____. *Collected Works, Vol. III* [*The Day Emily Married, Tomorrow, A Coffin in Egypt, Laura Dennis, Vernon Early, Getting Frankie Married—and Afterwards*]. Lyme, NH: Smith & Kraus, 1998.

_____. *Farewell*. New York: Scribner, 1999.

_____. *The Last of the Thorntons*. Woodstock & New York: Overlook Press, 2000.

_____. *Four New Plays*. Intr. Jerry Tallmer. Lyme, NH: Smith & Kraus, 1993.

Moore, Barbara & David G. Yellin, eds. *Horton Foote's Three Trips to Bountiful*. Dallas: Southern Methodist UP, 1993.

Wood, Gerald C., ed. *Horton Foote: A Casebook*. New York: Garland, 1998.

_____, ed. *Selected One-Act Plays of Horton Foote*. Dallas: Southern Methodist UP, 1989.

The Sane Face of Texas: Pursuing the Decent Life in Horton Foote's Films_____

Robert W. Haynes

Movies with Texas ingredients have long been popular, and their relevance to historical reality varies considerably. Don Graham, J. Frank Dobie Regents Professor of American and English Literature at the University of Texas, has asserted: "Texans have two pasts, one made in Texas, one made in Hollywood" (2). He has also commented of a 1966 Arthur Penn film that "*The Chase* set out to demonstrate among other things that Texans were about the lowest form of life in these United States" (76). This film originated in the work of Texas playwright and screenwriter Horton Foote, who, as a Texan himself (and, in fact, a direct descendant of one of the Texas pioneers who established the location of the new frontier state capital in what is now Austin), most definitely did *not* have a bias against his fellow inhabitants of the Lone Star State. Yet, as the film's history makes clear, the aesthetic concerns of Foote's original play and derivative novel were cast roughly aside as producer Sam Spiegel and screenwriter Lillian Hellmann intercepted Foote's story and ran with it toward the opposing team's goal line. Elsewhere in this volume, Roy J. Gonzáles, Jr., discusses the pre-film versions of *The Chase*, so here let it suffice to say that the film version, featuring a posse of major stars, demonstrates Graham's point about Hollywood's production of an alternate Texas history—in this case, a history twisted from the remnants of well-intentioned but superficial, didactic themes intended to demonize the oil-and-cows crowd as a result of the Kennedy assassination. Hellman possibly deserves to have it acknowledged that her own plan for the film was also sabotaged by Spiegel, which may not have been such a bad thing, but those interested can themselves consult the Hellman archive at the Harry Ransom Center in Austin to be sure.

The party most entitled to be offended by this cinematic train wreck was Foote himself, who had begun work on the original play during a period of what amounted to a self-imposed exile from the New York theater world in the late 1940s. Working at the King-Smith School in Washington, DC, Foote hoped to reinvigorate his dramaturgic career and to achieve the kind of popular success that had brought fame and fortune to his friends Jerome Robbins and Tennessee Williams during the Second World War. The play was produced on Broadway in April 1952, by which time Foote was already engaged in work with Fred Coe in a distinguished career as television writer, but it was not well-received, and Spiegel's decision to film the story, as Marion Castleberry notes, came after he read Foote's novelized version, which was published in 1956 (231). Spiegel's plans advanced slowly, and, in 1963, Horton Foote (who did not show up for the ceremony) was awarded an Oscar for the screenplay for *To Kill a Mockingbird* (1962). Later that same year, President John F. Kennedy was killed in Dallas. The assassination, shocking as it was, was soon followed by the televised murder of the alleged assassin by a Dallas strip-club operator. The fact that a Texan became president upon Kennedy's assassination appeared suspicious to many, and conspiracy theories still thrive in some quarters over half a century later. The Cuban Missile Crisis had occurred in 1962, and Lyndon Johnson's former friend and fellow Texan Billie Sol Estes had been much in the news after a 1962 newspaper report indicated his extensive involvement in bribery and fraud. Other contemporary news featured fierce opposition to the civil rights movement in the Deep South. In state universities in Georgia, Mississippi, and Alabama, racial integration was opposed, sometimes violently.

The Harper Lee novel *To Kill a Mockingbird* (1960) had featured a white southern family's resistance to bigotry, but, in William Faulkner's hometown of Oxford, Mississippi, black student James Meredith's admission to the University was met in 1962 with riots. In Alabama, Governor George Wallace, as promised, personally blocked a door (briefly) to prevent black students from enrolling. Black leader Medgar Evers was murdered in Mississippi in 1963, and, two months before President Kennedy's death, a terrorist bomb killed four children in an Alabama church. It is no wonder that Hellman felt obligated to express outrage, and possibly her revulsion to current violence and brutality found an outlet in her unsympathetic treatment of the story by the screenwriter who had helped make Atticus Finch (as played by Gregory Peck) a champion, if only a fictional one, of liberal thought in the South. The version of Texas that emerged from the Spiegel film satisfied no one, however, and Foote's unhappy experience with this project pushed him further in his inclination to avoid Hollywood and its tendency to abuse its writers. His main objection was that film writers were considered low-level employees with no right to control the cinematic use of their work or to enjoy appropriate rewards for it. His exclusion from the composition of the screenplay for *The Chase* was not necessarily objectionable in itself, but Hellman's attitude toward his original work appeared downright hostile, and when Foote was asked as a last, desperate measure to make saving adjustments to a script that had been taken from Hellman and further altered, he could only feel frustration and a sense that the work he had had in hand for many years had become something of a joke. As a man of the theater, he must also have felt the absurdity of a process so disrespectful of character, theme, and plot, especially when such remarkable (and expensive) acting talent had been enlisted for the film's cast.

Horton Foote's three primary successes in film deal with representations of the South, and each represents a different phase of twentieth-century southern history. His first widely-recognized work, the screenplay for *To Kill a Mockingbird*, reorganized Harper Lee's prose fiction into a dramatic form, expressing crucial concerns grounded in developments in civil rights. Jan Whitt describes Foote's modifications of Lee's novel in another chapter of this anthology. Foote's Oscar for this screenplay was the most substantial public recognition of his career to that date, but he was not present at the awards ceremony. He explained his absence by saying that he had not thought he would win, and, though he reiterated this assertion many times over the years, it seems possible that in the violent and troublesome climate of that time, he might have drawn retaliation upon himself or his family by reminding the world of his contribution to a film that focused on racial injustice. After all, Foote's large family was based in Texas and the South, and the obloquy piled on Atticus Finch in the film for defending Tom Robinson reflected a reality much more recent than the 1930s. Those who recall living in the South in the 1960s will never forget the uncertainty and anxiety of those years, but Horton Foote, who was born in 1916, the year of the notorious lynching referred to as "the Waco Horror," knew an even earlier time when there were few limitations on the unfair treatment of African Americans. He would, in fact, describe such a period later in his life, during the 1970s, as he composed the second play (*Convicts*) of his *Orphans' Home Cycle*. This play was produced in a 1990 film version starring Robert Duvall and James Earl Jones.

The frustrating operation of injustice in Lee's novel and in the subsequent film would have evoked sympathy from those seeing or remembering either work after Kennedy's assassination, for the expected clarification of the sequence of events and of responsibility for the shooting was obscured by the subsequent events, and even of those who were pleased by the president's death, many soon found themselves stunned by his successor's sudden and effective support of civil rights. Lyndon Johnson's quotation of the civil rights anthem "We Shall Overcome" in Congress in March, 1965, seemed to promise a restoration of sanity in American society, and the hitherto unenthusiastic federal protection given those advocating recognition of civil rights was invigorated. The rational and decent stance of an Atticus Finch seemed then to advocates of change to have been endorsed by an authority greater than that of the political opportunists and white supremacists who fought elimination of long-standing discriminatory racial codes. Lee's film had made a kind of reluctant rifleman of Atticus, but his marksmanship was restricted, in a slightly ludicrous scene, to the shooting of a mad dog. The film's other memorable discharge of firearms is reported from afar, when news arrives of Tom Robinson's suicidal escape attempt and death. With President Johnson's Civil Rights Bill, the government in effect took a positive step toward eliminating the kind of injustice that generated the desperation forced upon men like Tom Robinson by prejudice and a biased system, and such works as the film *To Kill a Mockingbird* contributed to the changes that brought such legislation into being. Horton Foote's home in the cotton-farming region near the Texas coast was very much a part of the agricultural South, and conflicts over minority rights in Wharton resembled similar conflicts across the Deep South. In her chapter of this collection, Rebecca Briley discusses some relevant issues, and it can be noted here that in his memoir *Farewell*, Foote tells of a Texas relative's experience with a lynching that is reminiscent of Tom Robinson's catastrophe (32–34). Thus despite the Mississippi setting of *Mockingbird*, it is still possible to perceive in the film a theme as critical for small-town Texas as for any region of the South.

The second film, *Tender Mercies* (1983), cast Robert Duvall in the part of a country musician/songwriter struggling with alcoholism and heartbreak. Rejected by the entertainment industry in which he had once made a name for himself, the singer finds himself slowly restored to vitality and to sanity by the simple life and by the love of a young widow and her son. The story is set in a world centered around a rural motel located on the Texas plains, and, within this world, the audience encounters a quiet reinterpretation of Texas, a state long celebrated as wild and violent and populated by heavily-armed vigilante-types short on due process and long on instant payback. The state Hollywood has put forward as intent upon stringing up rustlers, remembering the Alamo, and resolving differences with spectacular barroom brawls is gently excluded from this film managed by the famously tactful Horton Foote and the Australian director Bruce Beresford, and a kind of justice is done to a region where, although a history of violence has been more than merely evident, a powerful, quiet spirituality has also resided and still gives inspiration to many of its people.

A turning point in the film occurs when Mac Sledge, baffled and enraged by a hostile encounter with his country-star ex-wife, who has scornfully rejected a song he had hoped she would be interested in recording, drives away from the motel where he and his new wife Rosa Lee live. He drives aggressively, cursing at those who get in his way, and stops at a liquor store to buy a bottle. The camera shows a quiet conversation at the motel between Rosa Lee and her young son, and no more is heard from Mac until after Rosa Lee has put

Sonny to bed and switched off most of the lights. When she goes to bed and recites a scriptural passage in prayer, she hears the truck outside, and Mac enters.

Mac announces that he is not drunk, Rosa Lee offers him some soup, and their marriage continues almost as if nothing had happened. In fact, Rosa Lee tells Mac she wanted to learn one of his songs so she could surprise him by singing it for him. They talk briefly about his songs, and Mac brings out some manuscripts and begins to play his guitar and sing. The scene continues:

> MAC: (*Singing.*) ... If you'll just hold the ladder,
> Baby, I'll climb to the top.
> (*Pause*)
> Sing it.
> ROSA LEE: I can't.
> MAC: Why? (*Moves the songs to one side.*) Come here. Come over here.
> ROSA LEE: You just walked right out of here.
> (*They embrace.*) (*Three Screenplays* 121–122)

The scene ends with a minimum of reproof, yet Rosa Lee makes her point effectively. She is committed to Mac, and she expects that commitment to be respected. Her prayer from the Psalms, the book attributed to the ancient musician/songwriter and giant-killer David, broke off just as she was about to recite the following verse: "Remember, O Lord, thy tender mercies and thy loving-kindnesses; for they have been ever of old" (25:6). Rosa Lee's interrupted prayer would have extra significance for those able to ascertain its context, and the gentle dignity of her love makes it clear that in rejecting his crazed life of lonely self-centeredness, Mac is advancing in spirituality and sanity and in a love for others that justifies acceptance of himself. Rosa Lee is his third wife, and he had been physically violent with Dixie, his second wife. However, in this scene, he has put aside selfish irresponsibility and is a better man for it. His griefs are not over by any means, but he is now, as part of a caring family, better able to sustain suffering as well as to appreciate the moments of its absence. Foote has commented that, as an alcoholic, Mac

Sledge still faces a life of challenge, and possibly Mac's distrust of happiness is, in a world of pain and change, the beginning of wisdom, but, battered as he is, he clearly recognizes that good things have happened to him and that more are likely to follow.

Foote's third outstanding film, *The Trip to Bountiful* (1985), took a play that had been first presented on television in 1953 and subsequently developed into a stage play for Broadway, where it did not prosper, and re-shaped it into a version made effective by the inspired interpretation of the leading part by Geraldine Page, who received an Academy Award for her playing of the role of Mrs. Watts. Foote's screenplay also received an Oscar nomination.

The cinematic Texas of film tradition drew value from the representation of a frontier in which virtue was often the heroic fortitude of individuals who, at risk of life and limb, stood against those who opposed the encroachment of civilized customs and forcibly asserted their sovereignty upon them. Often this theme was complicated by the fact that heroic individuals tend to find themselves at odds with conventional authority and thus are placed in opposition both to the practitioners of brute tyranny and those who wish to enforce a social code, which protects the weak against the strong. In Foote's drama, however, the hero is of a different kind. Just as Atticus Finch refuses to fight when an adversary spits in his face, and just as Mac Sledge's most urgent fight is against whiskey, so the heroics of the protagonist of *The Trip to Bountiful* fail to stun the audience with spectacle.

Terry Barr has argued that a main concern of Horton Foote as artist is the establishment of the ordinary individual as the central figure in his drama, with this concern manifesting an effort to correct those literary efforts, which celebrate prodigious abilities or an individual destiny that fascinates by virtue of its rarity or its uniqueness. It is true that Foote's characters include no Hamlet, Oedipus, Tamburlaine, Theseus, St. George, Lucifer, Childe Harold, or Hedda Gabler, and his nobly philosophical Atticus Finch and his almost diabolical Ab Snopes are figures he has drawn already endowed with character from the authors who originally conceived them. Foote did develop his art in a modernist environment, which generated fitful revulsion both against aristocratic pretension and the absurd claims of equality often made despite the presence in the United States of conspicuous social inequality. He saw and appreciated the monstrous power of ideological totalitarianism that shaped the lives of so many in the twentieth century. Sympathizing strongly early in his career with Eva Le Gallienne's doomed but heroic efforts to establish the theater as a fundamental part of American daily life, he recognized the power of plays engaging dimensions of that life and sought to make it clear that the work of the theater is not simply to celebrate the predicaments of those described by Aristotle as "better than we are" (*Poetics* 1448a). Yet it would be simplistic to maintain that Horton Foote sought inspiration in the uninspired, for what Foote actually did was to identify extraordinary qualities or character or insight in such a way that his audience remembers that these do occupy and enrich the world around us. Although the horrifying predicament of an Oedipus still demands our deep and wordless sympathy, there are also more familiar and immediate predicaments that the theater should bring vividly to our minds, such as those presented in the stories of Will Kidder, Horace Robedaux, and Carrie Watts.

Foote's own devoted allies have at times inadvertently obstructed the artistic purpose of his work, though something similar can no doubt be said of all dramatic writers, since the theater does require a kind of team spirit and collaboration, with a measure of self-sacrifice, to bring about its intended achievement. Yet when things go well, the playwright often gains more than is lost in this process, especially if gifted actors are involved in the development of the work. The adoption of a part by a Geraldine Page or a Robert Duvall is bound to enhance the writer's contribution, but, in film, as Dixon McDowell has pointed out, "The realism of Foote's writing requires controlled and unobtrusive direction" (140). And, he continues, "In Horton Foote's movies, the director must stay with the metaphoric and poetic; the 'sensational' and 'theatrical' will destroy the material and betray the director" (141). It might be added that, given the extensive public association of Texas with rowdyism and violence, not to mention buffoonery and flim-flammery, the filmmaker dealing with Texas matters must also consider to what extent his work will counterpoint the accepted impressions of his audience.

In the film of *Bountiful*, the characters are arguably ordinary, but as their lives are opened onstage, it is not their ordinariness that we see, but rather something of the extent of their spiritual existence. In the apartment in Houston, Ludie and his mother seem besieged by debilitating forces, whereas the vain and lazy Jessie Mae is right at home, dominating the others with the protection of her little pleasures and an easy manipulation that shows her husband to be a good-natured dupe. When Mrs. Watts has escaped Houston at last and is talking to her new friend Thelma on the bus to Harrison, she comments on her daughter-in-law: "I bet she told you I was crazy.... Poor Jessie Mae, she thinks everybody's crazy that don't want to sit in the beauty parlor all day and drink Coca-Colas" (*Three Screenplays* 185)." Sanity, one supposes, has something to do with values, and Mrs. Watts' values are radically different from Jessie Mae's. As she continues, however, she expresses a suspicion that her son shares some of her own devotion to the rural world they both came from. She goes on: "You know, I think Ludie knows how I feel about getting back to Bountiful, because once when we were talkin' about something we did back there in the old days he burst out crying. He was so overcome he had to leave the room." Ludie later does confess that he remembers his childhood in Bountiful and feels that his life in the city has been a failure, but, possibly as a result of his mother's forbidden expedition to her old home, the air is finally cleared between them, he no longer pretends to have forgotten their shared memories, and he shows signs of becoming more resolute, less vulnerable to the city's threats, and perhaps even able to cope with his wife's selfishness in a beneficial way.

As Horton Foote sought a way to make a film of this story, he had thirty years of experience with it to guide his inclinations, but, since both film and theater are highly collaborative, he did not get his way in all respects, and one feature of *The Trip to Bountiful*, a favorite of many viewers, works against the dramatic unity of the film. I believe Foote himself saw this problem but was overruled in the process of the film's production.

The movie begins with a combination of sweetness and light, as a beautiful female voice sings the old hymn "Softly and Tenderly," and on the screen, a young woman and her child frolic through a fine field of Texas bluebonnets. Both memorable and charming, this opening establishes a theme as the chorus of the hymn resonates sweetly, and the woman's happy connection with nature is intensified by the innocent vigor of her loving child. The voice sings:

Come home, come home,
Ye who are weary, come home.
Earnestly, tenderly, Jesus is calling,
Calling, O sinner, come home.

So far, so good, but as the story goes forward, with the young mother from the flower-decked farm having become an old woman penned up with her frustrated son (the former child among the bluebonnets) and her son's bitchy wife in a cheap apartment in Houston, the impact of that opening scene, which is followed by the image of Mrs. Watts humming the melody in the apartment, becomes vague and problematic. It is true, undeniably, that Carrie Watts wants to go home, but we hear no more of a summons to her from the founder of Christianity. In fact, the not-very-complex metaphorical implication of the phrase "Come home" is the normal Christian invitation to join the ranks of the faithful who will be given eternal life in Heaven. Though Mrs. Watts definitely believes that Heaven awaits her in the next life, she equally certainly does not think that Jesus is calling her to come home to her abandoned village southwest of Houston. And sin does not specifically enter the picture at all. No wonder Foote objected to the beautiful opening, just as elsewhere he warns about music as a potentially distracting element in film.

Here it is difficult not to conclude that the opening of this film, harmonious and engaging as it seems, is something of a stunt, which undermines the artistic purpose of the film, generating a disunity that would have been avoided had Foote's original choice of Mrs. Watts' favorite hymn been retained. That song, titled "No, Not One," or "There's Not a Friend Like the Lowly Jesus," a homelier, less familiar hymn, which suggests the general inadequacy of human relationships, speaks more comprehensively of Mrs. Watts' life of disappointment and betrayal and her strength in overcoming bitterness and despair. The strikingly cinematic opening is oddly more congruent with the outlook of the Hollywood-obsessed Jessie Mae than with that of the more sympathetic characters Mrs. Watts and Ludie. Though the performances by the gifted chief actors do much to offset this strangely inappropriate opening, this scene remains a sugar-coated poison pill, as it both suggests a false explanation of Mrs. Watts' motive (patronizing her in the process) and indicates a devout skepticism on the director's part with respect to the audience's capacity to understand *why* Mrs. Watts wants to go home. Is the assumption that the audience requires a sweet musical voice reiterating that Mrs. Watts is running away to Bountiful, poor foolish thing, because she thinks she has been divinely commanded to do so? Alas, the truth is that the nursing homes of America are full of senior citizens who want to go home, and it is not at all unusual for them to try to escape. In fact, it is more than likely that some readers of this essay may anticipate the urgency of a similar situation.

Horton Foote's film connects its Texas characters to nature in such a way as to demonstrate their individual modes of response. Carrie Watts is unthinkingly committed to keeping her own nature attuned to the cycles of external nature. Jessie Mae dissociates herself from nature as fully as possible. Though born a country girl, she devotes herself to urban life and the fantasies generated by the urban culture of the cinema. It is Ludie who is the Texas Everyman, slow, capable of great strength but vulnerable to artificiality, divided between love for his intuitive, compassionate, and self-sacrificing mother and, rather oddly, in this case, love for his shrewish, grasping, selfish wife. His spiritual salvation seems to depend upon whether he can balance his loves and invest his heart's energies in a just and tolerable way. Though his choice presents itself as one between the past and the future, his sudden moment of self-assertion at the end of the play suggests that he may realize he has faced a false dilemma and that familial negotiations often work out better when abstractions (and childishness) are put aside.

The key moment just preceding this suggestion of hidden potential in Ludie draws great power from an improvisation by Geraldine Page, who, when confronted by her arch-enemy Jessie Mae, who is outraged by her mother-in-law's temporary escape with her pension check, gently and lovingly kisses Jessie Mae on the cheek, an electrifying gesture that suddenly clarifies the high spiritual plane on which old Mrs. Watts lives at her best. In fact, the closing scene of the film suggests that, even for Jessie Mae, there is some hope of redemption. The terms of a truce in the Watts apartment have been set out and agreed upon, and no one really doubts that Mrs. Watts' life is drawing to a close. No one will expect Jessie Mae to develop the intense spirituality of her mother-in-law, but the actress Carlin Glynn manages to give a glimpse of hope for improvement in her character as the film winds down. Jessie Mae's sense that she alone in the world is sane in her tastes and preferences is made absurd by contrast as she stands at the old farmhouse with her somehow-wiser husband Ludie and the mother-in-law who has, after all, made a kind of victory of homecoming.

Both films, *Tender Mercies* and *The Trip to Bountiful*, engage the frontier myth of Texas to reformulate it, for the honky-tonk glories of Mac Sledge's drunken past and the pastoral labors of Mrs. Watts' agricultural youth have given way to a world of new challenges, where heroic fortitude, internalized and humbled, is called on to operate compassionately, and the worst enemy is the inadvertence or lethargy or vagueness of one's own spirit. Thus each of these works indicates ways heroic resolution can confront the traps and distractions with which twentieth-century Texas replaced the more spectacular, but no less dangerous, enemies of its frontier citizens.

Don Graham's assertion that one kind of Texas history was made by Hollywood is true enough, but Horton Foote's work in film after *Mockingbird* and the Steve McQueen film *Baby, The Rain Must Fall* (1965) embodies something of an escape from Hollywood's meretricious and fad-serving processes. Foote's preoccupation with the lives and history of his hometown, a small, cotton-farming city southwest of Houston, enabled him to understand Harper Lee and her novel so well as to produce a screenwriting classic, and though

Texas gets no credit for that, it probably should. His departure from his familiar region of Texas in *Tender Mercies*, a shift made proper by Australian Bruce Beresford's sense of familiarity with the open spaces featured in the film, actually serves to internalize the action, and the only heroics of the film are those that might have been performed by Sonny's father, who died in Vietnam. Yet there is a strength gathered within the small, but loving family living at the Mariposa Motel, and that strength quietly connects to the proper valuation of things for all involved.

The fact that the story of Mrs. Watts stayed with Horton Foote from his days as early television writer to the mid-1980s says much about the story's essence and of its author's abiding artistic concerns. Though Foote had long hoped that Lillian Gish would play Mrs. Watts in the film as she had on television and onstage in 1953, her age made it impossible by the time the film project was begun, and Foote's friend Geraldine Page, who had played in his 1958 *Playhouse 90* adaptation of Faulkner's "The Old Man," took the part, winning an Oscar for her performance. The part of the Texas past embodied in Page's now-legendary work in this film is not Hollywood stuff, but an exploration of a dimension of humanity that Foote's intense sympathy opens to the actor's own inspiration. Mrs. Watts wraps up the voyage of life with resolution, compassion, and humor, defying the pettiness of detractors and never ceasing to deal honestly with her own inner conflicts. In her wake, she leaves, along with the lost handkerchiefs and purses and loves that have marked her passing, eddies of the invigorating sea air that brings life to Bountiful. Her hymns will long echo in the minds of those close to her, even in that of her nervous daughter-in-law.

Acknowledgments

The acknowledgments listed in the separate chapter by Robert W. Haynes also apply to this essay.

Works Cited

Aristotle. *The Poetics*. Trans. W. Hamilton Fyfe & W. Rhys Roberts. Loeb Classical Library. Cambridge, MA: Harvard UP, 1932.

Barr, George Terry. "The Ordinary World of Horton Foote." Diss. U of Tennessee, Knoxville, 1986.

Castleberry, Marion. *Blessed Assurance: The Life and Art of Horton Foote.* Macon, GA: Mercer UP, 2014.

Graham, Don. *Cowboys and Cadillacs: How Hollywood Looks at Texas.* Austin: Texas Monthly Press, 1983.

McDowell, S. Dixon. "Horton Foote's Film Aesthetic." Ed. Gerald C. Wood. *Horton Foote: A Casebook.* New York: Garland, 1998.

Foote, Horton. *Collected Plays: Volume II* [*The Trip to Bountiful, The Chase, The Traveling Lady, The Roads to Home*]. Intr. Robert Ellerman. Lyme, NH: Smith & Kraus, 1996.

_____. *Farewell: A Memoir of a Texas Childhood.* New York: Scribner 1999.

_____, screenwriter. *Tender Mercies.* Dir. Bruce Beresford. Perf. Robert Duvall. EMI, 1983.

_____, screenwriter. *The Trip to Bountiful.* Dir. Peter Masterson. Perf. Geraldine Page. Island, 1985.

_____, screenwriter. *To Kill a Mockingbird.* Dir. Robert Mulligan. Prod. Alan J. Pakula. Perf. Gregory Peck. Universal, 1962.

_____. To Kill a Mockingbird, Tender Mercies, *and* The Trip to Bountiful: *Three Screenplays by Horton Foote.* New York: Grove Press, 1989.

Lee, Harper. *To Kill a Mockingbird.* New York: Lippincott, 1960.

RESOURCES

Chronology of Horton Foote's Life_____

1916	Albert Horton Foote, Jr., is born in Wharton, Texas, to Albert Horton Foote, Sr., and Harriet Brooks Foote.
1925	Death of Tom Brooks, Horton's grandfather.
1932	Horton Foote graduates from high school at sixteen.
1933	Foote departs for Pasadena, California, to study acting at the Pasadena Playhouse. He sees Eva Le Gallienne in three Henrik Ibsen plays in Los Angeles.
1935	Foote finishes his Pasadena second year in spring and departs for Martha's Vineyard, where he will assist with drama at the Phidelah Rice Institute of Drama. He plays the lead part in a production of Paul Green's play "The No 'Count Boy." In the autumn, he moves to New York to seek acting jobs.
1936	Rosamond Pinchot introduces Foote to Tamara Daykarhanova and pays his tuition for study with the Russians.
1937	Mary Hunter invites Foote and several of his friends to join the American Actors Company (AAC). He gets a non-speaking part on the Franz Werfel show *The Eternal Road*.
1938	The AAC produces Euripides' *The Trojan Women*.
1940	Agnes de Mille suggests that Foote try his hand at writing plays, and Foote writes a one-act. The play, "Wharton Dance," is staged by the AAC with two one-acts by Thornton Wilder, and the program is favorably reviewed by Arthur Pollock.

1941	Foote returns to Texas to write his first full-length play, *Texas Town*, which is staged in New York. *NYT* drama critic Brooks Atkinson writes a favorable review.
1942	Foote's play *Out of My House* is performed in New York. Late in the year, another play, *Only the Heart*, is produced.
1943	Foote decides to revise *Only the Heart* and goes to California for a few weeks to work on it.
1944	*Only the Heart* opens on Broadway, closing after forty-seven performances. Foote accepts a position as Doubleday bookstore manager and meets Lillian Vallish there.
1945	Foote marries Lillian Vallish, and the couple accepts positions at the King-Smith School in Washington, DC.
1948	A performance of *Only the Heart* is broadcast on television.
1949	The Footes return to New York.
1950	Horton begins writing for *The Gabby Hayes Show* (Fall 1950–Winter 1951). Birth of the Footes' first child, Barbara Hallie.
1951	"Ludie Brooks" broadcast. Foote accepts more television assignments.
1952	Broadcasts of *The Old Beginning* and *The Travelers*. Staging of *The Chase* on Broadway (thirty-one performances). Birth of Albert Horton Foote, III.

1953	Broadcasts of *The Trip to Bountiful* and eight other teleplays. Expanded version of *Bountiful* produced on Broadway for thirty-nine performances.
1954	Broadcasts of *The Dancers* and *The Shadow of Willie Greer*. *The Traveling Lady* produced on Broadway for thirty performances.
1955	Broadcast of *The Roads to Home*. Birth of Walter Vallish Foote.
1956	Foote writes his first screenplay for *Storm Fear*. Broadcast of *Flight*. Publication of novel *The Chase*.
1957	Broadcasts of *A Member of the Family* and *The Traveling Lady*.
1958	Broadcast of *Old Man*.
1959	Birth of Daisy Brooks Foote.
1960	Broadcasts of *Tomorrow* and *The Shape of the River*.
1961	Broadcast of *The Night of the Storm*.
1962	Release of film *To Kill a Mockingbird*, screenplay by Horton Foote.
1963	At Academy Awards ceremony, Foote, not in attendance, is awarded an Oscar. Filming begins on *Baby, the Rain Must Fall* (based on Foote's play *The Traveling Lady*).
1966	Release of Sam Spiegel/Lillian Hellman adaptation of *The Chase*. The Footes move to New Boston, New Hampshire.

1972	Foote works on musical version of *Gone with the Wind* in London. He also writes the screenplay for the film *Tomorrow*, featuring Robert Duvall.
1973	Death of Albert Horton Foote, Sr.
1974	Death of Harriet Brooks Foote.
1974-75	Foote begins work on the plays that will become *The Orphans' Home Cycle*.
1977	Foote adapts Flannery O'Connor's short story "The Displaced Person" for television.
1978	*Night Seasons* produced.
1980	*In a Coffin in Egypt* produced. Foote adapts William Faulkner's short story "Barn Burning" for television.
1982	*The Man Who Climbed the Pecan Trees*, *The Old Friends*, *The Road to the Graveyard*, and *The Roads to Home* produced.
1983	Film *Tender Mercies* is released, winning Academy Awards for Foote and Robert Duvall.
1985	*The Trip to Bountiful* is released, winning an Academy Award for Geraldine Page and a nomination for Foote. The film version of *1918* is also released. Trilogy *Harrison, Texas* is produced.
1986	Film versions of *On Valentine's Day* and *Courtship* released.
1987	PBS production of *The Story of a Marriage*, a series based on three *Cycle* plays.

1988	*Land of the Astronauts* and *The Habitation of Dragons* produced.
1989	*Dividing the Estate* produced.
1990	Film of *Convicts* released.
1992	Death of Lillian Vallish Foote. Release of film *Of Mice and Men*, with Foote screenplay. Teleplay of *The Habitation of Dragons* broadcast.
1995	Production of *The Young Man from Atlanta*, which wins a Pulitzer Prize. Horton Foote Festival held at Brigham Young University.
1996	Film of *Lily Dale* presented on *Showtime*. Foote becomes member of the Theatre Hall of Fame.
1997	Broadcasts of teleplays *Alone* and *Old Man*. Foote wins Emmy for *Old Man*.
1999	Publication of *Farewell*, Foote's first volume of memoirs.
2000	Production of *The Last of the Thorntons*. National Medal of Arts presented to Foote by President Clinton. *The Carpetbagger's Children* produced.
2001	Publication of *Beginnings*, Foote's second volume of memoirs.
2002	*The Actor* produced in London. Foote appointed visiting distinguished dramatist at Baylor University.
2003	Fiftieth anniversary productions of *The Trip to Bountiful*.

2004	Horton Foote American Playwrights Festival held at Baylor University.
2006	Ensemble Studio Theatre's production of *The Traveling Lady* is nominated as Drama Desk "Best Revival."
2008	Production of *Dividing the Estate* wins Obie Award (screenwriting) for Foote. Horton Foote Center for the Study of Theater and Film opened at Carson-Newman College.
2009	Albert Horton Foote, Jr., dies in Hartford, Connecticut.
2010	Horton Foote Festival held in Dallas/Ft. Worth Metroplex, with exhibition of Foote materials at the DeGolyer Library. Release of film *Main Street*, with world premiere in Austin, Texas.

Works by Horton Foote

Plays

Wharton Dance (1940)

Texas Town (1941)

Out of My House (1942)

Only the Heart (1942)

Miss Lou (1944)

Daisy Lee (1944)

Goodbye to Richmond (1944)

The Lonely (1944)

Homecoming (1944)

People in the Show (1948?)

Themes and Variations (1948?)

The Chase (1952)

The Trip to Bountiful (1953)

The Traveling Lady (1954)

The Orphans' Home Cycle (nine plays written in the mid-1970s: *Roots in a Parched Ground, Convicts, Lily Dale, The Widow Claire, Courtship, Valentine's Day, 1918, Cousins, The Death of Papa*)

Night Seasons (1978)

In a Coffin in Egypt (1980)

Blind Date (1982)

The Man Who Climbed the Pecan Trees (1982)

The Old Friends (1982)

The Road to the Graveyard (1982)

The Roads to Home (three short plays, 1982*)*

Harrison, Texas (three short plays, 1985)

The Habitation of Dragons (1988)

Land of the Astronauts (1988)

Dividing the Estate (1989)

Talking Pictures (1990)

Laura Dennis (1985)

The Day Emily Married (1997)

Vernon Early (1998)

The Last of the Thorntons (2000)

The Carpetbagger's Children (2001)

The Actor (2002)

Getting Frankie Married—and Afterwards (2002)

The Orphans' Home Cycle (revised for a sequence of three three-hour productions, 2009)

Teleplays

Ludie Brooks (1951)

The Old Beginning (1952)

The Travelers (1952)

The Death of the Old Man (1953)

The Expectant Relations (1953)

John Turner Davis (1953)

The Midnight Caller (1953)

The Oil Well (1953)

The Rocking Chair (1953)

The Tears of My Sister (1953)

The Trip to Bountiful (1953)

A Young Lady of Property (1953)

The Dancers (1954)

The Shadow of Willie Greer (1954)

The Roads to Home (1955)

Flight (1956)

A Member of the Family (1957)

Old Man (1958)

The Shape of the River (1960)

Tomorrow (1960)

The Night of the Storm (1961)

The Gambling Heart (1964)

Keeping On (1983)

Alone (1997)

Old Man (1997)

Screenplays

Storm Fear (1956)

To Kill a Mockingbird (1962)

Baby, the Rain Must Fall (1965)

The Displaced Person (1977)

Barn Burning (1980)

Tender Mercies (1983)

The Trip to Bountiful (1985)

1918 (1985)

On Valentine's Day (1986)

Courtship (1986)

Convicts (1991)

Of Mice and Men (1992)

Habitation of Dragons (1992)

Lily Dale (1996)

Main Street (2010)

Other Works

Farewell: A Memoir of a Texas Childhood (1999)

Beginnings: A Memoir (2001)

Bibliography

Atkinson, Brooks. "American Actors Company Produces Horton Foote's 'Texas Town' in Sixteenth Street." *New York Times*. (30 Apr. 1941): 22. *ProQuest Historical Newspapers*. 18 Oct. 2015.

Barr, George Terry. "The Ordinary World of Horton Foote." Diss. U of Tennessee P, 1986.

_____."Horton Foote's TV Women: The Richest Part of a Golden Age." *Horton Foote: A Casebook*. Ed. Gerald C. Wood. New York: Garland, 1998. 35–47.

Benson, Sheila. "Horton Foote." *The Voice of an American Playwright: Interviews with Horton Foote*. Ed. Gerald C. Wood & Marion Castleberry. Macon, GA: Mercer UP, 2012. 199–205.

Brian, Crystal. "Horton Foote: Mystic of the American Theatre." *The Playwright's Muse*. Ed. Joan Herrington. New York: Routledge, 2002. 181–206.

_____. "The Roads to Home: Material, Method & Meditation in Horton Foote's *The Orphans' Home Cycle*." Diss. U of California P, Los Angeles, 1993.

_____. "'To Be Quiet and Listen,' *The Orphans' Home Cycle* and the Music of Charles Ives." *Horton Foote: A Casebook*. Ed. Gerald C. Wood. New York: Garland, 1998. 89–108.

Briley, Rebecca Luttrell. *You Can Go Home Again: The Focus on Family in the Works of Horton Foote*. New York: Peter Lang, 1993. American University Studies Ser.

Broughton, Irv. "Horton Foote." *The Voice of an American Playwright: Interviews with Horton Foote*. Ed. Gerald C. Wood & Marion Castleberry. Macon, GA: Mercer UP, 2012. 79–95.

Burkhart, Marian. *Horton Foote's America: A Critical Analysis of His Plays*. Minneapolis, MN: Mill City Press, 2014.

_____. "Horton Foote's Many Roads Home: An American Playwright and His Characters." *Commonweal* 115.4 (26 Feb. 1988): 110–115.

_____. "On *The Habitation of Dragons*," *The Horton Foote Review* 2 (2009): 66–76.

Canby, Vincent, "Nameless Menace in Latest by Foote." *New York Times* (30 Jan. 1995) C13, 16. *ProQuest Historical Newspapers*. 12 Dec. 2015.

Castellani, Victor. "Ibsen and U.S. Theater in the 1990s." *Proceedings: IX International Ibsen Conference, Bergen 5–10 June 2000*. Eds. Pål Bjørby & Asbjørn Aarseth. Øvre Ervik, Norway: Alvheim & Eide, 2001. 147–55.

Castleberry, Marion. *Blessed Assurance: The Life and Art of Horton Foote.* Macon, GA: Mercer UP, 2014.

_____. "Reflections on the American Theatre: A Conversation with Horton Foote." *Baylor Journal of Theatre and Performance* 1.1 (Fall 2004), 43–62. Rpt. in *The Voice of an American Playwright: Interviews with Horton Foote*. Ed. Gerald C. Wood & Marion Castleberry. Macon, GA: Mercer UP, 2012. 258–84.

_____. "Remembering Wharton, Texas." *Horton Foote: A Casebook.* Ed. Gerald C. Wood. New York: Garland, 1998. 13–33.

_____. "Voices from Home: Familial Bonds in the Works of Horton Foote." Diss. Louisiana State U, 1993.

_____ & Susan Christensen, eds. *Farewell: Remembering Horton Foote 1916–2009*. Dallas, TX: DeGolyer Library, 2011.

Christensen, Susan. "Selected Correspondence from the Horton Foote Collection, 1912–1991." Diss. U of Texas at Arlington, 2008.

_____. "'Dead Cold Light': Portrayal of Pandemic and War in Katherine Anne Porter's *Pale Horse, Pale Rider* and Horton Foote's *1918*." *The Horton Foote Review* 2 (2009): 54–65.

Cincotti, Joseph A. "Horton Foote: The Trip from Wharton." *Backstory 3: Interviews with Screenwriters of the 1960s*. Ed. Pat McGilligan. Berkeley, CA: U of California P, 1997. 114–134.

Clinkscale, Rebekah. "'Music of a Kind': Character and Song in *The Orphans' Home Cycle*." *The Horton Foote Review* 2 (2009): 4–15.

Davis, Ronald L. *Roots in Parched Ground: An Interview with Horton Foote*. DeGolyer Library Keepsake Series Number Seven. Rpt. from *Southwest Review* 73.3 (Summer 1988): 298–318. Rpt. in *The Voice of an American Playwright: Interviews with Horton Foote*. Ed. Gerald C. Wood & Marion Castleberry. Macon, GA: Mercer UP, 2012. 57–78.

Desser, David. "Transcendental Style in *Tender Mercies*." *Religious Communication Today* 8 (September 1985): 21–27.

DiGaetani, John L. "Horton Foote." *A Search for a Postmodern Theater: Interviews with Contemporary Playwrights*. Ed. John L. DiGaetani. New York: Greenwood, 1991. 65–71. Rpt. in *The Voice of an American Playwright: Interviews with Horton Foote*. Ed. Gerald C. Wood & Marion Castleberry. Macon, GA: Mercer UP, 2012. 102–9.

Donahoo, Robert. "Buried Memory: *1918* and the Uses of the Past." *The Horton Foote Review* 1 (2005): 21–33.

_____. "On *The Day Emily Married*: An Interview with Horton Foote." *The Horton Foote Review* 2 (2009): 77–94. Rpt. in *The Voice of an American Playwright: Interviews with Horton Foote*. Ed. Gerald C. Wood & Marion Castleberry. Macon, GA: Mercer UP, 2012. 285–300.

_____. "Remembering and Forgetting: History and Memory in Horton Foote's *The Last of the Thorntons*." *Journal of the American Studies Association of Texas* 34 (Oct. 2003): 1–13.

Edgerton, Gary. "A Visit to the Imaginary Landscape of Harrison, Texas: Sketching the Career of Horton Foote." *Literature/Film Quarterly* 17 (1989): 2–12.

Ellenberger, Matthew. "Illuminating the Lesser Lights: Notes on the Life of Albert Clinton Horton." *Southwestern Historical Quarterly* 88.4 (Apr. 1985): 363–386.

Fifer, Elizabeth. "Pathos and Humor in the Man's World of *The Widow Claire*." *The Horton Foote Review* 1 (2005): 43–54.

Flynn, Robert & Susan Russell. "Horton Foote." *The Voice of an American Playwright: Interviews with Horton Foote*. Ed. Gerald C. Wood & Marion Castleberry. Macon, GA: Mercer UP, 2012. 140–47.

Foote, Abram William. *Foote Family, Comprising the Genealogy and History of Nathaniel Foote, of Wethersfield, Conn., and His Descendants*. Vol. 1. Rutland, VT: Marble City Press, The Tuttle Co., 1907.

Foote, Horton. *Beginnings: A Memoir*. New York: Scribner, 2001.

_____. *Collected Plays: Volume II* [*The Trip to Bountiful*, *The Chase*, *The Traveling Lady*, *The Roads to Home*]. Intr. Robert Ellerman. Lyme, NH: Smith & Kraus, 1996.

_____. *Collected Works, Vol. III* [*The Day Emily Married, Tomorrow, A Coffin in Egypt, Laura Dennis, Vernon Early, Getting Frankie Married—and Afterwards*]. Lyme, NH: Smith & Kraus, 1998.

_____. *Convicts. The Orphans' Home Cycle*. New York: Grove Press 1989.

_____. The Death of the Old Man. 1953. *Selected One-Act Plays of Horton Foote*. Ed. Gerald C. Wood. Dallas, TX: Southern Methodist UP, 1989.

_____. *Genesis of an American Playwright*. Ed. Marion Castleberry. Waco, TX: Baylor UP, 2004.

_____. *Farewell: A Memoir of a Texas Childhood*. New York: Scribner, 1999.

_____. *Horton Foote: Four New Plays*. Intr. Jerry Tallmer. New York: Smith & Kraus, 1993. Contemporary Playwrights Ser.

_____. *Lily Dale. The Orphans' Home Cycle*. New York: Grove Press, 1989.

_____. *Only the Heart*. New York: Dramatists Play Service, 1944.

_____. *The Orphans' Home Cycle*. New York: Grove Press 1989.

_____. The Prisoner's Song. *Selected One-Act Plays of Horton Foote*. Ed. Gerald C. Wood. Dallas, TX: Southern Methodist UP, 1989. 391–413.

_____. *Roots in a Parched Ground*. Foreword by Stark Young. New York: Dramatists Play Service, 1962.

_____. *"Roots in a Parched Ground," "Convicts," "Lily Dale," "The Widow Claire": The First Four Plays of "The Orphans' Home Cycle."* New York: Grove Press, 1988.

_____. *Selected One-Act Plays of Horton Foote*. Ed. Gerald C. Wood. Dallas, TX: Southern Methodist UP, 1989.

_____. *Horton Foote's "The Shape of the River": The Lost Teleplay about Mark Twain*. Ed. Mark Dawidziak. New York: Applause, 2003.

_____, screenwriter. *Tender Mercies*. Dir. Bruce Beresford. Perf. Robert Duvall. EMI, 1983.

_____, screenwriter. *The Trip to Bountiful*. Dir. Peter Masterson. Perf. Geraldine Page. Island, 1985.

_____, screenwriter. *To Kill a Mockingbird*. Dir. Robert Mulligan. Prod. Alan J. Pakula. Perf. Gregory Peck. Universal, 1962.

_____. *"To Kill a Mockingbird," "Tender Mercies," and "The Trip to Bountiful": Three Screenplays by Horton Foote*. New York: Grove Press, 1989.

_____. *The Trip to Bountiful*. Ed. Moore and Yellin. *Horton Foote's Three Trips to Bountiful*.

_____. "A Young Lady of Property." *Selected One-Act Plays of Horton Foote*. Ed. Gerald C. Wood. Dallas, TX: Southern Methodist UP, 1989. The video of the 1953 broadcast is online at <https://vimeo.com/61639873>.

_____. *The Young Man from Atlanta*. New York: Dramatists Play Service, 1995.

_____. *The Young Man from Atlanta*. New York: Dutton, 1995.

Freedman, Samuel G. "From the Heart of Texas." *New York Times Magazine* (9 Feb. 1986) Sec. 6: 30–31, 50, 61–63, 73. Web. 1 Oct. 2015.<http://www.nytimes.com/1986/02/09/magazine/from-the-heart-of-texas.html.>

_____. Introduction. *"Cousins" and "The Death of Papa": Two Plays from The Orphans' Home Cycle*. New York: Grove Press, 1989. xi–xxvi.

Gallagher, Michael. "Horton Foote: Defying Heraclitus in Texas." *Southern Literary Journal* 32.1 (Fall 1999): 77–86.

Graham, Don. *Cowboys and Cadillacs: How Hollywood Looks at Texas*. Austin: Texas Monthly Press, 1983.

Guilliams, Rick. "Houston as Symbol of Displacement in the Urban Works of Horton Foote." *Lamar Journal of the Humanities* 27.2 (Fall 2002): 5–21.

Guare, John. "Conversation with Horton Foote." *The Voice of an American Playwright: Interviews with Horton Foote*. Ed. Gerald C. Wood & Marion Castleberry. Macon, GA: Mercer UP, 2012. 238–57.

Hachem, Samir. "Foote-Work." *Horizon* 29 (Apr. 1986): 39–41.

Hampton, Wilborn. "The Bodies Are Buried, So a Play Can Be Unearthed." *New York Times* (5 Aug. 2004): E1.

_____. *Horton Foote: America's Storyteller*. New York: Free Press, 2009.

Haynes, Robert. "Betrayal and Responsibility in Henrik Ibsen's *A Doll's House* and *Little Eyolf* and Horton Foote's *The Young Man from*

Atlanta." *Baylor Journal of Theatre and Performance* 4.2 (Fall 2007): 57–68.

_____. "Departure, Arrival, and Varieties of Silence: Narration and Dramaturgy in Horton Foote's *Beginnings* and *Farewell.*" *Southwestern American Literature* 34.2 (Spring 2009): 29–44.

_____. "The Kidders and the Disappointment Club: A Critical Theme in Horton Foote's *The Young Man from Atlanta,*" *Journal of American Drama and Theatre* 18.1 (Winter 2006): 24–33.

_____. *The Major Plays of Horton Foote: "The Trip to Bountiful," "The Young Man from Atlanta," and "The Orphans' Home Cycle."* Lewiston, NY: Mellen, 2010.

_____. "The Nature of Nature in Horton Foote's *The Trip to Bountiful.*" *Southwestern American Literature* 31.2 (Spring 2006): 9–17.

_____. "Woman Escapes: An Ibsenian Theme in Horton Foote's Play *The Trip to Bountiful.*" *The Horton Foote Review* 2 (2009): 40–53.

Hildner, Jeffrey. "Everlasting Grace." *The Voice of an American Playwright: Interviews with Horton Foote.* Ed. Gerald C. Wood & Marion Castleberry. Macon, GA: Mercer UP, 2012. 301–7.

Hunter, Mary. Foreword. *Only the Heart.* By Horton Foote. New York: Dramatists Play Service, 1944.

King, Kimball. "Performing *The Death of Papa*: A Review." *Horton Foote: A Casebook.* Ed. Gerald C. Wood. New York: Garland, 1998. 131–35.

Koszyn, Jayme. "Interview with Horton Foote." *The Voice of an American Playwright: Interviews with Horton Foote.* Ed. Gerald C. Wood & Marion Castleberry. Macon, GA: Mercer UP, 2012. 189–98.

Krampner, Jon. *The Man in the Shadows: Fred Coe and the Golden Age of Television.* New Brunswick, NJ: Rutgers UP, 1997.

Lee, Harper. "A Word." *To Kill a Mockingbird* [screenplay]. New York: Harcourt Brace & World, 1964.

Lusky, Richard. "Intergenerational Relations in Two Works by Horton Foote: *The Trip to Bountiful* and *Alone.*" *The Horton Foote Review* 1 (2005): 1–19.

Martin, Carter. "Horton Foote's Southern Family in *Roots in a Parched Ground.*" *Texas Review* 12 (Spring–Summer 1991): 76–82.

McDowell, S. Dixon. "Horton Foote's Film Aesthetic" *Horton Foote: A Casebook*. Ed. Gerald C. Wood. New York: Garland, 1998.

McLaughlin, Buzz. "Conversation with Horton Foote." *The Voice of an American Playwright: Interviews with Horton Foote*. Ed. Gerald C. Wood & Marion Castleberry. Macon, GA: Mercer UP, 2012. 148–62.

Mendell, Dean. "Squeezing the Drama out of Melodrama: Plot and Counterplot in *Laura Dennis*." *Horton Foote: A Casebook*. Ed. Gerald C. Wood. New York: Garland, 1998. 189–201.

Middleton, David L. "Winning, Losing, and Compromising: The Screenwriter Contends for Personal Turf." *The Voice of an American Playwright: Interviews with Horton Foote*. Ed. Gerald C. Wood & Marion Castleberry. Macon, GA: Mercer UP, 2012. 3–18.

Moore, Barbara & David G. Yellin, eds. *Horton Foote's Three Trips to Bountiful*. Dallas: Southern Methodist UP, 1993.

Nathan, George Jean. *The Theatre Book of the Year 1942–1943*. 1943. Rutherford, NJ: Fairleigh Dickinson UP, 1971.

_____. *The Theatre Book of the Year 1943–1944*. New York: Knopf, 1944.

Nichols, Lewis. "The Play: *Mamie Borden*." Review of early version of Horton Foote's *Only the Heart* (formerly *Mamie Borden*). *New York Times*. (7 Dec. 1942): 22. Web. 18 Oct. 2015.

_____. "The Play: Pistol Packin' Mama." Review of Horton Foote's *Only the Heart*. *New York Times*. (5 Apr. 1944): 17. Web. 18 Oct. 2015.

O'Quinn, Jim. "Eye of the Beholder." *The Voice of an American Playwright: Interviews with Horton Foote*. Ed. Gerald C. Wood & Marion Castleberry. Macon, GA: Mercer UP, 2012. 185–8.

Oxman, Steven. "Chi puts best Foote forward." *Variety* (10 Mar.–16 Mar. 2008): 410, 4. *Arts Module*, 48.

Pacheco, Patrick. "Remember Me: In their searches for a lost time, playwrights Neil Simon and Horton Foote reveal two distinct visions of America." *Daily News-City Lights*. (4 Jan. 1987): 5.

Pollock, Arthur. "Actors at Work over a Garage: Plays by Paul Green, Thornton Wilder Done by the American Actors Company." *The Brooklyn Daily Eagle*. (16 Apr. 1940): 15. Web. 15 Oct. 2015. <http://bklyn.newspapers.com/image/52777103>.

Porter, Laurin. "The Horton Foote Collection at the DeGolyer Library." *Resources for American Literary Study* 26.1 (2000): 64–74.

_____. "An Interview with Horton Foote." *The Voice of an American Playwright: Interviews with Horton Foote.* Ed. Gerald C. Wood & Marion Castleberry. Macon, GA: Mercer UP, 2012. 110–26. Rpt. in *Studies in American Drama, 1945–Present* 6.2 (1991): 177–94.

_____. "Houses Divided: The Legacy of Slavery in *Convicts, The Last of the Thorntons,* and *The Carpetbagger's Children."* The *Horton Foote Review* 2 (2009): 16–26.

_____. "Memory and the Re-Construction of the Past: Horton Foote's *Carpetbagger's Children." The Horton Foote Review* 1 (2005): 35–42.

_____. *Orphans' Home: The Voice and Vision of Horton Foote.* Baton Rouge: Louisiana State UP, 2003. Southern Literary Studies Ser.

_____. "Subtext as Text: Language and Culture in Horton Foote's Texas Cycle." *Horton Foote: A Casebook.* Ed. Gerald C. Wood. New York: Garland, 1998. 109–29.

_____. "Unpublished Interview." *The Voice of an American Playwright: Interviews with Horton Foote.* Ed. Gerald C. Wood & Marion Castleberry. Macon, GA: Mercer UP, 2012. 223–37.

Price, Reynolds. "Introduction: New Treasure." *"Courtship," "Valentine's Day," "1918": Three Plays from The Orphans' Home Cycle.* New York: Grove Press, 1987. ix–xiii.

Rather, Dan. "Horton Foote Tribute: Storyteller of Texas." *The Voice of an American Playwright: Interviews with Horton Foote.* Ed. Gerald C. Wood & Marion Castleberry. Macon, GA: Mercer UP, 2012. 206–8.

Roberts, Jerry. "Horton Foote and *Tomorrow." The Voice of an American Playwright: Interviews with Horton Foote.* Ed. Gerald C. Wood & Marion Castleberry. Macon, GA: Mercer UP, 2012. 169–84.

Rooney, David. *"Dividing the Estate." Variety Review Database.* Variety Media, LLC, Nov. 2008. Web. 12 Dec. 2015.

Roussel, Peter. "Profiles from Houston: Horton Foote." *The Voice of an American Playwright: Interviews with Horton Foote.* Ed. Gerald C. Wood & Marion Castleberry. Macon, GA: Mercer UP, 2012. 163–8.

Shackelford, Dean. "The Female Voice in *To Kill a Mockingbird*: Narrative Strategies in Film and Novel." *Mississippi Quarterly* 50 (Winter 1996–1997): 101–13.

Sherman, Howard, et al. "Working in the Theatre: Horton Foote's America." *The Voice of an American Playwright: Interviews with Horton Foote*. Ed. Gerald C. Wood & Marion Castleberry. Macon, GA: Mercer UP, 2012. 308–30.

Skaggs, Calvin. "Interview with Horton Foote." *The Voice of an American Playwright: Interviews with Horton Foote*. Ed. Gerald C. Wood & Marion Castleberry. Macon, GA: Mercer UP, 2012. 19–27.

Smelstor, Marjorie. "'The World's an Orphans' Home': Horton Foote's Social and Moral History." *The Southern Quarterly: A Journal of the Arts in the South* 29.2 (Winter 1991): 7–16.

Smith, Amanda. "Horton Foote: A Writer's Journey." *Varia* (July–August 1987): 18–20, 23, 26–27.

Sterritt, David. "Horton Foote: Filmmaking Radical with a Tender Touch." *Christian Science Monitor* (15 May 1986): 1, 36.

Sutton, Meredith. "American Dance-Drama Collaborations: Martha Graham, Valerie Bettis, and Horton Foote." *The Horton Foote Review* 1 (2005): 55–63.

Toft, Marie, ed. *Drama Criticism: Horton Foote (1916–2009)*. Detroit: Gale, Cengage, 2011. 42, 57–170. *Literary Criticism Online*. 12 Dec. 2015.

Underwood, Susan. "Singing in the Face of Devastation: Texture in Horton Foote's *Talking Pictures*." *Horton Foote: A Casebook*. Ed. Gerald C. Wood. New York: Garland, 1998. 151–62.

Watson, Charles S. "Beyond the Commercial Media: Horton Foote's Procession of Defeated Men." *Studies in American Drama, 1945–Present* 8.2 (1993), 175–187.

_____. "Past and Present Cultures in Recent Drama." *The History of Southern Drama*. Lexington, KY: UP of Kentucky, 1997. 192–201.

_____. *Horton Foote: A Literary Biography*. Austin: U of Texas P, 2003.

Wood, Gerald C., "'A Certain Kind of Writer': An Interview with Horton Foote." *Literature Film Quarterly* 14.4 (1986), 226–237.

_____. "Boundaries, the Female Will, and Individuation in *Night Seasons*." *Horton Foote: A Casebook.* Ed. Gerald C. Wood. New York: Garland, 1998. 163–77.

_____. "Horton Foote." *Film Voices: Interviews from Post Script.* Ed. Gerald Duchovnay. Albany, NY: State U of New York P, 2004. 317–328.

_____, ed. *Horton Foote: A Casebook.* New York: Garland, 1998.

_____. "Horton Foote: An Interview." *The Voice of an American Playwright: Interviews with Horton Foote.* Ed. Gerald C. Wood & Marion Castleberry. Macon, GA: Mercer UP, 2012. 127–39.

_____. *Horton Foote and the Theater of Intimacy.* Baton Rouge: Louisiana State UP, 1999.

_____. "Horton Foote's Politics of Intimacy." *Journal of American Drama and Theatre* 9.2 (Spring 1997): 45–57.

_____. "Horton Foote at the American Actors Company, *Dance Observer*, and King Smith Productions: Nothing More Real than the Human Heart." *The Horton Foote Review* 1 (2005): 65–78.

_____. "Loving Mac, Beth, and John: Grace in the Plays and Films of Horton Foote." *Religion and the Arts* 10.3 (2006): 374–390.

_____. "The Nature of Mystery in *The Young Man from Atlanta*." *Horton Foote: A Casebook.* Ed. Gerald C. Wood. New York: Garland, 1998. 179–188.

_____. "Old Beginnings and Roads to Home: Horton Foote and Mythic Realism." *Christianity and Literature* 45.3–4 (Spring–Summer 1996): 359–372.

_____. "The Physical Hunger for the Spiritual: Southern Religious Experience in the Plays of Horton Foote." *The World Is Our Culture: Society and Culture in Contemporary Southern Writing.* Ed. Jeffrey J. Folks & Nancy Summers Folks. Lexington: UP of Kentucky, 2000. 244–258.

_____. "Variations on the Monologue: Brian Friel's *The Faith Healer* and Horton Foote's *The Carpetbagger's Children*." *The Horton Foote Review* 2 (2009): 27–39.

_____ & Marion Castleberry, eds. *The Voice of an American Playwright: Interviews with Horton Foote.* Macon, GA: Mercer UP, 2012.

Wright, Tim. "A Conversation with Horton Foote." *Image: A Journal of the Arts and Religion* 20 (Summer 1998): 45–57. Rpt. in *The Voice of an American Playwright: Interviews with Horton Foote.* Ed. Gerald C. Wood & Marion Castleberry, eds. Macon, GA: Mercer UP, 2012. 209–22.

_____. *Dancing with Shadows: Stylistic Attributes of Impressionism in Selected Works by Horton Foote.* Diss. Regent U, 1996.

_____. "More Real than Realism: Horton Foote's Impressionism." *Horton Foote: A Casebook.* Ed. Gerald C. Wood. New York: Garland, 1998. 67–87.

Young, Stark. Foreword. *The Traveling Lady.* By Horton Foote. New York: Dramatists Play Service, 1955.

About the Editor

Robert W. Haynes, professor of English at Texas A&M International University in Laredo, Texas, teaches early British literature and Shakespeare. At his university, he has served as Faculty Senate president, and he has received the Scholar of the Year Award from the College of Arts and Sciences. His book *The Major Plays of Horton Foote* appeared in 2010, and grants from TAMIU have enabled him to do research on Foote in archives at the Library of Congress, the Harry Ransom Center, and the DeGolyer Library at SMU. As R. W. Haynes, he has published poetry in many journals in the United States and abroad, and some of his fiction and drama has also recently appeared.

Contributors

Terry Barr received his PhD in English from the University of Tennessee, Knoxville, in 1986. His dissertation, "The Ordinary World of Horton Foote," was the first full-length study of Foote's life and work. Barr's essay, "Horton Foote's TV Women: The Richest Part of a Golden Age," was published in *Horton Foote: A Casebook* (1998), edited by Gerald C. Wood. Barr's and Wood's interviews with Foote are part of the collection *The Voice of an American Playwright* (Mercer University Press), edited by Gerald C. Wood and Marion Castleberry.

Since 1987, Barr has taught the modern novel, film and American culture, and creative nonfiction at Presbyterian College in Clinton, South Carolina. His nonfiction has appeared in a variety of journals, including *American Literary Review, Sport Literate, Full Grown People, Red Truck Review, Blue Bonnet Review,* and in the collection *Half-Life: Jew-ish Tales from Interfaith Homes,* edited by Laurel Snyder. His essay collection *Don't Date Baptists and Other Warnings from My Alabama Mother* will be published in 2016 by Red Dirt Press. He lives in Greenville, South Carolina, with his wife and two daughters.

Crystal Brian is professor of theater at Quinnipiac University (QU). She earned her MFA in acting and her PhD in theater history and criticism from the University of California, Los Angeles. She is the founder and artistic director of the QU Theater for Community, a production company dedicated to exploring issues of social justice and building community through theater. She has published widely on the work of Pulitzer Prize-winner Horton Foote and is coeditor of "Playwrights Teach Playwriting." She has also published articles on applied theater and theater for social change. She coauthored the play *Gathering Shells* with Vietnam veteran and poet, Allan Garry. The play was produced at Quinnipiac and, subsequently, in professional production in New Haven and New York. A reading of the play was held in Spain in November 2015 as part of the Peace Prize Laureate's conference. She is now writing a play about the Second World War and those who left Texas in 1941 to serve in the Pacific—specifically, New Guinea—in the Navy and the Marines. Her papa, Jack Brian, was in New Guinea for five years when he was seventeen and came back to Texas when he was twenty-two. The play is about the farm in the Texas Panhandle and everything that happened to him as a farmer because of that war.

Rebecca Luttrell Briley received her PhD in English and drama from the University of Kentucky, where she was inducted into the Alpha Chapter of Phi Beta Kappa. An English-Speaking Union scholar to the University of London, she studied twentieth-century literature, theatre, and culture. Her dissertation on Horton Foote, "You Can Go Home Again: The Focus on Family in the Works of Horton Foote," was published by Peter Lang in 1993. She also contributed a chapter on Foote's adaptations to Gerald Wood's *Horton Foote: A Casebook* (Garland 1998). Other academic publications include papers delivered at the International Journal of Arts and Sciences in Malta, "Actors Speak Louder than Words: Using Theatre to Teach ESL" (2010), and in Rome, "Looking at *Hamlet* through Oxfordian Glasses" (2011), as well as "Who Was Shakespeare and Why It Matters" in the *Language, Literature, and Linguistics (L3) Journal*, Singapore, 2012. She chairs the Shakespeare Session at the MMLA and has presented papers there on Brian Friel, Markus Zusak, and Bobby Sands. A Fulbright scholar to England, Briley has lived and taught all over the world, including Germany, Cyprus, Lithuania, and the Marshall Islands, returning recently to chair the English Department at Midway University in her home state of Kentucky. Creative publications include a book of poetry, *Bean Si Bones* (2009), as well as various poems, stories, and articles in a variety of literary journals and magazines. An award-winning director, she is also the author of several plays, including a musical adaptation of *Mrs. Wiggs of the Cabbage Patch* (2001). Her current projects include an illustrated children's book, a novel planned as a sequel to *The Great Gatsby*, and a memoir on her teaching experiences in Cyprus. She enjoys leading study tours to Ireland and the British Isles.

Robert Donahoo is professor of English at Sam Houston State University. In 2014, he codirected the NEH Summer Institute, "Reconsidering Flannery O'Connor" with Marshall Bruce Gentry, and is currently working with Gentry and John Cox on an O'Connor volume for the MLA series, *Approaches to Teaching*. He coedited *Flannery O'Connor in the Age of Terrorism: Essays on Violence and Grace* (2010) with Avis Hewitt and has published articles on O'Connor in numerous journals and essay collections. His previous publications on Horton Foote have examined *1918*; *Convicts*; *The Last of the Thorntons*; and Foote's adaptation for PBS, *The Displaced Person*, and he has also published an interview with Foote focused on *The Day Emily Married*. Additional publications include articles concerning southern novelists Larry Brown and Clyde Edgerton and essays on Tolstoy's *Resurrection* and postmodern science fiction. A past president of the Flannery O'Connor Society, he is currently working on a monograph focused on O'Connor and southern history.

Elizabeth Fifer is professor of English at Lehigh University, teaching contemporary American drama and world literature. She has written on three plays by Horton Foote, *The Widow Clare*, *Convicts*, and *1918*, as well as on other contemporary dramatists and authors. Her work has appeared in such journals as *The Horton Foote Review* and *The Eugene O'Neill Review*. She is the author of *Rescued Readings*, which focuses on the works of Gertrude Stein (Wayne State University Press).

Cynthia Franco is a librarian and certified archivist at DeGolyer Library, part of Southern Methodist University in Dallas, Texas. She processed the papers of Horton Foote, wrote the finding aid available online, and has published an article on Horton Foote in *The Handbook of Texas*. She presented a paper on the Horton Foote Archive at the 2013 College English Association Conference in Savannah.

Roy J. Gonzáles, Jr., is currently pursuing graduate studies in English at Texas A&M International University in Laredo, Texas. Although only recently introduced to Horton Foote, he finds the playwright's work powerful and elegantly restrained. He hopes that through scholarship such as that in this volume, more students will discover Foote and his work, especially some of his lesser-known writing, including the novel adaptation of *The Chase*.

Xueying Wang is a PhD candidate at Nanjing University in China, formerly a visiting scholar at George Washington University (2013) and Southern Methodist University (2014). Currently, she works on American dramatic literature and Horton Foote's plays in particular. She leads the research on Foote's plays in China. Her interest in Foote's plays grew from the time when she was reading American plays extensively in order to select her dissertation topic. Through correspondence with Professor Robert Haynes, she learned that the DeGolyer Library at Southern Methodist University sponsored scholars and students doing research in the Horton Foote Archive. The travel grant from the library made her "trip to Bountiful" possible. She aims to translate Foote's works into Chinese and build up a Chinese Horton Foote database for Chinese readers and literary critics.

Jan Whitt, recipient of the 2013 Edward R. Murrow Teaching Award and the 2014 Boulder Faculty Assembly Excellence in Research and Creative Work award, is a professor of literature and media at the University of Colorado at Boulder. She has published numerous journal articles on American literature, media studies, popular culture, and women's issues. Her books include *Allegory and the Modern Southern Novel, Burning Crosses and Activist Journalism: Hazel Brannon Smith and the Mississippi Civil Rights Movement, Dangerous Dreams: Essays on American Film and Television, Rain on a Strange Roof: A Southern Literary Memoir, Reflections in a Critical Eye: Essays on Carson McCullers, Settling the Borderland: Other Voices in Literary Journalism,* and *Women in American Journalism: A New History. The Redemption of Narrative: Terry Tempest Williams and Her Vision of the West* is in press. A book about Truman Capote's *In Cold Blood* is in progress.

Gerald C. Wood is distinguished emeritus professor of English from Carson-Newman University, where he served as director of the Horton Foote Center. Wood edited a collection of one-act plays by Horton Foote for Southern Methodist University Press (1989) and the Garland casebook on Foote (1998). His critical study *Horton Foote and the Theater of Intimacy* (LSU, 1999) was nominated for the George Jean Nathan and C. Hugh Holman Awards. *The Voice of an American Playwright: Interviews with Horton Foote,* which he coedited with Marion Castleberry, was published in 2012 by Mercer University Press. He also wrote *Conor McPherson: Imagining Mischief* for the Liffey Press (Dublin, Ireland, 2003) and edited *Neil LaBute: A Casebook,* published in 2006 by Routledge Press. His *Smoky Joe Wood: The Biography of a Baseball Legend* (U of Nebraska P, 2013) won the Seymour Medal in 2014.